CUSTOM CURRICULUM

Can I Really Know Jesus?

Why Be a Christian?
Darrell Pearson and Mark Oestreicher

Face to Face with Jesus
Paul Borthwick and John Duckworth

Extreme Closeup
Paul Borthwick and Mark Syswerda

NEXGEN®
Building the New Generation of Believers

An Imprint of Cook Communications Ministries
Colorado Springs, Colorado

Can I Really Know Jesus?

© 2003 Cook Communications Ministries

All rights reserved. Except for the reproducible student sheets, which may be copied for ministry use, no part of this book may be reproduced in any form without the written permission of the publisher, unless otherwise noted in the text.

Unless otherwise noted, Scripture quotations are from the Holy Bible, New International Version (NIV), © 1973, 1978, 1984 by International Bible Society. Used by permission of Zondervan Publishing House.

Published by Cook Communications Ministries
4050 Lee Vance View
Colorado Springs, CO 80918
www.cookministries.com

Editorial Manager: Doug Schmidt
Product Developer: Karen Pickering
Series Creator: John Duckworth
Series Editor: Randy Southern
Cover Design: Granite Design
Interior Design: Becky Hawley Design, Inc.

Unit 1: Why Be a Christian?
© 2003 Cook Communications Ministries
Editor: Randy Southern
Writers: Darrell Pearson and Mark Oestreicher
Option Writers: Eric Potter, Nelson E. Copeland, Jr., and Ellen Larson
Inside Illustrator: John Hayes

Unit 2: Face to Face with Jesus
© 2003 Cook Communications Ministries
Editor: Randy Southern
Writers: Paul Borthwick and John Duckworth
Option Writers: Randy Southern, Nelson E. Copeland, Jr., and Ellen Larson
Inside Illustrator: John Hayes

Unit 3: Extreme Closeup
© 2003 Cook Communications Ministries
Editor: Sharon Stultz
Writers: Paul Borthwick and Mark Syswerda
Option Writers: Stan Campbell, John Duckworth, Sue Reck, and Randy Southern
Inside Illustrator: Joe Weissmann

Printed in the U.S.A.

Contents

How to Customize Your Curriculum   5

Unit One: Why Be a Christian?

Talking to Junior Highers about Why to Be a Christian   9

Unit One Publicity Clip Art   12

SESSION 1
I Doubt It!   14

SESSION 2
What Does It Cost and What Do I Get?   30

SESSION 3
Accepted by God, Rejected by Others   44

SESSION 4
Blind Faith   60

SESSION 5
The Price Jesus Paid   74

Unit Two: Face to Face with Jesus

Talking to Junior Highers about the Real Jesus   89

Unit Two Publicity Clip Art   92

SESSION 1
Does He Feel the Way I Do?   94

SESSION 2 Does He Have a Sense of Humor?	110
SESSION 3 What Kind of Friend Is He?	126
SESSION 4 Is He Tough Enough?	142
SESSION 5 Does He Really Love Me?	160

Unit Three: Extreme Closeup

How You and God Can Stay Connected	175
Unit 3 Publicity Clip Art	178
SESSION 1 Why Read the Bible?	180
SESSION 2 Why Pray?	196
SESSION 3 Why Praise God?	212
SESSION 4 Why Fellowship?	226
SESSION 5 Why Serve Others?	240

How to Customize Your Curriculum

We know your time is valuable. That's why we've made **Custom Curriculum** as easy as possible. Follow the three steps outlined below to create custom lessons that will meet the needs of *your* group. Let's get started!

 Read the basic lesson plan.

Every session in this book has four to six steps designed to meet five goals. It's important to understand these five goals as you choose the options for your group.

Getting Together

The goal for Getting Together is to break the ice. It may involve a fun way to introduce the lesson.

Getting Thirsty

The goal for Getting Thirsty is to earn students' interest before you dive into the Bible. Why should students care about your topic? Why should they care what the Bible has to say about it? This will motivate your students to dig deeper.

Getting the Word

The goal for Getting the Word is to find out what God has to say about the topic they care about. By exploring and discussing carefully-selected passages, you'll help students find out how God's Word applies to their lives.

Getting the Point

The goal for Getting the Point is to make the leap from ideals and principles to real-world situations students are likely to face. It may involve practicing biblical principles with case studies or roleplays.

Getting Personal

The goal for Getting Personal is to help each group member respond to the lesson with a specific action. What should group members do as a result of this session? This step will help each person find a specific "next step" response that works for him or her.

Consider your options.

Every **Custom Curriculum** session gives you 14 different types of options. How do you choose? First, take a look at the list of option categories below. Then spend some time thinking and praying about your group. How do your students learn best? What kind of goals have you set for your group? Put a check mark by the options that you're most interested in.

 Extra Action—for groups that like physical challenges and learn better when they're moving, interacting, and experiencing the lesson.

 Media—to spice up your meeting with video, music, or other popular media.

 Heard It All Before—for fresh approaches that get past the defenses of students who are jaded by years in church.

 Little Bible Background—to use when most of your students are strangers to the Bible or haven't yet made a Christian commitment.

 Extra Fun—for longer, more "festive" youth meetings where additional emphasis is put on having fun.

 Fellowship and Worship—for building deeper relationships or enabling students to praise God together.

 Mostly Girls—to address girls' concerns and to substitute activities girls might prefer.

 Mostly Guys—to address guys' concerns and to substitute activities guys might prefer.

 Small Group—for adapting activities that might be tough with groups of fewer than eight students.

 Large Group—to alter steps for groups of more than 20 students.

 Urban—for fitting sessions to urban facilities and multiethnic (especially African-American) concerns.

 Short Meeting Time—tips for condensing the meeting. The standard meeting is designed to last 45 to 60 minutes. These include options to cut, replace, or trim time off the standard steps.

 Combined Junior High/High School—to use when you're mixing age levels but an activity or case study would be too "young" or "old" for part of the group.

 Sixth Grade—appearing only in junior high/middle school volumes, this option helps you change steps that sixth graders might find hard to understand or relate to.

 Extra Challenge—appearing only in high school volumes, this option lets you crank up the voltage for students who are ready for more Scripture or more demanding personal application.

Customize your curriculum!

Here's a simple, three-step plan to customize each session for your group:

1. Choose your options.

As you read the basic session plan, you'll see icons in the margin. Each icon represents a different type of option. When you see an icon, it means that type of option is offered for that step. The five pages of options are found after the Repro Resource student pages for each session. Turn to the option noted by the icon and you'll see that option explained.

Let's say you have a small group, mostly guys who get bored if they don't keep moving. You'll want to keep an eye out for three kinds of options: Small Group, Mostly Guys, and Extra Action. As you read the basic session, you might spot icons that tell you there are Small Group options for Step 1 and Step 3—maybe a different way to play a game so that you don't need big teams, and a way to cover several Bible passages when just a few kids are looking them up. Then you see icons telling you that there are Mostly Guys options for Step 2 and Step 4—perhaps a substitute activity that doesn't require too much self-disclosure, and a case study guys will relate to. Finally you see icons indicating Extra Action options for Step 2 and Step 3—maybe an active way to get kids' opinions instead of handing out a survey, and a way to act out some verses instead of just looking them up.

2. Use the checklist.

Once you've picked your options, keep track of them with the simple checklist at the end of the option section (just before the start of the next session plan). This little form gives you a place to write down the materials you'll need too—since they depend on the options you've chosen.

3. Get your stuff together.

Gather your materials; photocopy any Repro Resources (reproducible student sheets) you've decided to use. And...you're ready!

Unit One: Why Be a Christian?

Talking to Junior Highers about Why to Be a Christian

by Darrell Pearson

Sometimes I'm not sure why I'm a Christian. Sometimes it just seems like the thing to do. Maybe I'm a Christian because most of my friends are Christians. Or perhaps it's due to the way my parents brought me up. Or maybe it's because the Christian life is familiar and comfortable. My life is not always filled with the spiritual vitality that could land me a guest spot on the *700 Club* or turn my city upside down with excitement. Often I'm just acting the part, being a Christian because I've, well, *always* been a Christian (or so it seems).

Sounds like a junior high kid talking. Junior highers are really not much different from us, if we're honest about it. Many of them are Christians—or pretend to be Christians—because their friends are, because their parents have trained them well, or because it's the life they've always known. The "I'm-so-pumped-because-I've-just-found-the-Lord" mentality of the new Christian is generally left for high schoolers; junior highers who are new to the faith have a hard time articulating their discovery or really understanding the new joy. Sometimes, junior highers are not sure why they are Christians.

Junior highers, almost without exception, will come to grips with this problem in the eighth or ninth grade. Studies have shown that ninth grade is the time when students choose the Christian life or decide it's time to start sleeping in on Sundays. It's the first time that they've ever really considered the option of not accepting the faith. For once in their lives they are in the position of making the decision themselves. And that fact is very puzzling, frightening, and threatening to those of us who are trying desperately to pass on the faith to the next generation.

My own parents were scared to death of my rejection of the faith (though they didn't tell me at the time). My dating a non-Christian girl and my resultant drift away from the church led them to question my youth pastor about what they could do. His advice? Give him time....

The Secret of Life in 25 Words or Less

I think most Christian adults have an extremely difficult time articulating what their faith means to them. Isn't that strange? We spend hours, days, months, years in study to grow as Christians; yet most of us (including us full-time youth directors) couldn't answer the simple question "Why are you a Christian?" in a few words. Why is this? You would think it would be the easiest thing in the world to do, but it isn't. Maybe the process is so ongoing and so lifelong that we just can't get an easy handle on it ourselves. So why are we so threatened by junior highers questioning their faith?

They're Too Much Like Us

I think most of us would agree that it's difficult for adults to believe and follow Christ. By the same token, it's equally difficult to watch students struggle with their faith. Helping and observing someone else struggle with the same difficulty you face is not easy.

I remember the first time my daughter Hilary was hurt by other kids calling her a name. It hurt to watch her struggle to understand why the kids did this, partly because it brought up so many memories buried in my own mind. (When you're the shortest kid in a school of three thousand, you get called a few names!) I didn't want her to go through these problems, but she had to. I could help as she dealt with the comments, but I couldn't keep her from experiencing life. When she gets older, she, too, will be in the ninth grade, and will start to wonder if it's worth being a Christian. It's still hard for me to follow Christ, and it will be hard to watch her as she chooses what to do. Strange paradox: I know that I struggle with following Jesus, but I have a hard time accepting that my child might do the same.

So, Why Are You . . . ?

Come up with *something*! Can you answer the great question? If not, you need to be able to. Not being able to give an account to students for the central motivation in your life is a pretty sad state.

When I was starting my youth ministry career I interned at a church in Iowa. One of the volunteers asked me one day, "How much do you love the Lord?" She expected an eloquent exposition I'm sure, but got a dumbfounded response that puzzled her. I spent years trying to answer that question. I still am. But I think now I could give a much clearer response about why I choose to follow Christ. With maturity, I've learned His provision for my life, my unworthiness, His grace. *Now* I think I could answer her question better. Junior high students are at the most critical age to make a decision about following Christ. Will they hear some wise words from us?

Be Like Me, For I Am Like . . . Christ!

That's what Paul said, even though it sounded a little haughty. He knew that even though it wasn't healthy for people to become overdependent upon a personality, to some extent a committed Christian is the best picture of Christ that others will see. What picture of Christ do your students see in you? If you are striving to be Christlike, your junior highers will never forget that image. I know. It's why I'm a follower today.

My college years involved the common search-and-destroy method of faith building: search for other answers, slowly let your faith die. It wasn't until I was halfway through college that I realized that all of the wonderful non-Christian friends I had associated with for two years had one desire for my life, which was for me to drink alcohol. The realization that this was their level of great concern for me prompted me to start looking for new friends. Where could they be found? Why, in the people who had always cared for me in the first place, the people from my Christian past I had grown up with. A look back at these people brought me back to the journey, because I knew they cared. Did you have a similar time in your life? A story of drifting and recovery? I'll bet in your return to the faith, there were people involved, maybe ones from your past.

That's the role you want to fill for your students. In the midst of their throwing pencils out the window, making cutting remarks about the Bible, belching at three in the morning on a retreat, they are somehow formulating a picture of the Christian faith for the future—and it's based on you, the nearest portrait of Christ they might ever see.

A Reason to Live

As students process the ideas and concepts in their lives that give direction to where they are going, they will most likely develop a growing awareness that their lives must revolve around some purpose. In the early years of middle school/junior high, those purposes are very simple: developing a self-image, growing a desire for material things, developing power, learning success in relationships, becoming independent. As kids move into high school, their ability to consider broader issues will lead them to discover that there are more important things in this world to build their lives around. They, just like us, will need a purpose for their lives. What will help them discover the greatness of following Christ is a close study of the leaders who, because they have chosen to follow Him, were willing to spend time with hard-to-love junior high students.

Darrell Pearson is co-founder of 10 to 20, an organization dedicated to presenting high-involvement events for teenagers. Formerly youth director at the First Presbyterian Church in Colorado Springs, Darrell spent most of his eleven years there directing the junior high program. He's co-authored Creative Programming Ideas for Junior High Ministry *(Youth Specialties), and written and presented the national-touring program* Next Exit. *He also speaks frequently to youth groups and leaders around the country. He lives with his wife and three daughters in Colorado Springs, Colorado.*

Publicity Clip Art

The images on these two pages are designed to help you promote this course within your church and community. Feel free to photocopy anything here and adapt it to fit your publicity needs. The stuff on this page could be used as a flier that you send or hand out to kids—or as a bulletin insert. The stuff on the next page could be used to add visual interest to newsletters, calendars, bulletin boards, or other promotions. Be creative and have fun!

Is This What It Means to Be a Christian?

What does it mean to be a Christian, anyway?
Is it really worth it? What if it's not for real?
We're starting a new course called *Why Be a Christian?*
Come and find the answers you need.

Who:

When:

Where:

Questions? Call:

Unit One: Why Be a Christian?

Doubt Busters

Think about it.

You won't believe your eyes!

Check it out.

SESSION 1

I Doubt It!

YOUR GOALS FOR THIS SESSION:
Choose one or more

☐ To help kids identify some of the spiritual doubts they might have.

☐ To help kids understand that having honest doubts is not sinful.

☐ To help kids choose one doubt to attack, using the "SCRAM" method.

☐ Other:_____

Your Bible Base:

John 20:24-30
Acts 17:10-11

I DOUBT IT!

STEP 1

The "I Doubt It" Game

Divide your group into two teams. Explain that you're going to read a list of world records. Some are actual records and others are made up. Each team has to decide whether the record is real or fake. If the team thinks the record is fake, team members should shout out "I doubt it!" as loud as they can. If the team thinks the record is real, members should keep quiet.

Point to Team 1, read the first statement, and give team members a chance to make up their minds. Award one point for each correct response (or lack of one). Go back and forth between the two teams until you've gone through the list. Declare a winning team and have members cheer for themselves. Here is the list of records.

1. **A man rode a 145-mile wheelie on a motorcycle.** *(Real.)*
2. **One man was struck by lightning seven different times.** *(Real.)*
3. **A woman kept a Hula Hoop going for 193 consecutive hours.** *(Fake.)*
4. **The largest Easter egg hunt involved over 72,000 eggs.** *(Real.)*
5. **The longest bicycle ever made held 47 riders.** *(Fake.)*
6. **The longest tunnel is 105 miles long.** *(Real.)*
7. **The biggest pumpkin ever grown was almost 6 feet high.** *(Fake.)*
8. **Two men played tennis for 8 days straight without sleeping.** *(Fake.)*
9. **Twenty-eight snow skiers did a back flip while holding hands.** *(Real.)*
10. **The biggest ice-cream sundae was 10 feet tall.** *(Real.)*
11. **One man received a 10,000 year prison sentence.** *(Real.)*
12. **A man ate 42 bananas in 3 minutes.** *(Fake.)*

U N I T   O N E

Dozens-O-Doubts

(Needed: Copies of Repro Resource 1, pencils)

Before passing out copies of "Dozens-O-Doubts" (Repro Resource 1) and pencils, ask group members to react to this comment: **When a person has doubts about his or her faith, he or she may not be a true Christian.**

Ask a few kids to explain their answers. You may want to point out that this may very well be true in some situations. In other cases, a person might be asking honest questions that deserve honest answers.

Hand out copies of Repro Resource 1 and instruct group members to put a check in the box that best describes their thoughts and feelings about each doubt.

After about five minutes, regroup and ask for a few responses to the following questions.

Which doubts on this list never bother you?
Which ones bug you a lot?
What are some other doubts kids have about God and Christianity that weren't on this list?

Then say: **Take a look at what you checked off for the last doubt on the sheet: "I doubt that it's OK to have doubts." Do you sometimes wonder if God will "zap" you if you have doubts or questions about Him or the Bible?**

Doubting Thomas

(Needed: Bibles)

Choose one of your kids who's a good sport to roleplay a quick conversation with you. Ask this kid to tell you about the best vacation he or she ever went on, or some other memorable event. As he or she talks to you, interrupt with comments such as these: **Oh, really?**

OPTIONS

EXTRA ACTION
LARGE GROUP
LITTLE BIBLE BACKGROUND
MOSTLY GIRLS
URBAN

Are you sure? or even a rather skeptical sounding **Hm-m-m.** Sound extremely doubtful of whatever the person says. When the kid has finished talking, it would be a good idea to assure him or her that you believed his or her story—honest!

Then ask: **How would you feel if people doubted *everything* you said?**

But what if a friend had a serious question about something you said, how would you prove it was true? (You could try to find some evidence or another person to back up what you're saying. You'd want to show that what you're saying is accurate and true.)

Explain that you're going to be looking at two instances in the Bible to see how the apostles and Jesus Himself reacted to people who had doubts about their message. Remind group members to keep in mind the last doubt on the "Dozens-O-Doubts" worksheet—"I doubt that it's OK to have doubts."

Have group members turn in their Bibles to Acts 17:10-11. Fill in the details by explaining that Paul, Silas, and Timothy were traveling from city to city instructing people about their faith. Have a volunteer read aloud the two verses. Then ask: **What was going on in Berea? If these people were so noble, why did they check out Paul's message? Why didn't they just accept what Paul was saying?**

You might want to mention that Berea was a large, cosmopolitan city (today it's a ski resort!). People who lived there were open-minded and probably had heard all sorts of ideas—from the weird to the wacky to the wise. These people probably wanted to be sure Paul wasn't a religious kook.

Was it OK for them to do check out what Paul said? Give kids a chance to express their opinions. If necessary, point out that these individuals went to the right source, Scripture, to check out Paul's message.

Next, ask group members to turn in their Bibles to John 20:24-30. Have a volunteer read aloud this passage. Set the stage by explaining that Jesus had already died on the cross, had been buried, had risen from the dead, and had appeared to all the disciples—except Thomas.

Say: **Meet the original Doubting Thomas. Thomas wasn't a traitor like Judas Iscariot, but sometimes he gets a bad rap. How would you describe Thomas?**

Call on two or three kids who are familiar with this story to describe Thomas. For example, Thomas was a realist. He wasn't going to believe anything he hadn't seen. Thomas may have been timid or afraid, but with good reason. He and the other disciples had just witnessed Jesus' gruesome death, and word was out that the religious leaders wanted to kill the disciples too.

Look at the way Jesus handled Thomas's doubt. What does this tell you about Jesus? (Jesus accepts us—doubts and all. He wants to help us stop doubting and believe.)

UNIT ONE

Explain: **Jesus didn't yell at Thomas and tell him it was wrong for him to doubt. In fact, Jesus did the opposite—He wanted to help Thomas work through his doubts and believe.**

Refer to Repro Resource 1 again. Point to the last doubt ("I doubt that it's OK to have doubts") and ask: **Based on what we've been talking about, would you change your answer to this last doubt?**

Pause for a minute to give kids a chance to reevaluate their responses, and then say: **Remember these two things: It's not un-Christian to have doubts, and Jesus can help us get the doubt out!**

SCRAM

(Needed: Copies of Repro Resource 2, chalkboard and chalk, or newsprint and marker)

Ask group members what they would say to someone who is pesky (like a younger brother or sister) to get rid of him or her. If they don't come up with this themselves, suggest the command, "Scram!"

Have your group members shout, "Scram!" several times, teasing them with comments such as, **Oh, that's not loud, I can hardly hear you,** and **Is that really as loud as you can yell?**

Then pass out copies of "The SCRAM Doubt-Removal System" (Repro Resource 2). You'll need a chalkboard and chalk, or newsprint and a marker for this exercise. Write the letters S, C, R, A, and M down the left side of the board.

Explain that the S stands for "Seek God's help." Instruct your group members to write this next to the S on their sheets while you write it on the board.

Say: **Before tackling any doubts, we have to pray—even if you have doubts about prayer. Just do it! Ask God to help you work through your doubts. He promises us He will!**

Next, explain what the C stands for: "Call it what it is." Have kids write this next to the C on their outlines while you write it on the board. **We need to be really honest with ourselves about our doubts. Sometimes it's easier to pretend we don't have**

doubts than to admit that we do. If you have doubts about God's forgiveness, tell God. Be specific. God can take it!

Then tell your group members that the *R* stands for "Read what the Bible says." Again, have group members write this on their outlines while you write it on the board.

The Bible is God's main way of communicating with us, so we need to read His Word. Maybe you could read one of the Gospels, like the Book of John, or a book like Ephesians.

Take a minute to review the first three steps in the method. Have group members turn their papers over. Then ask them what the *S*, *C*, and *R* stand for.

And the *A* stands for "Ask people you trust." This step helps out when those doubts refuse to budge. It's important to get the input of other people who love God. These people may have struggled with some of the same doubts you're struggling with, and you can learn from their experiences and advice. Or someone like a youth leader or pastor can help you understand what the Bible has to say.

Review the first four letters. Then tell your group members that the last letter, *M*, stands for "Make a decision and move on." Have your group members write this on their outlines as you write it on the board.

There comes a point when you need to make a decision about specific doubts. Either you've found enough help from the Bible and other sources that you can put a doubt behind you and move on—or you might need to keep applying the SCRAM Doubt-Removal System to get the doubt out.

It might take time for you to work through some doubts, but keep working at it. Some people lug around the same doubts all their lives only because they never do anything about them.

Review the whole process until you're confident your group members can remember the five points.

UNIT ONE

STEP 5

Pick a Doubt

(Needed: Different colored markers)

Set out several markers and ask kids to choose two different colors. Then have group members skim the "Dozens-O-Doubts" list from Repro Resource 1.

Explain: **Use one color and put a star next to your top three doubts. Next, use the second color, and write the word "SCRAM" in big, bold letters over the one doubt you want to confront.**

Quickly go over the SCRAM method one last time: Seek God's help; Call it what it is; Read what the Bible says; Ask people you trust; and Make a decision and move on.

Take care of the first step in the process by leading group members in prayer. Challenge kids to practice the SCRAM method on their chosen doubts.

WHY BE A CHRISTIAN?   REPRO RESOURCE 1

Dozens-O-Doubts

	BIG TIME	SOME	A LITTLE	NOT!
1. I doubt God exists.				
2. I doubt Jesus Christ is really God's Son.				
3. I doubt God really cares about me.				
4. I doubt that Jesus never sinned.				
5. I doubt that heaven really will be all that great.				
6. I doubt that hell exists.				
7. I doubt a loving God would send people to hell.				
8. I doubt that God listens to everyone's prayers.				
9. I doubt God answers my prayers.				
10. I doubt the Bible doesn't have mistakes.				
11. I doubt that demons and angels exist.				
12. I doubt that miracles, like raising people from the dead, ever happened.				
13. I doubt that it's very important for me to read the Bible.				
14. I doubt God has good plans for my life.				
15. I doubt that God understands what my family is like.				
16. I doubt God can forgive some of the things I've done.				
17. I doubt that going to church is very important.				
18. I doubt God is with me all the time.				
19. I doubt that I'll ever be able to say no to some temptations.				
20. I doubt the story of Creation is accurate.				
21. I doubt Jesus will ever come back—at least not in my lifetime.				
22. I doubt God really cares about all the bad stuff going on in the world.				
23. I doubt that it will matter much if I wait a few more years to "get serious" about God.				
24. I doubt that it's OK to have doubts.				

NOTES

WHY BE A CHRISTIAN? REPRO RESOURCE 2

THE SCRAM Doubt-Removal System

S

C

R

A

M

NOTES

OPTIONS
SESSION ONE

STEP 3

One way to increase our understanding of the Bible is to read it imaginatively—that is, to imagine how the people involved in the stories of Scripture might have felt in various situations. Help your group members do this by having them write skits based on the passages in this step. Have group members pair up for this activity. Instruct the pairs to make up conversations and reactions that might have taken place among the people involved in these Bible events. The skits should reveal the character of the people in the passage, their motivations, and how others might have reacted to what happened. Prod group members' creativity with questions like these: **What do you think the Bereans said about Paul's teaching? How might the people with Paul have reacted to the Bereans' skepticism? How would the disciples have responded to Thomas's doubts?** (For example, Peter might have said something like, "Are you calling me a liar?") Encourage the pairs to be humorous and accurate in their skits. Give them a few minutes to work; then have them perform their skits.

STEP 4

Since the SCRAM principles involve reading what the Bible says and asking people you trust, give group members an opportunity to respond to doubts by staging a debate. Determine one of the main doubts held by your group. Then divide into two teams. One team should prepare to argue *against* the doubt; the other should prepare to argue *for* it. For example, one team could argue that God doesn't exist; the other could argue that He does. Give the teams five minutes to prepare their arguments. Then give each side one minute to present its view and thirty seconds to respond to its opponent's view. Afterward, point out that belief is grounded in faith but has support in reason, revelation, and fact.

STEP 2

Depending on the maturity of your group members and their closeness, you may want to have all of them, rather than a few volunteers, share the results of their sheets. As a leader, you might want to get kids started by sharing your own doubts. It can be comforting for kids to know that they're not the only ones with doubts. Such honesty can also build unity and a sense of dependence on each other. For some of your group members, you may be one of the "trusted people" with whom they share their doubts privately. (See the "SCRAM" principles in Step 4.) Hearing you share your own doubts may inspire them to come to you with some of their more personal doubts.

STEP 5

If your group is small, you have the opportunity to apply two of the SCRAM principles ("read what the Bible says" and "ask people you trust") to your kids' most pressing doubts. Have each group member write his or her number-one doubt on a slip of paper. Collect the slips in a paper bag. Then pull out a slip and read the doubt. Ask volunteers to call out pertinent Bible passages and give their views as to why they believe, rather than doubt, this point. If possible, try to address the doubts on all of the slips.

STEP 1

The opening quiz would be difficult for a large group to do as a contest, since large teams would have trouble reaching a consensus about the statements. So try this variation. Read one of the statements aloud. If group members think it's a real record, they should stand up. If they think it's fake, they should remain seated. After group members have responded to each statement, give the correct answer. (You may want to figure out a "gullibility percentage" or have group members keep their personal score and applaud those with the best records.) To add excitement to the activity, eliminate those who are wrong after each round. Afterward, discuss group members' basis for choosing whether or not to doubt something.

STEP 3

Get more group members actively involved in the Bible study by breaking them into teams of four or five people. Have half of the teams look up the Acts passage and the other half look up the John passage. Instruct the teams to do profiles of the people in their passages, either of the typical Berean or of Thomas. Encourage them to think of the traits that these people exhibited. In creating the profiles, team members might write down a list of traits or they might use poster board and markers to make posters depicting the characters. Give the teams a few minutes to work. Then have each team share its list or poster and summarize its passage.

OPTIONS
SESSION ONE

HEARD IT ALL BEFORE

LITTLE BIBLE BACKGROUND

FELLOWSHIP & WORSHIP

STEP 2

Despite assurances that "it's OK to have doubts," kids who've been raised in the church may feel that adults, particularly church leaders, never have any doubts. After all, few kids have probably ever heard a pastor or speaker say, "I have a really hard time believing this principle." Address the feelings of these kids with the following questions. Ask: **Do you think your pastor ever has any doubts about the Bible or his faith? Why or why not? If he did have doubts, would you want him to share those doubts with the church? Why or why not? How do you think the church would respond if the pastor shared his doubts? How would you respond? How might a non-Christian visitor to the church respond?**

STEP 4

Some of your kids may be struggling with what appears to them to be circular logic: God exists because the Bible says so and the Bible is true because it's God's Word. Point out that, ultimately, belief is a gift from God, a matter of faith—but it's not a blind leap. There are evidences for the trustworthiness of Scripture and, while they might not absolutely *prove* the Bible is true, they can be persuasive. Get group members thinking about the problems of proof and persuasiveness by having them play a game in which they must prove their identity. Ask a volunteer to state who he or she is. The rest of the group members should ask for proof of the person's claims. As the volunteer offers various proofs (ID card, library card, testimony of friends, swearing on a stack of Bibles, etc.), have the rest of the group members "poke holes" in the evidence. Afterward, discuss which proofs offered by the person were most persuasive. It may have to do with the number and reliability of the witnesses. Explain that the Bible offers similar evidence. A book like Josh McDowell's *Evidence That Demands a Verdict* can be a big help to those with doubts.

STEP 3

To help group members better understand the passages, provide the following background in addition to the suggestions in the session. For the John passage, explain that when Jesus was crucified, His hands and feet were nailed to the cross and that a soldier stuck a spear in His side to make sure that He was dead. That's what caused the holes that Thomas wanted to see and touch. He wanted physical evidence that Jesus' crucified body had really risen. For the Acts passage, explain that Paul took many missionary journeys. In each city he visited, he first went to the Jewish synagogue, where he showed the people that Jesus was the Messiah about whom the Jewish Scriptures (our Old Testament) had prophesied.

STEP 5

Group members with little Bible background may have difficulty applying the SCRAM principles because they won't automatically know what the Bible says about various doubts. In fact, they may not even know how to find out what the Bible says. To help them with this problem, choose one or two doubts, such as "I doubt God exists," and show group members some passages that reveal what the Bible says about each doubt. For the "I doubt God exists" example, some possible passages might include Genesis 1:1 ("In the beginning God created . . .") and Exodus 3:14 (in which God says to Moses, "I am who I am"). If possible, bring in some Bible concordances and other resources and briefly demonstrate to your group members how to use them to find various words and topics in the Bible.

STEP 1

Use the following game either before or instead of the world records quiz. It will help group members learn more about each other and get them thinking about what makes a statement believable. Divide into two teams. Have group members make up three statements about themselves, two of which are true and one of which is false. Have a player from Team A read his or her statements; then have a player from Team B guess which one is false. If the player guesses correctly, Team B gets a point; if he or she guesses wrong, Team A gets a point. Keep playing until all of the players have read their statements. (If you have a large group, you may want to arrange for several smaller competitions.) Afterward, have group members discuss why they doubted or believed various statements.

STEP 5

Close the session with a time of prayer in which group members confess their doubts and ask God's help for belief. You can use all or some of the doubts on Repro Resource 1 or have group members come up with a list of their top ten doubts. Have different volunteers read aloud one of the doubts (from the sheet or your list); then have the group respond with the refrain "Lord, I believe, help my unbelief." End with a time of personal confession of doubts, either having kids pray silently or letting volunteers confess their own doubts aloud. During the prayer time, you may also want to read some of the claims that the Bible makes about God.

OPTIONS
SESSION ONE

Mostly Girls

Step 3
Instead of having group members describe Thomas, ask for two volunteers to roleplay the event in John 20:24-30. Ask one of the volunteers to play the role of Thomas and the other to play the role of Jesus. The rest of the group members will play other disciples and friends present at the scene. Ask that the characters ad-lib a conversation beyond what is told in the John passage. Suggest that the group members playing disciples and friends contribute to the skit by reacting to Thomas's doubt.

Step 5
Ask group members to select one item from "Dozens-O-Doubts" (Repro Resource 1). Have those who are interested in discussing the same items meet together and talk about how to help each other implement the SCRAM method with that doubt.

Mostly Guys

Step 1
Play "Sentinel" to help guys test their ability to determine whether someone's telling the truth. Have group members form two teams. One team will be the sentinels; the other will be the challengers. Give each of the challengers a slip of paper that says either "friend" or "foe." When a challenger approaches a sentinel, the sentinel will say, "Halt. Are you friend or foe?" The challenger will reply, "Friend." The sentinel must determine if the challenger is telling the truth. The sentinel gets a point for letting friends pass and for refusing foes. The challenger gets a point if the sentry lets a foe pass or refuses a friend. After all the challengers have played, switch roles. Wrap up the activity by discussing how the sentinels made their decisions. Did they guess? Did they look for certain clues? On what did they base their doubts?

Step 4
Before discussing the principles for dealing with doubts, help group members think about the criteria they already use for determining whether or not someone is trustworthy. Give each group member an index card and have him think of a hero or a person he respects and who he thinks can be believed. Instruct group members to make "hero" cards (modeled after baseball cards). On one side, they should write the hero's/heroine's name (and draw a picture of him or her, if they like). On the other side, they should list the person's "stats," the things that make this person believable. When they are finished, have volunteers share their cards. Discuss what causes us to trust people. (It may include their characters, examples of things they've said that proved true, their reputations, their positions, etc.) Use these ideas to help group members see the trustworthiness of the Bible's claims and of the counsel of other believers.

Extra Fun

Step 1
Play the following game to get group members thinking about the issues of believability and trust. Have group members form a circle. Choose a volunteer ("It") to stand in the center of the circle. While "It" closes his or her eyes, the people in the circle should pass around a marble (keeping both hands in front of them, palms down), trying to keep its location hidden. After 30 seconds or so, have "It" give a warning, then open his or her eyes and try to guess who has the marble. The people in the circle should do all they can to trick "It," but they must keep the marble moving. If "It" guesses correctly, the person caught becomes "It." If "It" guesses wrong, he or she has to try again. Afterward, discuss the difficulty of trying to decide who to believe and who to doubt.

Step 4
Briefly introduce each of the SCRAM principles, but don't pause for review. Instead, use a more interesting method of helping kids familiarize themselves with the principles. Have group members form teams of three or four. Instruct each team to come up with a creative and/or humorous presentation of the five SCRAM principles. One team may choose to present the principles in rap form. ("Yo, listen everybody, to our plan. It's got five parts, and they spell out 'Scram' . . .") Another team may put the principles to a TV theme song—*Gilligan's Island*, for instance. ("Just sit right back and you'll hear a tale, a tale of a plan called 'Scram'. . . . There's 'Seek God's help'; 'Call it what it is'; 'Read what the Bi-i-ble says'; 'Ask people you trust'; 'Make a de-cis-ion, and move on'—and your doubts will scram.") Other teams may use poems, jokes, limericks, cheers, cartoons, etc. They may keep the original words or rewrite the principles in their own words—whichever is more conducive to their creativity. When everyone is finished, have each team make its presentation.

OPTIONS
SESSION ONE

STEP 1
Bring in several tabloid newspapers, such as the *National Enquirer*. Have group members form two teams. Give each team several tabloids. Instruct each team to choose three headlines from the newspapers and then make up a fourth headline. Each team will then try to guess which of its opponent's headlines is made up. Play several rounds. Afterward, discuss how group members determined which headlines were made up. Use this activity to lead into a discussion of how we determine whether to believe something or not.

STEP 5
Here's a way for kids to apply two of the SCRAM principles ("read what the Bible says" and "ask someone you trust") to some of their doubts. Have group members form teams. Assign one doubt to each team. (You might want to take a poll to figure out the top five doubts of your group members and then assign those doubts.) Provide the teams with tape recorders or video cameras. Instruct each team to make a public-service message to help kids overcome the doubt assigned to the team. Encourage the teams to include relevant Bible verses and "expert opinions" or "endorsements" in their messages. When they are finished, play and discuss the messages.

STEP 1
Depending on the amount of time you have, you may need to either shorten this step by reading only half of the records or skip the step entirely and begin the session with the "Dozens-O-Doubts" sheet in Step 2. If you skip the step, you might want to be prepared to open the session with an anecdote about a time you (or someone you know of) doubted something that turned out to be true. Then, if you have time, you could ask one or two group members to share similar anecdotes.

STEP 4
If you're short on time, you may need to condense the activities in this step. Here are some suggestions. Don't ask kids what they would tell a pesky brother or sister and don't have them shout "scram." Instead, distribute Repro Resource 2 and list each of the five steps. You can save additional time by not pausing to review the steps. By presenting this information quickly, you will give kids more time to apply these principles to their own doubts in Step 5.

STEP 1
Here are some other records that may interest city teens.

1. Three New York City youths rode nearly 232 miles on the subway in almost 30 hours. (Real.)
2. Michael Jordan once leaped 40 feet to slam from midcourt. (Fake.)
3. The tallest hairstyle for a woman stood eight feet high. (Real.)
4. The tallest (8' 3/4") and smallest (28.3") adult living persons are both of African heritage. (Real.)
5. The biggest-selling rap song of all time is "End of the Road" by Boyz II Men. (Fake—It's not a rap song.)
6. Wilt Chamberlain once scored 100 points in one basketball game. (Real.)
7. In 1972, a fourteen-year-old weight lifter in Miami lifted 762 pounds. (Fake.)

STEP 3
For the conversation activity that begins this step, you may want to use a scenario other than "the best vacation" the person ever had. Many urban teens never leave the city, and a "vacation" is an almost-foreign concept to them. Instead, you might want to ask the person to talk about the best day he or she ever had.

OPTIONS
SESSION ONE

STEP 4
Since some high schoolers might find the SCRAM acrostic "beneath" them, skip the beginning of the step—especially the part in which kids yell "scram." Skip the sheet as well. Instead, have group members form teams. Instruct each team to come up with a list of steps for handling doubts. After five minutes, have the teams share their lists. List all of the steps on the board as they are named. Afterward, you may want to supplement the teams' ideas with the SCRAM principles (though not by that name).

STEP 5
If you skipped the SCRAM principles in Step 4, don't have kids write "SCRAM" over their main doubt. Instead, after they have highlighted their top three doubts, have them choose the main doubt they want to face. Then, on the back of Repro Resource 1, have them make a list of the steps they can take to face (and perhaps overcome) this doubt. Encourage them to use the different strategies developed in Step 4.

STEP 4
Help your sixth graders be more specific with the R and A on "The SCRAM Doubt-Removal System" (Repro Resource 2). After you write in the acrostic "Read what the Bible says" and "Ask people you trust," talk about ways to find out where to look in the Bible for specific information. On another section of the board, make a list of some Bible references, such as concordances, Bible dictionaries, and the names of a few specific books. Also write the names of some knowledgeable people in your church who would be receptive to a personal discussion with your group members.

STEP 5
Practice the "Call it what it is" step by asking each of your sixth graders to select one of the doubts from Repro Resource 1 to discuss. Distribute pencils and small pieces of paper. Instruct group members to write the number of the doubt they chose on the paper. Collect the papers and put them in a small container. Then draw the slips one at a time, and spend some time discussing the doubts that are identified.

DATE USED:
                    Approx. Time

STEP 1: *The "I Doubt It" Game* _____
- ❏ Large Group
- ❏ Fellowship & Worship
- ❏ Mostly Guys
- ❏ Extra Fun
- ❏ Media
- ❏ Short Meeting Time
- ❏ Urban

Things needed:

STEP 2: *Dozens-O-Doubts* _____
- ❏ Small Group
- ❏ Heard It All Before

Things needed:

STEP 3: *Doubting Thomas* _____
- ❏ Extra Action
- ❏ Large Group
- ❏ Little Bible Background
- ❏ Mostly Girls
- ❏ Urban

Things needed:

STEP 4: *SCRAM* _____
- ❏ Extra Action
- ❏ Heard It All Before
- ❏ Mostly Guys
- ❏ Extra Fun
- ❏ Short Meeting Time
- ❏ Combined Junior High/High School
- ❏ Sixth Grade

Things needed:

STEP 5: *Pick a Doubt* _____
- ❏ Small Group
- ❏ Little Bible Background
- ❏ Fellowship & Worship
- ❏ Mostly Girls
- ❏ Media
- ❏ Combined Junior High/High School
- ❏ Sixth Grade

Things needed:

SESSION 2
What Does It Cost and What Do I Get?

YOUR GOALS FOR THIS SESSION:
Choose one or more

☐ To help kids understand the cost and benefits of following Christ.

☐ To help kids realize that their commitment to Christ should be a wholehearted commitment.

☐ To help kids make a decision to follow Christ out of commitment to Him.

☐ Other:_____

Your Bible Base:

Mark 10:17-31
Luke 14:25-35
John 15:18-21

WHAT DOES IT COST AND WHAT DO I GET?

STEP 1

Survival Quest

(Needed: Copies of Repro Resource 3, poster board or newsprint, markers, pencils)

In this fun team effort, group members will have to make some choices about the necessities of life. Divide group members into teams of three or four. Pass out copies of "Survival Quest" (Repro Resource 3) to each team. Also give each team a couple of pieces of poster board or newsprint and markers.

Go over the situation at the top of the sheet together; then tell teams they have ten minutes to decide what supplies to take. Have them draw or write out their strategies for survival.

After a few minutes, interrupt with this scenario: **BOOM! There goes the plane. Believe it or not, things have gotten worse. Without enough water and food, your chances of survival are slim. There's no way you can make it to the town. Your only three concerns should be staying as cool as possible during the day, collecting as much water as possible, and signaling passing search planes.**

With this turn of events, which supplies do you absolutely need, and which ones can you leave behind?

Have teams rethink their strategies, and if necessary, come up with different plans of action. When kids have finished, regroup and give teams a chance to present their strategies. Keep track of which supplies are taken and which are left behind. You might want to take a group vote on the best strategy for survival.

Use the following information to supplement your discussion of which supplies would be useful and which would be useless.

Here are the items that would come in handy:
- *Plastic raincoat*—Could be used for collecting dew at night.
- *Plastic canteen*—Could be used to store the dew where it won't evaporate as you ration it out.
- *Bag of oranges*—Could supply additional water and energy.
- *Hand mirror*—Could be used for signaling planes during the day.
- *Flashlight*—Could be used for signaling planes at night.

Here are the items that could be left behind:
- *Can of lighter fluid*—What would you burn? What would you light it with?

UNIT ONE

- *Map and compass*—You'd die trying to get to a town that's 500 miles away.
- *Rattlesnake serum*—There are no rattlesnakes in the Sahara.
- *Loaded handgun*—There's nothing to shoot.
- *"Acme Desert Weasel Bait"* and *Acme's 101 Ways to Prepare Desert Weasel*—That terrible Acme company lives off the stupidity of tourists who don't know there's no such thing as a desert weasel.
- *Jumbo bag of Fritos*—They'd dry you out and make you more thirsty.

Say something like: **Being a follower of Jesus Christ is kind of like this survival quest. We have to make choices about what things to give up—like the Fritos and the Acme desert weasel books—in order to live the right way. There are other things God gives us—like hand mirrors and raincoats—that we may not always see the advantage of having right away, but are exactly what we need for living. In fact, if we try to make it on our own, we'll die. We need a rescuer like Jesus.**

Plus and Minus

(Needed: Index cards with plus signs and minus signs written on them)

For this activity, you'll need several index cards. Before the meeting, draw plus signs on half of the cards and minus signs on the other half. Have everyone sit in a circle, and then randomly hand out the cards to kids.

Explain: **If you have a plus sign on your card, think of one plus about being a Christian and write it on your card. If you have a minus sign, write one negative thing about being a Christian.**

Some of your kids might feel weird writing down negative things about being a Christian. If this is the case, have them write what *other* kids think are some of the negative things about being a Christian.

Let your kids work for a couple of minutes. Then ask someone who has a positive sign on his or her card to read one of the advantages, and toss the card in the middle of the circle. Others with the same response should rip up their cards. Do the same thing for someone with a negative sign. Go back and forth between the advantages and disadvantages, even if kids run out of cards to toss. When all the cards

are in the middle, count up the pluses and the minuses. At this point, it's all right if the negatives outnumber the positives. The positive group may have had a hard time coming up with advantages other than "going to heaven." If kids give vague, general responses such as "too many rules," press them to be more specific.

Afterward, say: **When you follow Christ, you have to count up the pluses and minuses, or the costs involved in following Him.**

The Price Is Right

(Needed: Bibles, slips of paper with Scripture references written on them, a ten-dollar bill, a five-dollar bill, a one-dollar bill, pieces of green construction paper with dollar amounts written on them [optional])

If you can, bring a ten-, a five-, and a one-dollar bill to this session. Or, if you're not feeling wealthy, write these same dollar amounts on three separate sheets of green construction paper.

Have group members move back into their teams from Step 1 or form three new groups. Give each team a slip of paper with one of the following passages to read. Explain that the teams are to come up with one or two "costs" involved in following Jesus.

Here are the passages:
- Mark 10:17-31
- Luke 14:25-35
- John 15:18-21

Give the teams a few minutes to work; then go over their findings. To do this, ask each group to describe what was going on in its passage and to name at least one cost involved in following Jesus. Also hand the reporting group the ten-, five-, and one-dollar bills (or green construction paper).

Explain: **Hold up the ten-dollar bill and call out "Too high," if you think the cost was too high. Hold up the one-dollar bill if you think the cost was too low. Hold up the five-dollar bill if you think the cost was just right.**

Give each group a minute to decide which amount to hold up and to explain the choice.

Use the following information to supplement your discussion of these hard teachings of Jesus.

Mark 10:17-31—This is the story of the rich young man (or ruler as he's described in Luke 18:18). The young man thought he could earn salvation, but Jesus taught that it was a gift to be received. Even though the young man sincerely kept the law, it was still an external kind of obedience. Jesus obviously cared for the young man and knew he was sincere; but He also wanted the man to realize the depth of God's commandments. Jesus' commandment to go and sell everything and give it to the poor may not apply to every single Christian; but in this case, the young man's major problem was his wealth—and it kept him from following Jesus.

Cost involved in following Jesus: Being willing to give up everything.

Luke 14:25-35—This passage describes the cost of being a disciple. In verse 26, Jesus used exaggeration to make His point: A person must love Him even more than immediate family members. The phrase "carry his cross" communicates the total commitment involved in following Christ. Since the cross was a symbol of death, that commitment includes dying for Christ's sake—but it also means self-denial, complete loyalty, and a willing obedience. Jesus doesn't want a blind, everything-is-going-to-be-wonderful-now commitment. Just as a builder estimates the cost or a king evaluates his military strength, a person must consider what Jesus expects of His followers—total commitment to Him.

Costs involved in following Jesus: Relationships with people can't be more important than Christ; suffering; self-denial; total commitment to God.

John 15:18-21—This passage contains some of Jesus' parting words to His disciples. Jesus reminds His followers that if the world (that is, the human system that opposes God's purposes) hates them, it's because the world hated Him first. Christians don't belong to the world's system anymore. They have new life in Christ and belong to Him. So guess what? People will treat Christians the way they treated Christ. But remember, it's a sign of belonging to Christ.

Costs involved in following Christ: Being unpopular and hated; persecution.

After all the groups have shared, say: **For every cost we talked about, we could have said that it was too high. Why do you think the cost in following Jesus is so high?** (Jesus wants to be sure that we are following Him completely. Our relationship with Christ has to be the most important relationship we have. He wants us to be ready to give up everything for Him, and even be prepared to suffer for His sake.)

To help kids understand the total commitment Christ demands, say: **Suppose you liked someone who really liked you, too, but he or she only wanted to be your boyfriend or girlfriend fifty percent of the time. The other fifty percent of the time, he or she wanted to someone else's girlfriend or boyfriend. How would you feel about this person's commitment to you?**

As kids describe their feelings, mention that a halfway commitment usually means no real commitment at all.

Explain: **The same thing can be said about our choice to follow Christ. We either do it all the way, or not at all. It's not a halfway commitment. That's why Jesus wants His followers to count the cost, and choose to follow Him one hundred percent. We've been talking about some serious stuff, but there are some pretty good trade-offs involved in following Christ.**

Let's Make a Trade

(Needed: Four assorted sizes of boxes, wrapping paper, slips of paper, envelopes)

Before the session, collect four assorted sizes of boxes (for example, a shoe box, a photocopy paper box, a grocery store box, and a shirt box). For each box, cover one side of it with wrapping paper (or some substitute). Also label the boxes 1, 2, 3, and 4.

On the opposite side of the box, write one of the benefits of following Christ. Here are some sample benefits you might want to use:
- Forgiveness—You don't have to live with a guilty conscience.
- Eternal life—You don't have to worry about death.
- Peace—God is in charge and is good even in bad times.
- Love and acceptance
- Help with problems

Next, write on slips of paper some of the "benefits" of not following Christ. For example:
- Popularity with a lot of different people
- Freedom to do whatever you want
- Don't have to go to church all the time
- No pressure to act a certain way
- Life is good just the way it is—no reason to change

Put these slips of paper in envelopes.

Instead of coming up with new benefits, you might want to reuse the negative cards from Step 2. If you do, just hand out the cards, without the envelopes.

To wrap up the session, ask for four volunteers to play "Let's Make a Trade." Hand out the envelopes and tell kids to open them and read what's inside. Meanwhile, set up the boxes, with the wrapped side facing your kids.

Play this part as a Monty Hall clone from the old game show "Let's Make a Deal." Explain how the trade works.

Each of you has one "advantage" of not being a Christian. Inside these boxes are some of the advantages of following Christ. So, would you like to trade what's in your envelope for what's behind Box #1, Box #2, Box #3, or Box #4?

Get the other kids to yell out which boxes the volunteers should choose. When a choice has been made, have the volunteer come up to the box, turn it around, and read the advantage to the rest of the group.

As a group, talk about the trade-offs. Ask kids what they would have to give up and what they would receive in return. For example, if a person traded freedom for forgiveness, he or she might not be able to do certain things anymore. But, when he or she blows it, God will forgive him or her—and the person doesn't have to live with a guilty conscience.

Say: **As Jesus said, each of us has to count the cost in following Him. Are the trade-offs worth it? I think so.**

Encourage kids to make a decision to follow Christ wholeheartedly. Close in prayer, thanking God for all the benefits of following Christ.

WHY BE A CHRISTIAN?   REPRO RESOURCE 3

Survival Quest

You and your tour group were flying in a small airplane over the Sahara Desert when your engine caught fire. You made an emergency landing in the middle of nowhere. You see nothing but sand in every direction. According to the map, the nearest town is about 500 miles away. The temperature is 111 degrees. Once you land, you discover that fuel is leaking near the flames, and the plane will explode any second.

You have to act fast before the plane goes up in flames, so you grab an armload (five items) of supplies from the plane. All the passengers are OK, with only minor cuts and scrapes—except for one, who appears to have broken a leg.

What supplies would you take from the plane? Circle five items from the following list:

- a plastic raincoat
- a can of lighter fluid
- a map of the region
- a compass
- a vial of rattlesnake serum
- a flashlight
- a loaded handgun
- an empty plastic canteen
- a can labeled "Acme Desert Weasel Bait"
- a small hand mirror
- a book titled *Acme's 101 Ways to Prepare Desert Weasel*
- a bag with three oranges in it
- a jumbo bag of Fritos Corn Chips

AS A GROUP, PLAN WHAT YOU'LL DO NEXT.

NOTES

OPTIONS
SESSION TWO

STEP 1 (Extra Action)

Adapt the opening "survival quest" activity to use as a trading game for your group members. Before the session, you'll need to prepare several index cards, each with one of the supplies from the plane (in the story) written on it. If necessary, write each supply item on two or more cards. You'll need two cards per group member. As group members arrive, distribute the cards. Then read the scenario from Repro Resource 3. Have group members look at the supplies written on their cards and decide whether those supplies would be useful or not. If not, they should trade cards with others, trying to get two useful items. The catch to this activity is that some of the most useful items (like the plastic raincoat) are not obviously useful. So some group members may trade away useful items without realizing it. After a few minutes, reveal which items are useful. Follow up the activity with the comments at the end of the step.

STEP 4 (Extra Action)

Get kids actively involved in examining trade-offs with the following activity. Have the group brainstorm a list of the advantages of being a Christian and a list of the advantages of not being a Christian. Give everyone a slip of paper and a pencil. Have half of your group members write down one advantage of being a Christian and the other half write down one advantage of not being a Christian. When they are finished writing, give them five minutes for free-for-all trading. Instruct them to try to get the best advantage possible. Afterward, discuss some of the trades. Ask: **What did you trade? What did you get? Why did you make the trade?** You may find that the kids who wrote advantages of not being a Christian get stuck with them. Discuss why that happened.

STEP 1 (Small Group)

Help your group members get to know each other better by having them answer a series of questions about trade-offs. Have group members form a circle. One at a time, have each person answer this question: **What would you have to get in return to convince you to give up eating sweets for a month?** After everyone has answered, try another question. Here are some other questions you might use: **What would you have to get in return to convince you to give up television for a month? What would you have to get in return to convince you to give up your Saturday nights for a month?** Afterward, explain that in this session you will discuss some of the costs and benefits of being a Christian.

STEP 4 (Small Group)

Encourage group members to choose one thing they could give up to follow Jesus more wholeheartedly. Begin by having them list various things that they could give up. If they have trouble coming up with ideas, get them started with some of the following suggestions: give up sleep so they have more time for devotions; give up songs, television shows, or movies that aren't God-honoring; give up some of their relaxation time to help others; etc. When the list is finished, have group members choose one idea from the list to apply to their lives. Then ask each person to share what he or she chose. Wrap up the session by having group members pray for the people to their left. They may pray either aloud or silently—whichever they would be most comfortable with.

STEP 2 (Large Group)

If you have too many kids to do the plus/minus index cards, you'll need to modify the activity. Have group members form teams of five. Assign half of the teams to come up with as many advantages of being a Christian as they can; assign the other teams to come up with as many disadvantages of being a Christian as they can. After five minutes or so, have the teams share their ideas. Make a master list on the board, using plus and minus columns.

STEP 4 (Large Group)

Review the lists you made in Step 2 of the advantages and disadvantages of being a Christian. If there aren't many advantages on the list, supplement them with the suggestions in the guide (forgiveness, eternal life, peace, love and acceptance, and help with problems). Then have group members form teams of four or five. Give each team ten index cards. Instruct the teams to write down five advantages and five disadvantages (one per card). Then have the teams arrange the advantages and disadvantages in pairs according to which ones would be worthwhile trade-offs. (For instance, the "love and acceptance" of being a Christian would be worth giving up the luxury of "not having as many rules to live by" as a non-Christian.) After a few minutes, have each team share and explain some of its matches.

OPTIONS
SESSION TWO

HEARD IT ALL BEFORE

LITTLE BIBLE BACKGROUND

FELLOWSHIP & WORSHIP

STEP 2

There is a tendency among many Christians, at least in the United States, to emphasize the benefits of Christianity and say little about the costs. Your kids may have heard the benefits all of their lives. Before thinking about them more, they need to be challenged with the costs. After all, as Christians we're not called to an easy life. Have your group members come up with a list of reasons *not* to be Christians. Focusing only on the negative may shock them enough to get them thinking. You might even wait until Step 4 to introduce the advantages of being a Christian.

STEP 4

Help your group members apply the Bible teaching of Step 3 to their own situations. Have group members form teams. Instruct each team to rewrite the Bible passages using modern examples for junior high students. (They could make them into skits.) Have the teams concentrate on one of the following questions: **What are you willing to give up? Who are you willing to give up? How much are you willing to give up?** For example, in one rewrite, Jesus might tell a young person to give away his or her Nintendo. After a few minutes, have the teams share their rewrites (or perform their skits); then talk about what Jesus might give in return.

STEP 2

Non-Christians and even young Christians might have difficulty coming up with advantages of being a Christian. After they've brainstormed a list of the disadvantages of being a Christian, you might want to suggest some advantages, such as eternal life, the comfort of knowing that God is always with you, the knowledge that God will forgive you if you mess up, etc. Be honest about the costs (or disadvantages) of being a Christian, but try to get group members to see that the benefits outweigh the costs.

STEP 4

Expand the discussion in this section to challenge your group members' thinking, especially if you have non-Christians in your group. After each trade-off is made in the game, get kids to discuss whether or not they think the trade was worthwhile. Try to create an atmosphere in which kids feel safe to express their views, even if you disagree with them. Try not to attack or judge their answers, especially if they think that being a non-Christian is more advantageous. After discussing the trade-offs, you might have kids think about what's wrong with some of the "benefits" of being a non-Christian.

STEP 1

Begin the session with the following icebreaker. Have group members pair off. Instruct the members of each pair to sit on the floor back-to-back, knees bent, elbows linked. Then have them stand up together. (Make sure the pairs have room to move.) With a little give and take, they should master this activity. After they do, have them try it in groups of three, four, and so on, as you have time. You may want to follow it up by discussing the give and take necessary to accomplish the task.

STEP 4

After discussing the trade-offs, encourage group members to think about what things they might give up to help them become more wholeheartedly committed to Christ. Encourage them to think about different areas of their lives, such as their use of time, their bodies, friends, entertainment, thoughts, etc. Distribute slips of paper and pencils. Have each person write one thing he or she will do to be more committed. Wrap up the session with prayer for these commitments. You could have kids pray aloud with the whole group or have them pair up and pray for their partners. You may even just want to have a time of silent prayer. Close the prayer time by thanking God that the benefits of following Christ outweigh the costs.

OPTIONS
SESSION TWO

STEP 3
Instruct the teams to list the "costs" on the board as they work through their assigned passages. After the teams have reported, ask group members if they know of other "costs" involved in serving Christ. Have them add any they can think of to the list. Then ask: **When you consider the "costs" involved in following Christ, does your commitment become stronger? Why or why not?**

STEP 4
After playing "Let's Make a Trade," talk about the benefits of being a Christian. Ask group members to choose two benefits they would use in talking to a friend who is not a Christian. Have them explain why they would talk about those benefits.

STEP 1
As an alternative to the survival quest, have your group members "buy" a car. Bring in advertisements for four different kinds of cars: a basic economy car, a luxury sedan, a family car, and a sports car. (If you can't find the ads, you could make up your own, giving the make and model, the price, and the features that are included in the price.) Have your group members examine the ads and decide which is the best buy. (They could do this individually, in pairs, or in teams.) Then have them discuss their decisions: which they thought was the best deal and why. (There will certainly be some interesting arguing.) Next, discuss the decision-making process. What factors did they take into consideration? (It will probably have a lot to do with costs versus benefits.)

STEP 2
Before discussing the advantages and disadvantages of being a Christian, get your group members to think about the advantages and disadvantages of commitments in general. For example, you might ask: **What does it mean to belong to a sports team? What might you have to give up? What do you get in return?** You might also have group members consider the advantages and disadvantages of having a girlfriend, being in the youth group, and being part of a family. Afterward, talk about the advantages and disadvantages of being a Christian.

STEP 1
Begin the session by having group members play a game of crab soccer (or a similarly goofy game). To play, you'll need an open space and a beach ball. Have group members form two teams. Set up some chairs as goals. Explain that the players have to "walk" crab style—on their hands and feet with their backs toward the floor—during the game. (Watch out for rug burns!) Use the game to introduce a discussion of what it means to be committed to a team. Ask: **What do you give up when you're part of a team? What do you get in return?** Explain that this session will focus on the costs and benefits of a commitment to Christ.

STEP 4
In keeping with the idea of trade-offs, add this twist to serving refreshments. Arrange to have five different kinds of refreshments—perhaps a drink, cookies, brownies, popcorn, and cupcakes. Divide your group into five teams. Give one kind of refreshment to each team. Let each team divide its food among its members (for example, five bags of popcorn per person). Then have group members trade their goods to get things that they want.

OPTIONS
SESSION TWO

MEDIA

STEP 2
Before the session have different adults and kids tape-record statements that express the advantages or disadvantages of being a Christian. For example, someone might say, "Being a Christian is great because you know you'll go to heaven" or "Christians have to follow a bunch of rules." Try to get at least five statements of each type. During the session, play the tape for your group members. As you discuss the statements, ask group members how common they think these views are and to what extent they agree with the comments. Also, you might ask group members to add some statements of their own.

STEP 4
Play a popular song that disparages Christianity and praises an alternative way of living. After listening to the song, discuss it with questions like the following: **What negative things does the song say about being a Christian? What positive things does it say about not being a Christian? To what extent do you think the song is right? What is the song missing? What is the real trade-off?** If you can't think of a contemporary song, you might play "Only the Good Die Young" by Billy Joel. In the song, he makes fun of a Catholic girl for believing in heaven and for choosing to remain a virgin.

SHORT MEETING TIME

STEP 1
To save time, you may need to skip this step or condense it. You can do the latter by not breaking into teams. Instead, distribute "Survival Quest" (Repro Resource 3), have the kids read the situation, and give them a few minutes to circle five items on the list. Have several volunteers share the items they chose; then discuss as a group which of the choices were best and why.

STEP 4
Condense this step by eliminating the "Let's Make a Trade" game. Instead, have group members brainstorm a list of the benefits of being a Christian and a list of the benefits of not being a Christian. Discuss the two lists in terms of trade-offs. Have the kids pair off the benefits in terms of opposites. Which side cancels out the other? Encourage group members to see that we gain more in being Christians than we lose.

URBAN

STEP 1
As an alternative situation, have your group members imagine that they are on a subway car a mile underground when it suddenly veers off the main track and onto an old one that hasn't been used for sixty years. As the subway shudders on the uncharted, unused, and tattered tracks, the driver announces **"We're going to crash!" BOOM!** After the crash, the subway car is in total darkness—but at least everyone is safe. You are now four miles underground. No one knows where you are, including you. To add insult to injury, the radio is broken and it's 25° Fahrenheit outside the car. Almost all of the items on Repro Resource 3 are found on this car, with these substitutions:

- roach spray (instead of rattlesnake serum)
- a fifty-foot rope (instead of a can labeled "Acme Desert Weasel Bait")
- ten old, moldy blankets (instead of a book titled *Acme's 101 Ways to Prepare Desert Weasel*).

STEP 4
When city teens say the cost of being a Christian in the city can be high, it's true. The result can be death itself. Have each of your group members add up on a piece of paper the cost he or she is *willing* to pay for living a Christian lifestyle. Instruct group members to make four columns on the sheet, labeled as follows: (1) Emotional Cost—what will happen to my state of mind; (2) Social Cost—what will happen to my relationship with friends and family; (3) Physical Cost—what will happen to my body; (4) Spiritual Cost—what will happen to my soul. Then, under each category, group members should write a number from 1 to 10 (with 10 being the highest), indicating how far they are willing to go for Jesus in that area. When they're finished, have them add up their costs. Use the following table in grading the scores: 4-10—bankrupt; 11-20—more safe than sorry; 21-30—getting faithful; 31-40—high spiritual value.

OPTIONS
SESSION TWO

Step 3

With a combined group, you may want to make the following adjustments to this step. First, eliminate the part in which kids wave money, since it probably won't go over well with high schoolers. Second, if possible, divide the teams according to age. Assign John 15:18-21 to your high school students. Given their more developed analytical skills, they will be better equipped to handle the fairly difficult concepts in this passage.

Step 4

Continue with the "cost" theme developed in Step 3. Although the costs to junior highers and high schoolers are fairly similar, they may not seem that way to the kids. If possible, have group members form teams according to age (with high schoolers together and junior highers together). Instruct the teams to brainstorm some of the costs of being a Christian in junior high or in high school. Encourage them to think about areas of their lives such as dating, going to parties, being cool, and being up on certain movies or music. After the teams come up with costs, have them brainstorm benefits. Then have them choose a cost and a benefit from their lists and make up a slogan, showing how the benefit outweighs the cost. For example, "It's better to be a Christian geek in high school than a cool goat for eternity." After a few minutes, have the teams share their lists and slogans.

Step 2

Some sixth graders may have difficulty describing what they consider the positive or negative things about being a Christian. Instead of distributing index cards to individuals, give one card to a team of two or three kids. Ask the team members to work together to decide what information they want to write on their card in response to the "+" or "–" sign on it. Explain that the information they write will be anonymous; after they've written on the card, they can toss it into the circle without reading it aloud. After all the cards have been completed, read them to the group; then discuss them together.

Step 3

Read through the Bible passages together as a group instead of having your sixth graders work in teams. Write the conclusions about the costs involved on the board. After the three conclusions have been listed, have your group members use the money to vote on the "cost" of following Jesus.

Date Used:

Approx. Time

Step 1: *Survival Quest* _____
- ❏ Extra Action
- ❏ Small Group
- ❏ Fellowship & Worship
- ❏ Mostly Guys
- ❏ Extra Fun
- ❏ Short Meeting Time
- ❏ Urban

Things needed:

Step 2: *Plus and Minus* _____
- ❏ Large Group
- ❏ Heard It All Before
- ❏ Little Bible Background
- ❏ Mostly Guys
- ❏ Media
- ❏ Sixth Grade

Things needed:

Step 3: *The Price Is Right* _____
- ❏ Mostly Girls
- ❏ Combined Junior High/High School
- ❏ Sixth Grade

Things needed:

Step 4: *Let's Make a Trade* _____
- ❏ Extra Action
- ❏ Small Group
- ❏ Large Group
- ❏ Heard It All Before
- ❏ Little Bible Background
- ❏ Fellowship & Worship
- ❏ Mostly Girls
- ❏ Extra Fun
- ❏ Media
- ❏ Short Meeting Time
- ❏ Urban
- ❏ Combined Junior High/High School

Things needed:

SESSION 3
Accepted by God, Rejected by Others

YOUR GOALS FOR THIS SESSION:
Choose one or more

☐ To help group members realize commitment to Christ will sometimes mean that we act differently.

☐ To help group members understand which of their beliefs are important enough to risk rejection for.

☐ To help group members take risks for Jesus, knowing that He understands their rejection.

☐ Other:_____
_____

Your Bible Base:

Matthew 3:1-12
Luke 3:1-20; 6:22-23

ACCEPTED BY GOD, REJECTED BY OTHERS

Invasion

(Needed: Copies of Repro Resource 4, pencils, drawing paper, markers)

Before the session, cut apart several copies of "Aliens!" (Repro Resource 4). To begin the meeting, divide kids into five teams. (Teams may be as small as two people.) Then read aloud the following scenario.

Last night a huge spaceship landed in a field outside the city, and alien creatures stepped off. Our city has been overrun with these creatures. They're trying to blend in with humans in restaurants, stores, malls, and movie theaters. This is a total joke because they don't blend in at all! Not only do they look different, they act completely different. Your job, as members of the "Alien Descriptor Task Force," is to describe the aliens to everyone. Here are your assignments. Distribute one or two assignment slips to each team.

After about five minutes, have each team appoint a spokesperson to report its discoveries to the rest of the group.

After all teams have reported, ask: **Based on the descriptions we've just heard of these aliens, how do you think earthlings will react to them?**

Alien Behavior

(Needed: Costumes and props as needed for characters)

For this step, you'll need to collect some costumes and props to portray the following characters:
- Obnoxious Oliver/Olivia—the Christian who crams religion down everyone's throat. This character is totally obnoxious and rude.
- Bigoted Bob/Babs—the Christian who's convinced that he or she has the corner on God's truth, and everyone else is wrong. This character is intolerant, insensitive, and impatient.

- Authentic Andy/Amanda—the Christian who truly wants to live for Christ. This character accepts other people, but takes a stand on important issues.

If you don't want to play all three characters yourself, get some other people to help you. Use your imagination and creativity in portraying these characters. Bring in props such as a huge Bible or nerdy-looking clothes.

You could play Obnoxious Oliver/Olivia like the Church Lady from "Saturday Night Live." Bigoted Bob/Babs could be like a Christian Archie Bunker from "All in the Family." You could play Authentic Andy/Amanda like some of your kids who truly love the Lord. The subject matter is how each character lets other people know that he or she is a Christian, and how he or she acts around people who may not know the Lord.

To introduce the activity, say: **Did you know that the Bible describes Christians as aliens and strangers? We didn't land in a field in a spaceship, but as God's people we may not always fit in with everyone else. But you have to wonder if some Christians don't fit in because of their own doing, not because of Christ's.**

One at a time, introduce the three characters to your kids. If you're playing all three roles yourself, introduce yourself in character and launch into an award-winning monologue. Turn around to make the character switch. If other people are playing the parts, conduct an interview that would make Barbara Walters proud.

When you've finished, say: **Clap, whistle, and stomp your feet if you think Oliver/Olivia did the best job in letting people know he or she is a Christian.**

Give kids a chance to react.

Clap, whistle, and stomp your feet if you think Bob/Babs did the best job.

Give kids a chance to react.

Clap, whistle, and stomp your feet, if you think Andy/ Amanda did the best job.

Give kids a chance to react.

After declaring a winner, ask: **How do you think people would react to these three different characters and their messages about Christ?** Chances are people would totally ignore the obnoxious and bigoted characters; thus, ignoring their message. People would be more accepting of the authentic, sincere character, but they still might reject his or her message.

We can be as sincere and as nice as we possibly can, but people still might not accept us. Why might this be true? (Some people just may not believe in God or Jesus. Some people may feel that beliefs are personal and shouldn't be discussed with others. Some people may think you're trying to change them, and may resist. Some people don't like to hear that they're sinners and need a Savior.)

ACCEPTED BY GOD, REJECTED BY OTHERS

Alien Prophet

(Needed: Bibles, dried locusts and honey [optional])

[OPTION: Before this session, try to find some edible dried locusts. Check with a wildlife and nature center, a health food store, or the neighborhood entomologist. If you find some, bring them to the meeting, along with some honey. Dare kids to eat the locusts and honey. (If you can't find any, substitute something else crunchy, like pork rinds.)]

Ask: **What would you think of a Christian who ate locusts and honey, wore weird clothes, lived alone, and went around town shouting, "Repent!"** (You'd think he or she was crazy. You might make excuses for him or her, telling your non-Christian friends that not every Christian is like that. You might not want this person to come to your church or hang out with you.)

Does anyone know who I just described? Let's hope no one says the pastor of your church! Some of your kids may have figured out that you were describing John the Baptist.

Have kids reassemble into their teams from Step 1. Ask the first three teams to turn in their Bibles to Matthew 3:1-12. Ask the other two teams to look up Luke 3:1-20. Give each team paper and pencils. Instruct the teams to read their assigned passages. As they read, go to each team and assign it the following questions.

Team 1: What do you think John the Baptist looked like? Use your imagination. Remember, he'd lived alone in the wilderness for a while.

Team 2: What was John the Baptist's message? How do you think people reacted to the message and the messenger?

Team 3: Who rejected John the Baptist? Why?

Team 4: Who accepted John the Baptist and listened to his message? Why do you think these people accepted John?

Team 5: What happened to John?

These two passages tell the same story. The Matthew passage describes John the Baptist and states that that his "brood of vipers" comment was directed toward the religious leaders. The Luke passage gives us a clearer picture of his message and his interaction with the crowd.

After about five minutes, have each team go over its answers. Use the following information to supplement the teams' responses.

Team 1—John the Baptist's clothes were made from camel's hair, and he wore a leather belt around his waist. Since he lived in the desert,

John the Baptist probably had a permanent tan. His skin may have been as leathery as his belt. He probably had long, tangled hair, and really didn't care how he looked.

Team 2—John the Baptist's message was short and to the point: Repent for the kingdom of God is near. He also warned the religious leaders to "produce fruit in keeping with repentance" (Matthew 3:8). People probably were all across the board in their reactions to John the Baptist; their reactions depended on whether they accepted him or rejected him.

Team 3—The religious leaders and establishment rejected John the Baptist. These were the people who held a lot of power. They didn't think they needed to repent, because they followed the law.

Team 4—These were the average people who were in the crowd, such as the tax collectors (who, in Jesus' day, were considered to be among the lowest of the low) and the soldiers—people who didn't have a lot of power or prestige. Perhaps these people knew they needed to repent. They probably had been looking forward to the Messiah's coming and hoped John the Baptist would lead them to the Messiah.

Team 5—John the Baptist sharply criticized Herod and the evil the ruler had done. Herod had divorced his wife to marry his niece, who was already married to his brother. Sounds like an afternoon soap!

Ask if anyone knows the final outcome of John the Baptist's imprisonment. (He was beheaded.)

Wrap up this look at John the Baptist with the following questions.

Do you think John the Baptist did or said anything to create his own problems? (John the Baptist didn't exactly win friends and influence the powerful people by calling them a "brood of vipers" and demanding they produce fruit in keeping with repentance. He was blunt, condemning, and overwhelming. He didn't go out of his way to be nice to people.)

Why do you think John the Baptist was so radical? (He obviously was on a mission from God [that is, the prophet Isaiah told about his coming]. He wanted to be sure people would listen to and understand his message.)

Why do you think John the Baptist didn't care if the religious leaders accepted him? (He wasn't looking for acceptance, but repentance.)

The Bible doesn't really say if John the Baptist felt hurt when he was rejected. Maybe he did, maybe he didn't, but he kept on telling people to turn from their sins and follow God—even if it meant death.

To Die For

(Needed: Copies of Repro Resource 5, pencils)

Who would you die for? Stand up if you'd die for your parents. Pause after each of the following items to allow kids to respond.
Your brothers or sisters?
Your best friend?
Your pet? Kids may be as goofy or as serious as they wish.
Then say: **Let's get a little more serious. You don't have to answer this question aloud, but would you die for your faith in God?**

Pass out pencils and copies of "To Die For" (Repro Resource 5). Read the instructions at the top of the page together. Then give group members about five minutes to complete the sheet.

When everyone has finished, ask: **Did this help you decide which of your beliefs were the most important, to-die-for beliefs?** Call on several kids to tell which beliefs they felt were important, and which ones weren't all that important to them.

If something is important enough to die for, do you think it's worth a little rejection?

Pain of Rejection

(Needed: Bibles, blank paper, markers)

Just for fun, show how you would reject the person sitting next to you. If you need to get things going, suggest these ways: plug one's ears, turn one's back on the person, walk away, or stick one's nose up in the air.

Ask: **Have you ever been rejected or made fun of because of what you believe?** Ask for a few volunteers to share examples.

Then say: **In real life, rejection isn't funny. If we're serious about following Christ, some people might reject us. Believe it or not, Jesus says this kind of rejection is a good thing.**

Have group members look up Luke 6:22-23. Ask someone to read it aloud.

Then ask: **What's your first reaction to these verses?** Hand out blank paper and markers, and encourage kids to write down the first thing that pops into their heads. At the count of three, have everyone hold up his or her paper.

Say: **Read aloud some of the things other people have written down. Do you agree or disagree with their reactions?** Give kids a minute to express their opinions.

What do you think the word "blessed" means? Some of your kids might suggest the word "happiness." That's true, but the word has a deeper meaning than just happiness. Blessed means having a sense of well-being, because the person trusts God, not the circumstances, for his or her happiness.

Explain: **Everything Jesus described in these verses eventually happened to Him. Jesus understands all about the pain of rejection. That won't magically take away the pain, but you can tell Him exactly how you're feeling when people reject you for His sake.**

Ask kids to close their eyes so they can make a personal decision, without being influenced by anyone.

Say: **I'm going to read three statements. When you hear one that you want to try, raise your left hand. You don't have to choose any of them, but keep your eyes closed. Here are the statements:**
- **I'm willing to take more risks for Jesus.**
- **I'll try not to create my own problems by being an obnoxious Christian.**
- **I'm willing to take a stand on important issues and to back off when the issue isn't all that important.**

Close in prayer, thanking the Lord for understanding the pain of rejection, and asking for His help in taking a stand for Him.

WHY BE A CHRISTIAN? REPRO RESOURCE 4

ASSIGNMENT #1

- Draw a picture of how the aliens look.
- How many hands or feet do they have, if any? What about their facial characteristics?

ASSIGNMENT #2

- Act out the way the aliens greet people and each other.
- How do they say good-bye?
- Show how they communicate their affection for each other. (For instance, humans hold hands. What do the aliens do?)

ASSIGNMENT #3

- Do the aliens make any strange noises? If so, imitate the noises.
- Do they smell like anything in particular? If so, describe the smell.
- Act out a conversation between two aliens. How do they talk? Does anything move or make sounds besides their mouths (if they have mouths)?
- How do they sleep? Act out an alien bedtime scene.

ASSIGNMENT #4

- Show what happens when the aliens get angry.
- Show how they express happiness or excitement.
- Act out what they do when they think something is really funny or really sad.

ASSIGNMENT #5

- Draw or describe the foods aliens eat.
- Act out any habits the aliens have that might offend humans or make them uncomfortable, but not grossed-out or mad.

NOTES

WHY BE A CHRISTIAN? REPRO RESOURCE 5

TO DIE FOR

Read each of the following statements. Next to each one, place a check mark in the box that best describes your commitment to that belief. For numbers 9 and 10, write in two issues of your own that you feel strongly about.

a = I don't believe this at all.
b = I believe this is true, but wouldn't take any grief for it.
c = I'd stick with this if only people I didn't like made fun of me.
d = I'd stick with this even if all my friends made fun of me.
e = I'd stick with this even if it meant physical harm to me.
f = I'd stick with this even if it meant death.

	a	b	c	d	e	f
1. Jesus is God.						
2. Jesus is the only way to heaven.						
3. Premarital sex is wrong.						
4. Getting drunk is a sin.						
5. I'm a Christian.						
6. Abortion is murder.						
7. Not everyone will go to heaven.						
8. Satan is real.						
9.						
10.						

NOTES

OPTIONS
SESSION THREE

EXTRA ACTION

STEP 2
Rather than acting out the three types of Christians yourself, have your group members do it. Divide them into three teams and assign one of the characters to each team. Write the basic description of the character (from the session) on a sheet of paper for each team. Each team should choose someone to play its character then come up with a monologue or skit starring this person. (You may want to bring in a box of props for group members to use for their presentations.) After all of the teams have performed, ask group members to vote on their favorite performance. Then discuss the different approaches to sharing your faith, using the questions in the session.

STEP 3
Have group members form five teams. Distribute markers and poster board to each team. Instruct the teams to read their assigned passages and discuss the accompanying questions. (You might want to write the team questions on the board.) Then have each team draw a comic strip based on its passage. The strip should answer the team's question—what John the Baptist looked like, how people might have reacted to him, etc. When the teams are finished, have them display and explain their strips. Continue the discussion with the questions in the session.

SMALL GROUP

STEP 1
You will need to modify the "Invasion" game to fit your group's size. Have your group members work in pairs. Allow the pairs to choose among the assignments on Repro Resource 4. (Make sure each pair has a different assignment.)

STEP 3
If your group is small, you'll need to modify the Bible study activity to accommodate fewer than five teams. You could do this in one of three ways. (1) You could have group members work in pairs, dividing the verses and questions among the different pairs. (2) You could assign individuals to read the passages and answer the appropriate questions. (3) You could read and study the passages as a group. As an alternate way of studying the passage, you could provide poster board and markers and have group members make a mural of John's life as presented in these passages. The mural could contain various scenes, representing his appearance, his message, and how various people reacted to him.

LARGE GROUP

STEP 2
For a large group, you might choose one of the following ways to spice up the presentation of the three types of Christians. (1) Before the session, recruit six volunteers. Divide them into three pairs. Explain that the pairs will be role-playing interviews. Assign one person in each pair to play one of the characters described in the session (Obnoxious Oliver/Olivia, Bigoted Bob/Babs, Authentic Andy Amanda). The other person in each pair will play the interviewer. Instruct each pair to come up with a two-minute interview in which the character can show his or her personality. (2) Ask for four volunteers to roleplay a talk show. One person will play the host of the show; the other three will each play one of the characters described in the session. To begin the roleplay, the host should introduce each character and let each make a few remarks to reveal his or her personality. Then the host should introduce a general topic and ask the guests to comment on it. For instance, the host might ask, "What do you think about _____?" (It could be any controversial issue.) "What would you say to the president [or some other highly visible person] about this topic?"

STEP 5
To facilitate honest and open discussion, have group members form teams of three or four for the beginning activities in this step (discussing times in which they have been rejected; responding to Luke 6:22-23; and reading and discussing others' reaction to those verses). Reassemble the large group to discuss what *blessed* means.

55

OPTIONS
SESSION THREE

HEARD IT ALL BEFORE

STEP 3
It's probably quite easy for your young people to side with John the Baptist, the "rebel" outsider. It's also probably easy to overlook the fact that he condemned the religious establishment. Challenge your kids to think about ways in which they belong to the "religious establishment" of today. Also challenge them to think of what a modern-day John the Baptist might say. Then, after they've read the passages and briefly shared their comments, have group members form teams. Instruct the teams to make up their own versions of a modern-day prophet. The teams should emphasize the prophet's appearance and message, and the response of people in your church and/or youth group to this prophet. After a few minutes, have the teams share their ideas.

STEP 5
Expand the discussion of Luke 6:22-23, challenging group members to think about what it means if they aren't rejected for Christ's sake. Point out that part of the blessing of being persecuted is that it's a sign that we're truly following Christ and consequently receiving the same treatment He did. Ask: **If you haven't been rejected for your Christianity, what does that say about the quality of your commitment?** Help your group members see that following Christ requires more than *knowing* the right answers; it requires sharing (and living) those answers loud enough that we get flak for it. Encourage your group members to consider what stands they can take to risk rejection.

LITTLE BIBLE BACKGROUND

STEP 1
Throughout this session, you'll need to be aware of and sensitive to non-Christians in your group. Since the session focuses on the rejection that Christians sometimes experience, non-Christians may feel excluded. There are a few places to be extra careful. For example, avoid using "we" in a way that refers specifically to Christians in Step 2. Also, you might want to skip the question **Would you die for your faith in God?** in Step 4.

STEP 3
Use one or more of the following suggestions to broaden your kids' understanding of the Bible. Explain that John the Baptist was Jesus' cousin, that he prepared people for the arrival of the Messiah (Jesus), and that many of his disciples later became Jesus' disciples. You might also explain the reference to Isaiah in Matthew 3 and Luke 3. When a king was scheduled to travel through an area, he sent people ahead (forerunners) to repair the road (make it straight, level it, and fill in the potholes). You might also explain that although Matthew and Luke are recording the same events, they emphasize different parts of the story. This is due to the fact that they are addressing different audiences with different purposes.

FELLOWSHIP & WORSHIP

STEP 1
Instruct group members to close their eyes and imagine what kind of alien they would want to be if they could. Then distribute paper and pencils and have group members write a description or draw a picture of their "alien selves." After a few minutes, have them read their descriptions or exhibit their pictures. Encourage them to explain why they would want to be that kind of alien. Then have them imagine how people might respond to such a creature.

STEP 5
Many of the psalms express the pain of rejection as well as the comfort of God's presence and His faithfulness to His people. Wrap up the session with a worship service based on the psalms. If group members have favorite psalms that are appropriate for the topic, use them. Otherwise, you might use some of the following: Psalm 23, which describes how God protects us from enemies, or Psalms 31, 35, 56, or 57, in which the psalmist talks about being beset by enemies and asks for God's protection. You could have individuals read the psalms (or pertinent portions of them) or do some group readings. You might want to close the service with a gospel song or hymn like "What a Friend We Have in Jesus."

OPTIONS
SESSION THREE

MOSTLY GIRLS

STEP 3
As you discuss John the Baptist and his lack of concern about acceptance, ask your group members whether they think girls or guys find it easier not to care about what other people think. Then ask group members to share how much they are affected by what other people think. Ask: **If personal acceptance has a higher priority for you than it should, what can you do about it?**

STEP 5
The possibility of rejection can be a very sensitive issue. Discuss the difference between being rejected because of your personality or appearance and being rejected because of your faith and your commitment to God. Ask: **When is it difficult to tell why you're being rejected? What can a person do when he or she feels rejected?**

MOSTLY GUYS

STEP 1
Play a game of "keep away," pitting "aliens" against "earthlings." To determine which students are the aliens, choose a physical characteristic such as being left handed, having dark hair, or being shorter than five and a half feet. All those who have that characteristic are aliens. After the teams have played "keep away" (using a ball or any other soft, non-breakable object you have around) for a while, discuss the game. Talk about how the opposing teams treated each other; then compare it to the way people often treat others who are different from them.

STEP 5
As you discuss rejection, have your group members concentrate on areas of potential rejection, areas in which following Christ might mean failing to be an "all-American guy." To do this, have your group members come up with a composite description of an "all-American guy." List group members' suggestions on the board as they are given. (Or, if someone in the group has an artistic bent, have him draw a basic figure and add details to reflect the various characteristics.) If your group members need help in coming up with suggestions, prompt them to think about what they're supposed to be like when it comes to drinking (e.g., being able to "hold their liquor"), language, sex, sports, schoolwork, and so on. When they've finished the composite description, discuss how being a Christian might affect a person's ability to be an "all-American guy."

EXTRA FUN

STEP 1
Begin the session with a party-mix game. Distribute paper and pencils. Instruct group members to each write down the name of a famous person (actor, politician, athlete, etc.). Then have them imagine that they are the people whose names they wrote. They should imagine that they're at a large party in Beverly Hills. As the party progresses, the people gradually group together in different parts of the mansion. (You could designate certain parts of the room as areas of the mansion. One corner could be the pool, another corner could be the ballroom, etc.) Have group members begin mingling. Explain that within five minutes each person should hook up with a group of at least three other people that his or her person would be likely to hang out with. After five minutes, have the members of each group introduce themselves and explain why they're in that group and why they're not in other groups. Discuss how similarities and differences affect the groups we form.

STEP 5
Try a more creative and fun way to introduce discussion of the word "blessed." You'll need at least seven "letter cubes" (dice that have letters on them instead of numbers) for this activity. (These letter cubes could be found in a game like "Boggle.") Make sure each cube has one of the letters of the word "blessed" on it and that together the cubes can spell out the entire word. Have each group member take turns rolling the cubes, trying to spell out "blessed." The object of the game is to spell out the entire word using the least number of rolls.

OPTIONS
SESSION THREE

MEDIA

Step 1
Bring in and show some short video clips of aliens from various movies. (Make sure you've screened the clips beforehand.) Have group members try to guess the movies. Here are some possibilities:
- *Star Wars*
- *Close Encounters of the Third Kind*
- *E.T.*
- *The Day the Earth Stood Still*
- *The Thing*
- *V*
- Any of the *Star Trek* movies

Step 2
Before the session, get some volunteers (perhaps members of your group or some adult volunteers) to script and perform a monologue for each of the three Christian character types. You might have the volunteers develop monologues on a similar subject. For example, you could have them all address the topic of junior high kids listening to heavy metal music. Record or videotape these monologues; then play them back for your group members at the beginning of this step.

SHORT MEETING TIME

Step 1
Rather than taking the time to have teams brainstorm descriptions of the aliens, read aloud the following description and have group members respond to it. Explain: **The aliens have three arms and three legs. Each of their hands has ten fingers on it; each of their feet has ten toes on it. They communicate with sounds that resemble human sneezes. They sleep upside down. They greet each other by kissing, using one of the three mouths on their faces.** Ask group members how they think people would respond if they met one of these aliens and why.

Step 4
Skip the opening questions of this step. On the "To Die For" sheet, rather than having group members check one of the letters next to each statement, simply have them circle the belief statements that they would be willing to die for. After a minute or two, ask a couple of volunteers to share which statements they circled and why.

URBAN

Step 3
Use the following questions to help group members determine how people in an urban society today would perceive John the Baptist.

Team 1: What do you think John the Baptist would look like today? What kind of clothes would he wear? Where would he live? What would he smell like? How would he act?

Team 2: How would people in today's urban society react to John the Baptist's message?

Team 3: What kind of people today would reject John the Baptist?

Team 4: What kind of people today would accept John the Baptist's message with no problems?

Team 5: What would happen to John the Baptist in today's society?

Also, when the activity is completed, you might have group members list persons in their own cultural history and/or contemporary experience who have prepared a way for other great leaders.

Step 5
Most urban young people need no introduction to the rejection mentioned in Luke 6:22-23. Instead, they need to be inspired to help eliminate the rejection others face. Ask: **Do you know people who have been rejected and need someone to share their pain with them?** Have group members write down the names of the people they know who have been rejected because of race, a disability, his or her personality or appearance, etc. Then have them choose one person to encourage or comfort this week. Then, as a group, choose one person for whom you can all do something this week. As you wrap up the session, have someone read aloud Acts 4:32-37.

OPTIONS

SESSION THREE

STEP 1

Instead of the alien activity, which some high schoolers might find too childish, have group members think about cliques and the idea of "belonging" at their schools. Have group members form pairs. (Ideally the members of each pair should be from the same school.) Distribute poster board and markers to each pair. Instruct the members of each pair to draw a map or diagram of their school, showing where different groups of kids hang out. Encourage the pairs to consider several different types of groups (jocks, druggies, brains, nerds, socialites, etc.). Give the pairs a few minutes to work. As the pairs explain their drawings, discuss them. Ask: **How do these groups form? How do they view each other? Why don't the members of different groups fit in with each other?** Encourage group members to think about the relationship between differences and acceptance or rejection.

STEP 5

To more specifically focus your discussion on rejection, ask your junior highers: **Have you or any of your junior high friends ever been rejected by a high schooler? If so, what happened? How did you or your friend feel? How did you or your friend handle the situation?** Ask your high schoolers: **Have you or any of your high school friends ever rejected a junior higher? If so, what happened? Why did you or your friend do it? How did you or your friend feel about it afterward?**

STEP 3

Adapt the Bible study plan so that your sixth graders are focusing on just one short passage in their teams. Have group members form three teams. Assign each team to read Matthew 3:1-12 and answer one of the first three team questions. (Assign each team a specific question.) Give the teams a few minutes to work; then have them share their responses. When they're finished, go through questions four and five together as a group.

STEP 4

Ask your sixth graders to consider filling in additional items as they work on "To Die For" (Repro Resource 5). After the kids have completed the sheet, give them each two pieces of paper and a pencil. On one piece they should write one "to-die-for" belief. On the other piece they should write a belief that isn't such a high priority. Collect the papers and make a list of the "to-die-for" beliefs and the low-priority beliefs. Refer to these lists as you ask group members to discuss some reasons behind their decisions.

DATE USED:

Approx. Time

STEP 1: *Invasion* _____
❏ Small Group
❏ Little Bible Background
❏ Fellowship & Worship
❏ Mostly Guys
❏ Extra Fun
❏ Media
❏ Short Meeting Time
❏ Combined Junior High/High School
Things needed:

STEP 2: *Alien Behavior* _____
❏ Extra Action
❏ Large Group
❏ Media
Things needed:

STEP 3: *Alien Prophet* _____
❏ Extra Action
❏ Small Group
❏ Heard It All Before
❏ Little Bible Background
❏ Mostly Girls
❏ Urban
❏ Sixth Grade
Things needed:

STEP 4: *To Die For* _____
❏ Short Meeting Time
❏ Sixth Grade
Things needed:

STEP 5: *Pain of Rejection* _____
❏ Large Group
❏ Heard It All Before
❏ Fellowship & Worship
❏ Mostly Girls
❏ Mostly Guys
❏ Extra Fun
❏ Urban
❏ Combined Junior High/High School
Things needed:

SESSION 4

Blind Faith

YOUR GOALS FOR THIS SESSION:
Choose one or more

☐ To help group members discover what it means to have faith.

☐ To help group members acknowledge that while it's difficult to believe in things they can't see, they still can trust God.

☐ To help group members understand that their faith is in a trustworthy God.

☐ Other: _____
_____

Your Bible Base:

Hebrews 11

BLIND FAITH

STEP 1

Mousetrap

(Needed: Two mousetraps, one long pencil, one-dollar bill, a bag or box [optional])

This is an excellent opener, but it takes some preparation. Purchase two mousetraps. Rig one of them so it can't be set off. In other words, hook it in the loaded position, so it cannot be sprung. You can do this by bending the trigger wire and slipping it through the hole in the catch.

Test the trap several times to make sure you've done this right. If you're not absolutely positive about it, don't use this activity. Otherwise you might have to call Jenny's parents and explain, "Well, about your daughter's fingers..."

Try to make your adjustment to the one trap as unnoticeable as possible. (Don't have the trigger wire sticking out at a strange angle.) Hide both traps out in the hallway in a big bag or box. Don't let any of your group members know you have the traps.

To start the session, ask for two volunteers to participate in a demonstration of faith. Excuse yourself and step out into the hall. Make sure kids can hear you but not see you. Set the first trap (the non-rigged one). Act as if you're worried about getting hurt (you might!). You could let the trap snap once while setting it so your group members hear it.

Bring this trap back into the room, carrying it very carefully so that it won't go off prematurely. (This will create some tension.) Give a long pencil to the first volunteer and ask him or her to show the power of the trap by setting it off. Make sure you are holding the trap by the base to avoid any unplanned pain! Also make sure that the volunteer holds the pencil by the very end, and puts it in the trap without putting his or her fingers in as well. The trap should snap shut quickly and powerfully on the pencil.

Then tell the group that you're going to set the trap for the second volunteer. Take the first trap back into the hall and let it snap shut once so it sounds like you're having a hard time setting it. Then take the second trap (the rigged one) and slip a folded dollar bill onto its bait holder. Bring the second trap out just as carefully as the first—making it seem as though it could go off at any moment.

Tell the second volunteer: **If you can get this dollar, it's yours. Trust me; you won't get hurt.** If the volunteer is too reluctant, encourage the person by reassuring him or her that you can be trusted. If the volunteer still won't take the bait, select a new volunteer.

UNIT ONE

After the dollar is taken, expose the whole setup to your group members, explaining that they just saw faith in action.

Ask: **How much faith did** (name of the second volunteer) **have to have in me?**

Suppose you knew ahead of time that the trap was rigged. How much faith would you have had? A lot? A little? About the same? If some kids say they would have had a lot of faith, ask them what made them have so much faith.

Seeing Isn't Always Believing

(Needed: One piece of paper)

Stand up if you agree with this statement: Seeing is believing. Ask whoever stands why he or she agrees with this statement.

Is there ever a time when you don't have to see something to believe it?

Wad up a piece of paper and hold it up in the air. Ask: **If I let go of this paper, what will happen to it?** (It will fall to the ground.)

How do you know it will drop or fall? (Gravity will cause it to.)

Stand up if you've seen gravity before. Pay attention to which group members stand.

Now stand if you've never seen gravity. Again, pay attention to which group members stand.

Then explain: **None of us has ever seen gravity! It's an invisible magnetic force. We've all seen the effects of gravity, but no one's ever seen gravity itself.**

Drop the wad of paper. Then tear a small piece from the wad, lay it in the middle of your palm, and lift your hand to your mouth.

Ask: **What would happen to this piece of paper if I blow it?** The group comedian might say something like, "It'll burn up from your breath!" But most kids will probably point out that the paper will fly away.

Explain: **Just as with gravity, none of us has ever seen wind, but we've all seen the effects of wind.** Blow the piece of paper off your hand. **In a way, God is like this. None of us has seen God.**

Ask: **Is it easy or hard for you to have faith in a God you can't see? Why?**

BLIND FAITH

STEP 3

The Sure Thing

(Needed: Slips of paper, copies of Repro Resource 6, pencils, Bibles)

Distribute slips of paper and pencils to your group members. Explain: **We're going to play a game called "Dictionary." In this game, I choose a word, and you write a definition for that word. Once all the definitions have been collected, we'll read them aloud. Then you'll choose the one you think is the correct definition. The word I want you to define is "faith."**

As kids write down their definitions, you write one too, based on Hebrews 11:1. It might be a good idea to rephrase it in your own words, in case any of your group members have memorized the verse.

When kids have finished, collect the definitions and add yours to the pile. Have kids take turns choosing a definition and reading it aloud. After each one has been read, have group members vote on whether they think that particular definition is the right one. Keep track of the votes. Reread the definition that received the most votes.

If it's the definition from Hebrews 11:1, ask: **How many of you knew that definition was in the Bible? Listen to how God's Word defines or describes faith in Hebrews 11:1: "Now faith is being sure of what we hope for and certain of what we do not see."**

If it's not the statement from Hebrews 11:1, ask: **Why did you pick this definition?**

After a few kids explain their reasoning, say: **Listen to how the Bible describes faith in Hebrews 11:1: "Now faith is being sure of what we hope for and certain of what we do not see." It's a little weird to talk about being sure of things we can't see, but instead of going on and on, the author of Hebrews decided to describe real-life examples of people who were sure of what they hoped for and certain of what they couldn't see.**

Before the session, you'll need to cut apart copies of "Faith Hall of Fame" (Repro Resource 6). Have group members form teams of two or three. Distribute one or more slips to each team.

Explain: **You might recognize some of these Faith Hall of Fame inductees. Some of them are pretty famous. For your inductee, read the assigned passage from Hebrews 11 and his or her "stats." Then decide whether it was easy or hard for**

this person to have faith, and come up with one reason why this person should be honored in the Faith Hall of Fame.

Give the teams about ten minutes to work. Then ask each team the following questions as it makes its presentation.

What is the name of your inductee?
Tell us one significant stat about your inductee.
Was it easy or hard for this person to have faith?
Why should your inductee be honored?

Use the following information to supplement the teams' responses.

- Noah should be honored because he trusted God and did the right thing, even when everyone thought he was crazy. Noah was right in the end.
- Abraham should be honored because he trusted God even when God seemed to go against His word. Abraham had confidence in God's promise.
- Moses should be honored because he followed God's plan for His people, instead of having a cushy life in the palace of the pharaoh. He led all those people out of Egypt and parted the Red Sea—with God's help, of course.
- Joshua should be honored because he trusted God's plans for Jericho and destroyed the city.
- Rahab should be honored because she had faith to take the God of Israel at His word. She wanted to be identified with the one true God.
- Gideon should be honored because he trusted God in spite of his weaknesses and led a small army to a huge victory over the Midianites.

Ask: **What do these inductees have in common?** (They accomplished fantastic things for God. They trusted God even when they didn't know how things would turn out. They obeyed God.)

Say: **These people are like the superstars of the Bible. Everything turned out great for them; so does that mean faith makes everything turn out all right? Why or why not?** Point out that if you take Hebrews 11 at face value, it does appear that faith guarantees a happy ending—until you read verses 35-40.

Explain: **This might come as bad news for some of you, but trusting God doesn't guarantee that life is going to be great. Look at the list of unnamed people in Hebrews 11:35-40, who are also in the Faith Hall of Fame. What happened to some of them?** (They were tortured, imprisoned, stoned, sawed in two, killed by the sword, went about destitute, persecuted, and mistreated. They wandered in deserts, mountains, and caves.)

Then say: **There comes a point when someone says, "Based on what I know about God, I'm going to trust Him." All of these Faith Hall of Fame inductees got to that point, where they believed God, no matter what. He's the sure thing.**

BLIND FAITH

STEP 4

The Real Thing

(Needed: Chalkboard and chalk or newsprint and marker)

Do you think you might end up in the Faith Hall of Fame? Why or why not? Most of your kids probably will say no.

You could get the impression from Hebrews 11 that only the super-spiritual are honored for their faith. But did you know that this group includes a murderer (Moses)**, a cheat** (Jacob)**, a prostitute** (Rahab)**, and a coward** (Gideon)**?**

But all of these people got to the point where they believed God, no matter what. That's real faith in the sure thing—God Himself.

Ask two kids who like to perform for a crowd to help you out with two short improvisations.

Explain: **I'm going to give these two a scene to act out. When I say "stop," the rest of you will have a chance to give some advice and explain why they can trust God.**

To the actors, say: **For the first improv, talk about doubts you have about God. You wonder if God cares about you, and worry about bad things happening to you. Ready? Start talking.**

After about a minute, yell "stop." Then get the rest of the group members to call out answers and advice they might have. Use the following suggestions to supplement group members' ideas.
- It's OK to trust God even if you have doubts.
- Even if things are bad, God is in control.
- We should put our trust in God, not in circumstances and appearances.

If your group members get into these improvs, get two different kids to do the second one.

Say: **For the second improv, talk about wanting God to prove Himself in a big way. If God would do something spectacular, then you would have faith in Him. Ready? Start talking.**

Again, go for another minute, then yell "stop." Have group members call out answers and advice. Use the following suggestions to supplement group members' ideas.

UNIT ONE

- God doesn't need to prove Himself. After all, He is God.
- Bible people such as Joshua and Daniel did see some amazing things happen, but even they didn't know what the outcome would be. They obeyed God and trusted His plans.
- Many other people have trusted God even when things have gone from bad to worse.

Picture-Perfect Faith

(Needed: Instant camera, film, construction paper, poster board, glue, markers)

Say: **You don't have to be perfect to have faith, and your faith doesn't have to be perfect. The more you trust God, the more your faith grows. You see, God shows us enough about Himself in the Bible and in Jesus, who came to earth as a man, to let us know that He's in control and that He's trustworthy. We can trust God with the big picture.**

Take out an instant camera and start snapping pictures of your group members. You may want to have group members take pictures of each other, too.

Once all the pictures have been developed, explain what you're going to do with them. Say: **We're going to make a collage of our pictures. Mount your picture on a piece of construction paper and write a caption to describe faith in God. When you've finished, we'll glue the pictures on the poster board.** (Caution: Don't cut apart the instant pictures as the chemicals used to develop them are included in the picture and can be harmful.)

Encourage kids to be as creative as they want in designing the collage. If they'd like, kids can use a pencil to accent different features of their photos, or draw right on them. When the collage has been put together, ask kids to read and explain the captions. Remember to compliment their creativity.

Close this session in prayer, thanking God for being trustworthy.

Faith Hall of Fame

INDUCTEE: NOAH - Hebrews 11:7
Stats: Noah walked with God even when no one else did. He believed God would send a flood. He followed God's plans completely and built an ark even when everyone laughed at him.

Was it easy or hard for Noah to have faith? _____

Why should Noah be honored in the Faith Hall of Fame?
_____

INDUCTEE: ABRAHAM - Hebrews 11:8-12, 17-19
Stats: Abraham believed God's promise to make him a great nation. He packed his bags and family and headed out to an unknown destination. He trusted God's promise of a son even though it was beyond reason. He obeyed and trusted God even when God told him to give up his one and only son.

Was it easy or hard for Abraham to have faith? _____

Why should Abraham be honored in the Faith Hall of Fame?
_____

INDUCTEE: MOSES - Hebrews 11:23-29
Stats: Moses chose to identify with God's people even though he had it made in Pharaoh's palace. He kept the Passover that God had commanded. He obeyed and trusted God to help him lead over two million people out of slavery in Egypt.

Was it easy or hard for Moses to have faith? _____

Why should Moses be honored in the Faith Hall of Fame?
_____

INDUCTEE: JOSHUA - Hebrews 11:30
Stats: Joshua trusted God even though the strategy to defeat Jericho sounded ridiculous. He obeyed God's command even though it made him and the people look foolish.

Was it easy or hard for Joshua to have faith? _____

Why should Joshua be honored in the Faith Hall of Fame?
_____

INDUCTEE: RAHAB - Hebrews 11:31
Stats: Rahab realized that the one true God was the God of Israel. She risked her life to hide the spies that came into Jericho. She trusted Joshua's God and was rescued while the rest of the city was conquered.

Was it easy or hard for Rahab to have faith? _____

Why should Rahab be honored in the Faith Hall of Fame?
_____

INDUCTEE: GIDEON - Hebrews 11:32-34
Stats: Gideon believed God's purpose for choosing him, even though he thought he was a nobody. He followed God's unusual battle plans and took risks for God because he knew God would be with him.

Was it easy or hard for Gideon to have faith? _____

Why should Gideon be honored in the Faith Hall of Fame?
_____

NOTES

OPTIONS
SESSION FOUR

EXTRA ACTION

STEP 3

Before the session, cut apart several copies of Repro Resource 6. Distribute the slips to your group members so that each person has several slips with the same character on them. (For instance, one person should have several slips that have "Noah" on them; another person should have several slips that have "Rahab" on them; etc.) The object of the game is for group members to trade slips with each other until they each have slips for all six characters on it. The first person to get all six slips is the winner. The catch is that group members won't know how many different slips they have to get. Don't tell them how many different characters they're looking for. Let them keep going until someone thinks he or she has all the slips. However, if a person comes to you with less than six different slips (thinking he or she has them all), he or she is out of the game. To make the game more interesting, you might cut up fewer slips of some characters, making those slips rarer and more valuable than the others.

STEP 5

Have group members form pairs. Instruct each pair to come up with a situation in which someone might need to exercise his or her faith in God or a situation in which that faith might be tested. Then instruct the pairs to think of ways to pantomime their situation to the rest of the group. After a few minutes, have the pairs act out their situations one at a time, while the rest of the group tries to guess the situations. Afterward, discuss how people could strengthen their trust in God in each of the situations.

SMALL GROUP

STEP 4

With a small group, you can handle the discussion of doubts in one of several ways. One is to have your group members make a list of the doubts that people might have about trusting God. After group members have suggested several doubts for the list, discuss as a group ways of responding to the doubts. If possible, try to counter each doubt with a biblical truth. (You can use the same method for discussing ways that we often want God to prove Himself to us. [For example: "If I get an 'A' on this test, then I'll know that God really cares about me."]) Another way to address the topic of doubts, especially if you sense that your group members are struggling with them, is to have each group member write a doubt on a slip of paper. Then collect the papers, read them aloud (keeping them anonymous), and let the group respond to them.

STEP 5

With a small group, you have the luxury of less-threatening surroundings for personal sharing. Take advantage of this fact as you wrap up the session. Explain to your group members that in the Old Testament, the people who trusted God often had their faith strengthened through experience. Recognizing God's work in their lives probably helped them have stronger faith later. Encourage your group members to strengthen their own and each other's faith by sharing experiences or evidence of God's work in their lives. Remind them that they don't have to have earth-shattering examples (like defeating an army with a few hundred men). You might get them started by sharing an experience or two of your own.

LARGE GROUP

STEP 4

Rather than having just two pairs of group members act out a scene, divide the group into teams. Instruct each team to make up a skit or conversation that addresses doubts about God or someone wishing that God would prove Himself in some way. The conversation should include at least one person expressing doubts and at least one person responding with biblical truth. Give the teams a few minutes to work; then have each team act out its conversation. After each team has performed its skit, have the rest of the group offer other suggestions about what to do in the situation. If you think the teams will have difficulty coming up with situations on their own, you may want to do some brainstorming as a group before dividing into teams.

STEP 5

You can make this activity more manageable for a large group. Bring in three instant cameras and assign three photographers to take pictures. Have group members form three teams. Assign a photographer and camera to each team. Also distribute construction paper, glue, and markers to each team. Instruct the photographers to take pictures of the members of their teams. When the pictures are developed, have the teams create collages with them. Team 1 should create a collage illustrating how to battle doubt. Team 2 should create a collage illustrating the fact that God is in control of everything. Team 3 should create a collage illustrating faith in God. Give the teams a few minutes to work; then have them share what they came up with.

OPTIONS
SESSION FOUR

HEARD IT ALL BEFORE

STEP 2
The gravity and wind illustrations may be old hat for kids who've "heard it all before." Instead of covering them one more time, have your group members consider how much faith (of all kinds) plays a part in life. Stimulate their thinking with the following question: **What would happen if you couldn't trust your doctor?** After group members have responded, ask the same question, substituting different people in their lives: cashiers, teachers, cafeteria workers, police officers, pastors, teammates, and so on. You might also point out that the business world depends on trust between people. For example, you couldn't order things by mail if the company didn't trust that you'd pay your bill.

STEP 4
Have group members form teams. Instruct each team to write a letter to "a wise person," expressing doubts about God (such as whether or not He really cares) or desires that God would prove Himself in some way. Encourage the team members to come up with doubts that are as realistic, persuasive, and tough to answer as possible. When everyone is finished, have each team trade letters with another team. The teams will then read the letters they've received and write a response. When they're finished, have the teams share the letters and responses.

LITTLE BIBLE BACKGROUND

STEP 3
To help your group members develop their knowledge of the Bible, provide them with the following Old Testament references for the faith heroes listed on Repro Resource 6.

- Noah—Genesis 6–9
- Abraham—Genesis 12:1–25:18
- Moses—the Books of Exodus, Leviticus, Numbers, and Deuteronomy
- Joshua—Numbers 13:1–14:38; Joshua 1:1–24:33
- Rahab—Joshua 2:1-24; 6:23-25
- Gideon—Judges 6–8

Have group members form teams of three or four. Assign each team one of the characters on Repro Resource 6. Instruct the teams to look up some of the accompanying references to supplement the "stats" of their assigned character on the sheet. With people like Noah, Gideon, and Rahab, the teams could read or skim the entire story; with people like Abraham, Moses, and Joshua, however, the teams should focus on one or two significant events (God's calling of Moses at the burning bush, for example). Encourage the teams to locate these significant events by using the subtitles in their Bibles. (Assist them if necessary.) Encourage the teams to summarize the stories as they present their characters to the group.

STEP 4
Kids with little Bible background may have no problem listing doubts about God, but they may have difficulty coming up with advice concerning those doubts. Consequently, they may not be able to improvise conversations. Instead, do this part as a group discussion. Have your group members brainstorm a list of doubts. (Be aware that some kids may be revealing their own doubts.) Discuss these doubts one by one, asking group members to offer advice and supplementing group members' suggestions with your own ideas. (You will probably need to carry the conversation in this activity.)

FELLOWSHIP & WORSHIP

STEP 1
Have group members form pairs. Instruct the members of each pair to come up with a list of as many things as they can think of that they've put their trust in since they woke up this morning. Encourage them to be as wacky, creative, and extreme as possible in their ideas. If they have trouble getting started, use some of the following suggestions.

- **When you brushed your teeth this morning, you put your trust in the fact that the toothpaste manufacturer didn't accidentally put drain cleaner in the toothpaste tube.**
- **When you got in the car to come to the meeting, you put your trust in the fact that no one had tampered with the car's brakes.**
- **When you walked outside, you put your trust in the fact that gravity wouldn't suddenly stop, sending you hurtling into space.**

The pair that comes up with the most ideas wins. Afterward, have the partners discuss why they trust some things without even thinking about them, but have difficulty trusting other things.

STEP 5
As you wrap up the session, point out that God has given us other Christians to help and encourage us in our faith. To remind group members of their responsibility to each other, create a collage of your own. While group members are working on their own collages, take a picture of each person and arrange the pictures so that group members look like they're posing for a group photo. (For fun, you might want to have your group members try to arrange themselves so that they look like the "group photo" in the collage.) Keep the collage displayed in your meeting area as a reminder of the help other Christians can offer when we struggle with our faith. Then close the session with prayer, praising God for giving us other Christians to help and encourage us.

OPTIONS
SESSION FOUR

STEP 4

It's usually easier to *talk* about faith in a group than it is to *practice* it when you're alone. Therefore, spend some time talking with your group members about "alone times." Ask: **If you are alone and worried about a major problem, which of the suggestions from these roleplays might help you? Why?** Encourage group members to write down and take home any pertinent ideas.

STEP 5

Your group members may prefer to write captions for another person's picture rather than for their own. Therefore, after you've given group members the pictures you took of them, have them trade pictures with one or two other people in the group. In writing captions for the pictures, suggest that group members use statements such as "Sally showed faith in God when she . . ."

STEP 1

Introduce the idea of trust with the following game. Before the session, prepare a stack of cards. Each card in the stack should say either "own color" or "other color." You'll also need a supply of white balloons, blue balloons, and toothpicks. To begin, clear an area in the room. Divide the balloons among group members so that there is an equal number of blue balloons and white balloons. Have each group member blow up his balloon and fasten it behind him by taping or tying it to his belt or belt loop. Then have each group member draw a card (keeping its message secret) and take a toothpick. The object is for group members to pop balloons of the color indicated by their cards. However, as group members are popping others' balloons, they must keep from getting their own balloons popped. The difficulty is that they don't know who to trust. The last person with an unpopped balloon wins. Afterward, discuss the difficulties of the game, especially of not knowing who to trust.

STEP 3

Instead of having them play "Dictionary," get your group members thinking about how faith relates to being a man. Point out that our society often emphasizes self-sufficiency, especially for guys. Men aren't supposed to need other people for help or support. Instead, they are supposed to be able to solve their own problems. Get group members thinking about these expectations by having them answer "does" or "doesn't" to the following questions: **(1) A real man does/doesn't ask for directions. (2) A real man does/doesn't depend on others to help him. (3) A real man does/doesn't admit that a problem could be bigger than he can handle.** Continue discussing other pressures on males to be self-reliant. Then explain that many men in the Bible were heroes of faith because they knew that real men trust God.

STEP 1

In your meeting area, create a maze or obstacle course of chairs. Have group members form pairs for a race. Explain that one member of each pair will be directing his or her partner (who will be blindfolded) through the maze. However, the person doing the guiding will not be able to talk to or touch his or her partner. Give the members of each pair a minute or two to come up with a series of nonverbal signals to indicate directions. (For instance, two hand claps might indicate "take two steps forward"; one foot stomp might indicate "turn right.") Then blindfold one person in each pair. When you say, **Go,** his or her partner will begin directing him or her through the obstacle course. (If possible, you might want to bring a stopwatch to time the pairs' efforts. You might even want to award prizes to the pair that completes the course in the shortest amount of time.) Afterward, discuss the importance of being able to trust your partner's guidance.

STEP 5

End the session on a fun note with another blindfold game. Have your group members form a loose circle with two people in the middle. The two in the middle should be blindfolded. Each should have a rattle. One of them will be the pursuer; the other will be the pursued. The object of the game for the pursuer is to capture (tag) the pursued. The object of the game for the pursued is to elude the pursuer. The rules of the game are simple. When one shakes his or her rattle, the other must rattle back immediately. (The players will use the rattle sounds to determine the location of each other.) The pursuer may only initiate the rattling five times. If he or she has not tagged the pursuer ten seconds after the fifth rattle, he or she loses. Let the group members on the sideline keep track of the number of rattles, make distracting comments, and move around to change the boundaries. Continue switching pairs until everyone has had a chance to play.

OPTIONS
SESSION FOUR

MEDIA

STEP 3

Have group members form teams of two or three. Assign one of the characters from "Faith Hall of Fame" (Repro Resource 6) to each team. Explain that you're going to make an audiotape or videotape for the Faith Hall of Fame display. Instruct the teams to think about what their character would say to junior high kids about faith. Have them write a 30-60-second statement, choose a team member to read it, and then record or videotape the statement. When everyone is finished, play the teams' tapes and discuss them as a group.

STEP 5

Instead of making a collage of instant-camera prints, bring a video camera and make a group faith video. Have each group member make up a personal description of faith, about 15-30 seconds long. Then record group members giving their descriptions. Not only can you use the tape in this session, you can play it for your group periodically over the next few months and years to see if group members' opinions have changed.

SHORT MEETING TIME

STEP 1

If you're short on time, you can skip this step or try a simpler and quicker alternative. Ask for three volunteers. Instruct one of them to fall backward, keeping his or her eyes closed and remaining stiff as a board. Instruct the other two to catch the person. Afterward, discuss how trusting the first volunteer was. Did he or she flinch, bend, or try to catch himself or herself at the last minute? Then discuss what kinds of things determine how much faith you have in the people catching you (e.g., how strong they are, how dependable they are, etc.).

STEP 5

If you don't have time to take pictures of your group members and make a group collage, try creating a group autograph sheet instead. You'll need a large sheet of poster board and several different-colored markers. Instruct each group member to write on the poster board his or her personal definition or description of faith and then sign his or her name. Afterward, go through the definitions and descriptions, asking group members to comment on or clarify what they wrote.

URBAN

STEP 3

After discussing the "Faith Hall of Fame," inform your group members that they will be involved in the "First Annual Faith Academy Awards" in your church or community. Explain that your youth group will be awarding certificates to people who have exemplified godly faith and have modeled the Christian life for all urban teens. Give your group members a few minutes to brainstorm a list of people in the church or community to nominate for the awards. Point out that the process of election ought to use the same fourfold criteria your group members used in choosing "Faith Hall of Fame" inductees. Discuss the list of names your group members come up with. Then narrow your choices down to the specified number of awards you want to present. You might want to consider making these award presentations publicly by inviting the recipients to your next youth group meeting (or church service). You might even consider listing the recipients' names in the local community newspaper.

STEP 4

With an urban group, you might want to consider using the following two improvisational situations.

- **For the first improv, talk about how faith in God's power and individual action can help a "crack head"** (drug addict) **get away from drugs and into treatment to get his or her life in order.**

- **For the second improv, talk about why some Christians are very poor and others are very rich.** In their discussion, instruct the volunteers to address this question: "Is it because the rich Christians pray more and the poor ones have a lack of faith, or is there another reason?"

OPTIONS
SESSION FOUR

STEP 2

The illustrations of gravity and the wind may seem easy (or overly familiar) to your high school students. So instead of using these illustrations, get group members thinking about the relationship between belief and sight by staging a debate on this proposition: "Seeing is believing." Have group members form two teams. One team will argue that the proposition is true; the other will argue that it's false. Give the teams a few minutes to come up with some arguments to support their positions. Then allow each team an opportunity to present its view. (A minute or two should suffice.) Give each team an opportunity to respond to its opponent. After some debate, help your group members see how this issue relates to belief in God. Point out that although we can't see God, we can see evidence of His existence and results of His activity.

STEP 5

Read the following list of situations in which a person might have difficulty trusting God. After you read each one, have group members call out whether the situation would probably affect a high schooler or a junior higher more, and why. Afterward, have your group members offer suggestions on how a person might increase his or her trust in God in each situation. If possible, have your junior highers offer suggestions for the high school situations and your high schoolers offer suggestions for the junior high situations. The situations are as follows:

- **Getting into a good college**
- **Going to school the day after you get a bad haircut**
- **Finding a summer job**
- **Finding a boyfriend or girlfriend**
- **Taking a test you're nervous about**
- **Telling your parents you flunked a class**
- **Not making a sports team/cheerleading squad**

STEP 3

Before your sixth graders work on "Faith Hall of Fame" (Repro Resource 6), have them form six teams. Give each team the name of one of the Faith Hall of Fame inductees. Instruct each team to tell the story of its inductee to the rest of the group. In its story, however, each team should include one piece of misinformation. After each story is told, have the rest of the group members try to identify what is true and what is not true about the inductee's experiences.

STEP 5

As your sixth graders are writing captions for their pictures, talk about the things we do to show our faith in God. Ask: **In what way is reading the Bible and praying demonstrating faith? What about things like showing respect for teachers and parents?**

DATE USED:

Approx. Time

STEP 1: *Mousetrap* _____
❏ Fellowship & Worship
❏ Mostly Guys
❏ Extra Fun
❏ Short Meeting Time
Things needed:

STEP 2: *Seeing Isn't Always Believing* _____
❏ Heard It All Before
❏ Combined Junior High/High School
Things needed:

STEP 3: *The Sure Thing* _____
❏ Extra Action
❏ Little Bible Background
❏ Mostly Guys
❏ Media
❏ Urban
❏ Sixth Grade
Things needed:

STEP 4: *The Real Thing* _____
❏ Small Group
❏ Large Group
❏ Heard It All Before
❏ Little Bible Background
❏ Mostly Girls
❏ Urban
Things needed:

STEP 5: *Picture-Perfect Faith* _____
❏ Extra Action
❏ Small Group
❏ Large Group
❏ Fellowship & Worship
❏ Mostly Girls
❏ Extra Fun
❏ Media
❏ Short Meeting Time
❏ Combined Junior High/High School
❏ Sixth Grade
Things needed:

SESSION 5

The Price Jesus Paid

YOUR GOALS FOR THIS SESSION:
Choose one or more

☐ To help group members realize the price Jesus paid for their sins.

☐ To help group members understand God's plan of salvation.

☐ To help group members respond to Christ by choosing to follow Him.

☐ Other: _____
_____

Your Bible Base:

John 18—19
Galatians 2:20

STEP 1

The Punishment Fits the Crime

(Needed: Two chairs, table, an adult volunteer, extra props [optional])

Open the session with a courtroom simulation designed to help group members understand what we mean when we say "Christ paid the penalty for our sin."

You can act out this simulation simply with two chairs and a table. But the more you can make your meeting place look like a courtroom, the better it will be. Some ideas for props include elevating the judge's desk and chair, giving the judge a gavel (or hammer) and a robe to wear, roping off a seating area as a jury box, and using a podium for a witness stand.

In addition to the props, you need to recruit someone to play the part of the judge. Ideally, this person should be another adult, but not one of your other leaders. You also could ask a high school student that your junior highers don't know very well. This person should have a little acting ability and a knack for improvising. Also, the simulation calls for the judge to be slapped, so your willing victim should agree to go along with this. *Don't* use one of your own junior highers.

You and your recruit should run through the simulation together, to get an idea of what will happen and what to say. You'll play the part of the bailiff.

One final preparation step is to think of a junior higher—someone who will be at the meeting—who can be the accused. Don't tell this person what you're up to; but make sure you choose someone who feels comfortable in front of the group and who can take a joke. It might be a good idea to choose a boy, because your group members might feel a bit more sympathetic toward a girl—and you *want* the group to reach a verdict of guilty.

As group members arrive for this session, direct them to sit in the "jury area." Explain to them that they will be the jury in a very serious criminal case.

Then announce: **All rise, this court is now in session. The honorable Judge _____ presiding.** The judge enters and takes his or her lofty seat. Then the group may be seated again.

You, the bailiff, read the charges: **The charges against the defendant are as follows: failure to clean his room, disobeying his parents, not paying attention in school, spending too much** money on junk, and resisting arrest. The name of the charged is _____.

Bring the accused to the witness stand. The judge will then list the charges again, giving more detail for each one. Here is where your judge can have some fun. He or she should embellish the charges, making them sound as if they were the most horrible crimes a person could commit. The judge should provide evidence, false as it may be, to prove that these charges are true.

When all the charges have been read, the judge instructs the jury (the rest of the group members) on the severity of the charges and urges them to make a decision that is fair and just.

As mentioned previously, you want the jury to reach a guilty verdict. Most junior highers will come to this conclusion very rapidly. If you think you might have a sympathetic jury on your hands, inform a couple of key kids beforehand to sway the group to a guilty verdict. After the verdict is reached, the jury reports to the judge who, in true courtroom manner, beats the gavel and pronounces the defendant guilty.

The judge should pause, look over some notes, and then give his or her decision on the penalty: **A verdict of guilty has been reached. The penalty for these crimes is a hard slap across the face. The sentence will be served now.**

As the bailiff, you should walk over to the defendant, ask him to stand, and in full view of the audience, wind up as if to slap him across the face. Just before you swing (the defendant probably will be ducking anyway), the judge should yell out: **Wait! It's true that this guy is guilty. It's also true that the punishment must be carried out. But because I care for him, I will take his punishment for him.**

The judge should descend from his or her chair, take off his or her robe, and solemnly walk over to you. In full view of the group, slap him or her across the face. The slap needs to be hard enough to surprise the group members, yet not hard enough to hurt the judge beyond a little stinging. Be sure to take off any rings, and be very careful to avoid the person's ears.

While it's tempting to alter this part of the simulation with a funny punishment, it is important that the punishment be something *none* of the kids in the group want. If the punishment is doing some crazy stunt, there would undoubtedly be some in the group who would wish they were up front getting the attention. Again, if the judge is played by a leader or a friend or peer of your group members, then some of the impact may be taken away—your group members might think it's funny.

Once the punishment has been administered, the judge should walk out of the room without saying a word. Quickly step forward and start discussing the simulation immediately.

Ask: **What are you thinking right now? Did the defendant deserve to get slapped? Why?**

Did the judge deserve to get slapped? Why or why not?

Why do you think the judge took the defendant's punishment for him?

Did anything bother you about the judge taking the punishment instead of the guilty person? (It didn't seem fair for the innocent person to be punished while the guilty person got off. Guilty people should pay some kind of price—that's how life works.)

Did this scene remind you of anything? Some of your kids may mention Jesus taking the punishment for our sin, which would be absolutely right.

Whipping Boy

There's a story about a prince who had a "whipping boy." Whenever the bratty prince did something wrong, his whipping boy would get whipped.

Suppose you had a grounding boy who got grounded each time you did something wrong. What do you think of the concept? It probably sounds like a great concept to your kids.

How do you think a person would end up as a whipping boy? (The person probably was forced into it, because he didn't have any rights or say in the matter. Or maybe the whipping boy was paying back some wrong *he* had done.)

In a way, Jesus was like the world's whipping boy, but there's a major difference. He *chose* to take the punishment for our sins because we were totally helpless to do anything about it ourselves.

UNIT ONE

STEP 3

No Pain, No Gain

(Needed: Bibles, copies of Repro Resource 7, pencils)

Have your group members turn to John 18 and 19. Say: **I know some of you have heard or read the story of Jesus' death before; but whether it's the hundredth time or the first time you've heard the story, pay attention to the details.**

Read aloud John 18:1-5, 12-13, 19-24, 28-40; 19:1-19, 28-30. It might be a good idea to put some lightly penciled check marks in your Bible ahead of time next to the verses you'll be reading, so you won't have to stop every few verses to check the references.

When you've finished reading, pass out copies of "Did You Know?" (Repro Resource 7) and pencils. Work through the sheet with your group, reading each statement and letting group members check the boxes. (Some of the items have been taken from the other Gospel accounts.) This should be a rather serious time as you help your group members focus on what Jesus did for them. Feel free to stop at any point and discuss questions they may have.

Then say: **Whoa! This is heavy stuff to think about. How do you feel about what Jesus suffered for us?**

Why do you think Jesus went through all this? Did He want to do this? Did He deserve to die? As kids talk about these questions, reassure them that Jesus wasn't a masochist (someone who enjoys pain), but His suffering had a purpose—to take away the sins of the world.

Say: **Jesus' pain was our gain. What were some of the things we gained? When you think of a gain, tell it to the person next to you; then the two of you should stand up and say the gain together.**

If you'd like, mention some of the following gains to different kids to get things started:
• Our sins are forgiven.
• We can have a right relationship with God.
• We can have eternal life.
• We become children of God.

Explain: **One thing we have to understand is that we're not forced to accept Jesus' payment for our sin. We have to make that choice ourselves.**

OPTIONS: LARGE GROUP, HEARD IT ALL BEFORE, LITTLE BIBLE BACKGROUND, MOSTLY GIRLS, SHORT MEETING TIME, URBAN, SIXTH GRADE

THE PRICE JESUS PAID

STEP 4

The Choice

(Needed: Bibles, index cards, pencils)

OPTIONS

You probably know your group members well enough to know who has and hasn't made a decision to accept the free gift of salvation offered to us by Jesus' death on the cross. If you think there are some kids who don't know the Lord, take some time to explain how they can become part of God's family. Here are some steps to help you.

- God wants everyone to enjoy the best life possible and experience His love (Jer. 31:3).
- But everyone has blown it in a big way—this is called sin and rebellion against God (Rom. 3:23).
- This would separate us from God forever—and we, the guilty ones, deserve to pay the penalty (Rom. 6:23).
- Only God could solve the problem, and He did. He sent His Son, Jesus, to die (John 3:16, 17; Rom. 5:8).
- But we're not forced to accept God's solution. We need to repent of our sins and personally commit ourselves to Him (Acts 20:21).
- We can have forgiveness. If a person receives Jesus as God's Son and believes that God raised Jesus from the dead, God has promised that person eternal life (John 1:12; Rom. 10:9; 1 John 5:11).

Distribute index cards. Have each person turn to Galatians 2:20 and write the verse on one side of the card. After your group members have finished copying the verse, discuss what it means. Then challenge kids to write a personal statement to God about following Him. Tell them you won't be collecting their responses; this is a matter between them and God.

Say: **Under the verse you just copied down, sign your name if you want the verse to be a true statement for you. Or just sign "Paul"—the writer of the verse—if you're not ready to make this kind of a commitment.**

By having all group members write something, no one should feel pressured to answer in a certain way. Have group members put their cards in their Bibles or pockets. *Don't* collect the cards.

Close your time in prayer, thanking Jesus for paying the price for our sin and making salvation possible.

Many junior highers think they need to accept God's forgiveness over and over again. You might want to have one or two adults ready to talk privately with anyone who wants to become a Christian or who has doubts about his or her commitment to Christ.

NOTES

WHY BE A CHRISTIAN?

REPRO RESOURCE
7a

Did You Know?

Check one of the boxes after each statement.

	I knew that.	I didn't know that.
1. Jesus was turned in by one of His close friends and disciples.		
2. All of Jesus' disciples deserted Him the night He was arrested.		
3. The guards blindfolded Jesus and punched Him.		
4. Jesus never said or did anything to defend Himself while the guards were beating Him.		
5. The guards made fun of Jesus and spit on Him.		
6. The religious leaders had Jesus beaten in their presence. One official hit Jesus in the face.		
7. Jesus was handed from one politician to another because they didn't want to deal with Him.		
8. His own people wanted Jesus killed and an accused murderer released from jail, rather than the other way around.		
9. Jesus was whipped (flogged). The whip probably had nine leather strands with bits of metal or bone embedded in the ends. The whip was flung onto the person's back—so that all the sharp objects stuck—and then pulled down to tear the skin and muscles off the back.		
10. A robe was stuck on Jesus' raw back to mock Him as a king.		

Check one of the boxes after each statement.

	I knew that.	I didn't know that.
11. The "crown of thorns" was most likely made of stiff, two- or three-inch thorns that stuck right into Jesus' head.		
12. Jesus was forced to carry His own cross. Crossbeams alone weighed forty pounds. The cross was made of very rough wood, and rested on Jesus' torn back as He carried it.		
13. Jesus had a big spike pounded through each wrist and one through both feet.		
14. The cross was lifted by soldiers and dropped into a hole in the ground, tearing Jesus' flesh around the spikes.		
15. Death on a cross occurs by suffocation—the victim can't breathe.		
16. Jesus had to hang His weight on the spikes in His wrists until He needed a breath. Then He'd push up on the spike in His feet, scraping His back against the wood, just to take a breath.		
17. The whole time Jesus hung on the cross people made fun of Him.		
18. Jesus may have been naked on the cross.		
19. Jesus could have said at any moment, "OK, that's enough." He could have chosen to stop what was happening to Him.		
20. The soldiers pierced Jesus' side with a spear after He was dead.		

OPTIONS
SESSION FIVE

STEP 1
Have group members form two teams for a competition. The competition could be any game in which individual team members have an opportunity to score a point for the team. A contest in which teams take turns shooting paper wads at a trash can would work well. The object of this activity for you, the leader, is to set up a situation in which one team member can win or lose the game for his or her team. For instance, when the last team member in line steps up to shoot, announce: **This final shot is worth ten points. If _____ hits it, his (or her) team wins!** Ideally the person will miss the shot. (If he or she hits it, continue the game until you have a "goat"—someone who loses the game for his or her team.) In setting up people to win or lose the game, make sure you select group members wisely. Don't choose someone who might be humiliated by the experience. After the "goat" has missed the shot, give his or her teammates an opportunity to come up with a suitable "punishment" for the person. (The punishment should be "wacky," but should not be embarrassing for the person.) Afterward, discuss whether the person deserved the punishment.

STEP 2
Instead of using the "whipping boy" analogy, bring in an inflatable "punching bag figure" (the kind that is weighted at the bottom so that it bounces back when it's hit). Say: **Imagine what it would be like to have a punching bag that took all of your punishments for you. For instance, rather than grounding you for getting home late, your parents would take out your punishment on the punching bag.** Have kids briefly discuss the benefits of such an arrangement. Then have volunteers demonstrate what kind of punishment the punching bag might receive for each of the following offenses: lying, cheating, shoplifting, assault, making fun of others, disobeying parents, etc.

STEP 1
If you don't have enough group members for the courtroom simulation, try the following sentence-completion activity. Instruct your group members to think about how they would complete this sentence: "The most difficult thing I'd do for my best friend is . . ." Give them a few minutes to think. You might stimulate their thinking with questions like these: **Would you stay home for him if he was grounded? Would you take her science test for her? Would you let a street gang beat you up instead of him? Would you let the dentist drill your teeth instead of hers?** After a few minutes, have each person complete the sentence. Then discuss the idea of sacrifice and of accepting pain for others.

STEP 4
If you are confident that all of your group members are Christians, have them share their personal testimonies. Doing so can help them reaffirm their commitment to Christ. If some of your group members aren't Christians, then ask for several volunteers to share their testimonies. Encourage them to emphasize how they became Christians, what things convinced them, and their reasons for choosing to accept salvation. If you haven't done so already, you might share your testimony with the group.

STEP 3
When you get to the discussion of the gains that we receive from Jesus' pain, have group members form several teams. Instruct each team to brainstorm a list of gains. After a few minutes, reassemble the group and have each team share its list. As the teams share, you (or a volunteer helper) should compile their lists on the board. After all the teams have shared, instruct each team to choose one of the ideas on the board and come up with a bumper sticker slogan expressing that idea. After a few minutes, have each team share its slogan. Then vote as a group on which slogan is best and award prizes to that team.

STEP 4
To review the salvation message, have group members form teams. Assign one or more of the references listed in Step 4 to each team. Provide the teams with poster board, old magazines, scissors, glue, and markers. Instruct each team to read its assigned passage and then make a poster that conveys the message of the passage. The teams may clip headlines and pictures from the magazines, add their own drawings, and/or write whatever they want. When the teams are finished, put the posters together in a display that presents an explanation of how to become part of God's family. Wrap up the meeting with the Galatians 2:20 activity in the session.

83

OPTIONS

SESSION FIVE

STEP 2

Kids who've "heard it all before" certainly know of Christ's death and what it means for us. But how would they explain it to their non-Christian friends—in terms that their friends could understand and relate to? Have group members form pairs. Instruct the members of each pair to come up with an analogy for Christ's work on the cross. For example, one pair might say that Christ's giving His life on the cross is like having someone else run your extra laps when you're late for practice. Encourage the pairs to put some thought into their analogies. After a few minutes, have each pair share what it came up with. Then, as a group, decide which analogies would be most helpful in sharing Christ with non-Christian friends.

STEP 3

Kids who've sat through several Good Friday and Easter services probably know many of the horrible details of Christ's physical pain on the cross. Briefly review these details, asking your group members to name the various abuses and physical agony that Jesus endured during His trial and crucifixion. Then discuss which of the abuses/pains may have been hardest for Him to endure. If no one mentions it, suggest the agony of being separated from God the Father. ("My God, my God, why have you forsaken me?" [Mark 15:34].)

STEP 3

Bring in a bag of objects to use in making the Scripture passage more concrete for your group members. Before reading the passage, hold up each object and then set it on a table where it will be visible during the reading. The objects should include the following: a piece of metal, broken glass (perhaps in a plastic bag), a robe, a whip, thorns, a nail or spike, a piece of rough wood, the word "traitor" written on an index card or piece of paper, a police badge or military insignia (either real or fake). After you display each item, encourage group members to pay attention to where the item is mentioned or referred to in the story. For some of the items, the references will be obvious; for others, group members may have to wait until they fill out Repro Resource 7 to figure them out.

STEP 4

Use this idea at the beginning of the step to reinforce the idea of choice. Bring in a bag of candy. Explain to the group that you have some candy for everyone. Don't show it to anyone. Pause for a moment, listening for group members to respond. (Perhaps one of them might say something like "Hand it over.") Give candy only to those who respond to your offer in some way. Afterward, explain what you did and then give candy to the rest of the group.

You may also want to spend extra time on the explanation of Jesus' gift of salvation. List the references on the board and have volunteers read them aloud. Discuss Jesus' gift and how we can accept it. When discussing Galatians 2:20, you may need to explain what it means to be crucified with Christ. Explain that it means putting to death our sinful nature and its desires. (See Rom. 6:5-10; 7:21-25; 8:1-11 for further insight.)

STEP 1

Help your group members get to know each other better by having them play a guessing game about their worst punishments. Distribute pencils and index cards. Have group members think of the worst (or toughest) punishments they ever received. On their cards, they should write a brief description of what they did and how they were punished. Make sure they don't let anyone else see their cards. Collect the cards in a hat or paper bag. Then pull out a card and read it. Have the rest of the group members try to guess who wrote it.

STEP 4

End the session with a prayer/worship time based on Repro Resource 7. Assign one (or more) of the facts on the sheet to each person in your group. Have each group member paraphrase his or her fact as part of a prayer. For example, the person assigned statement #1 might say, "Jesus, You allowed one of Your close friends to turn You in." The rest of the group will then finish the statement with this refrain: "To pay for my sins." After each person reads his or her statement, the rest of the group will respond. Close the prayer with a statement such as, "Thank You for the gift of salvation that You paid for with Your life."

OPTIONS
SESSION FIVE

MOSTLY GIRLS

STEP 3
After talking about our gain because of Jesus' pain, ask your group members to consider whether there was any gain on God's part. Ask: **What about the personal relationship God can now have with us because of His Son's death? Do you think God considers this a gain? Why or why not?**

STEP 4
Go through the steps of becoming part of God's family even if you know that all of your group members have already accepted Christ's gift of salvation. The more they understand about the steps involved in this personal decision, the easier it will be for them to share this information with their friends. You may even want to distribute index cards and pencils and have group members write down the six steps as well as the accompanying Bible verses.

MOSTLY GUYS

STEP 2
You can make the whipping boy analogy even more vivid and active with the following game. You will need a bag of candy and a pillow. Have group members pair off. Then have the partners play a game of "paper, rock, scissors." Explain that the winner in each pair will be the prince and the loser will be the whipping boy. Have each pair approach you. Pick a number between one and ten and have the prince try to guess it. If he guesses right (or within one), give him a piece of candy. (The whipping boy gets nothing.) If the prince guesses wrong, give the whipping boy a "whipping," using the pillow. After all the pairs have played, discuss the game's fairness. Ask if any of your group members would be a whipping boy voluntarily. Then explain how Jesus is like a voluntary whipping boy.

STEP 4
Focus your discussion on the Galatians 2:20 passage, especially the part that talks about Christ living in us now in the flesh. Have your group members consider what this means for the average junior high guy. As a group, brainstorm a list of ways that Christ, living in us, can change how we live. (Or you could have group members form teams and give them five minutes to brainstorm as many ideas as possible.) If your group members have trouble coming up with ideas, stimulate their thinking by mentioning different aspects of their lives, such as how they think about girls, what kind of language they use, how they treat their studies, how they treat their parents, how they spend their money, etc. After discussing these changes, encourage your group members to choose one way that they could change in order to strengthen their commitment to Christ, and commit to applying that change in their lives.

EXTRA FUN

STEP 1
Play "The Punishment Is Right." Before the session make a list of misdeeds (not cleaning your room, hitting your little brother, talking back to your parents, taking money from your mom's purse, etc.). Assign a punishment for each, such as being grounded for two weeks, doing extra chores, getting spanked, etc. To play the game, bring a contestant to the front of the room, read a misdeed, and have him or her guess the punishment. If the person guesses an equal or less-severe punishment, he or she gets a prize (perhaps some candy). Let the group decide whether the contestants' guesses are equal to or less severe than the "official" punishment. For example, the group can decide if it's worse to lose television privileges for a week or to be grounded on Saturday night. After the game, discuss punishments, misdeeds, and fairness.

STEP 4
Use this idea to reinforce the idea that pain can lead to gain. Have the kids sing (or do some other difficult or embarrassing thing) in order to get refreshments. You can do this in one of a couple ways. (1) You could have group members choose a "pain" for each individual—singing the first bars of the "Star Spangled Banner," doing twenty pushups, making animal noises, etc. (2) You could have everybody sing a solo or duet (with the group humming the accompaniment tune). As a twist, if you have someone who really, really doesn't want to participate, ask for a volunteer to perform in his or her place.

OPTIONS
SESSION FIVE

STEP 1

Use the following activity to get group members thinking about crimes and punishments. Bring in several copies of some local newspapers (or at least the sections that give the crime and court reports). Instruct each group member to find at least one example of an accused criminal being sentenced for a crime. (If you have a large group, you may want to divide into teams instead of having kids work individually.) After a few minutes, have each group member explain what the criminal did and what sentence he or she received. Then have group members discuss whether they think the punishment fit the crime and why.

STEP 4

Help your group members get a clearer understanding of the message of salvation by presenting it in the form of infomercials. You will need to supply them with video cameras or tape recorders. On the board, list the references for each point in the salvation message. Have group members form teams. Assign each team one or more of the passages. Instruct each team to read its passage and come up with a way to express its message in the form of an infomercial (about one minute long). Give the teams a few minutes to work. When everyone is finished, have the teams present their infomercials in the order of the salvation message.

STEP 1

Instead of using the courtroom simulation, briefly discuss the idea of crime and punishment. Try one of the following ideas. (1) If there is a well-publicized crime and sentencing in the news in your area, discuss it, focusing especially on whether or not the punishment fits the crime. (2) Ask a couple of volunteers to describe a time when they got in trouble and explain how they were punished. Discuss whether or not they deserved the punishment and if it was fair. (3) Have group members imagine that one of their friends at school got caught cheating, but that *they* got the punishment instead of the friend. Would that be fair? What if they volunteered to receive the punishment?

STEP 3

You can simplify and shorten this step with one or more of the following suggestions. (1) Write the references on the board and let your group members read them on their own. (2) Give your group members a few minutes to fill out Repro Resource 7 on their own. Then have several volunteers share something new they learned. (3) Rather than having pairs stand up and shout the gains they think of, have group members call out their suggestions individually. List the suggestions on the board as they are named.

STEP 2

You might want to use the "whipping boy" analogy to make a statement about people that teens take advantage of. Misusing power and position at the expense of someone else is common among urban relationships. It seems that in almost every group of teens, someone usually ends up as a "whipping boy," the unpopular underdog that others tease and abuse. Have your group members think about the people they use as "whipping boys" and challenge them to "release" these people from this torture. You may want to go even deeper with this activity. The people who abuse their power in relationships are often those who have been abused themselves through power relationships (physical and verbal abuse, rape, incest, parental intimidation). If you think the time is right, distribute paper and pencils and have group members write down how they feel they've been abused by others. Instruct those who want to be freed as someone else's "whipping boy" to write "WB" along with their initials in the upper left corner of the paper. Then have group members fold their papers. As you collect them, assure group members that you will not read any of them unless "WB" is written in the corner.

STEP 3

Illustrate the totality of Jesus' pain. Write the following headings on the board: "Personal Life," "Family," "Community," "City," "Nation," and "World." Have group members come up with a list of the sins committed in each of these areas. After you've got several long lists of sins, point out that each one of these sins contributed to Jesus' pain on the cross. Jesus felt all this pain on the cross at one moment. That's pain!

OPTIONS
SESSION FIVE

STEP 1
If you decide not to do the courtroom simulation, introduce the idea of punishment by having group members discuss what punishments are appropriate for certain offenses. In particular, try to get them to discuss what punishments are appropriate for junior highers and what punishments are appropriate for high schoolers. You may spark a lively debate. You might also get group members talking about the different things they get in trouble for—using the car without permission, staying out too late, not doing homework, etc. Ask them whether their offenses deserve punishment. Use this discussion to introduce the topics of fairness, innocent suffering, and suffering for someone else.

STEP 4
If you are convinced that most of your group members are Christians, then concentrate on the Galatians 2:20 passage, especially the idea of Jesus living in us. Ask your group members to imagine these two situations: Jesus goes to junior high and Jesus goes to high school. Focus on the different aspects of your group members' lives by having them consider how Jesus would act on a date, as a member of a sports team, in math class, behind the wheel, etc. In what ways would He act the same as most kids? In what ways would He act differently? Why? (If your group is creative, instead of a discussion you could have them make up several skits—Jesus at the prom, Jesus in the junior high cafeteria, etc.) After discussing how Jesus might act, have group members think about areas in which they don't live as if Jesus is in them. Encourage them to think of a way to improve their commitment in those areas.

STEP 3
In talking about the gains we have because of Jesus' pain, ask your sixth graders to form teams of four. Give each team a large piece of paper and a marker. Have the team members decide together on a "gain" to write on the paper. After the teams are finished, have them display and explain their papers. You may want to tape the papers to the wall of your meeting area as a reminder to your group members of Jesus' pain and our gain.

STEP 4
Go through the steps of becoming part of God's family even if you know that all of your sixth graders have already accepted Christ's gift of salvation. The more they understand about the steps involved in this personal decision, the easier it will be for them to share this information with their friends. You may even want to distribute index cards and pencils and have group members write down the six steps as well as the accompanying Bible verses. If there's time, have your group members practice sharing the steps with each other.

DATE USED: Approx. Time

STEP 1: *The Punishment Fits the Crime*   _____
❑ Extra Action
❑ Small Group
❑ Fellowship & Worship
❑ Extra Fun
❑ Media
❑ Short Meeting Time
❑ Combined Junior High/High School
Things needed:

STEP 2: *Whipping Boy*   _____
❑ Extra Action
❑ Heard It All Before
❑ Mostly Guys
❑ Urban
Things needed:

STEP 3: *No Pain, No Gain*   _____
❑ Large Group
❑ Heard It All Before
❑ Little Bible Background
❑ Mostly Girls
❑ Short Meeting Time
❑ Urban
❑ Sixth Grade
Things needed:

STEP 4: *The Choice*   _____
❑ Small Group
❑ Large Group
❑ Little Bible Background
❑ Fellowship & Worship
❑ Mostly Girls
❑ Mostly Guys
❑ Extra Fun
❑ Media
❑ Combined Junior High/High School
❑ Sixth Grade
Things needed:

NOTES

Unit Two: Face to Face with Jesus

Talking to Junior Highers about the Real Jesus

by Paul Borthwick

As youth workers, one of our goals (whether we've articulated it or not) is to combat "dead" religion. We want to teach a faith that is practical, relevant, and life changing. In other words, we want group members to leave our ministries with a sense of the realness of the Christian faith. This is why it is so important to dedicate the weeks ahead to the study of the *real* Jesus.

What does Jesus of Nazareth have to do with junior highers of the twenty-first century? How does this historical figure of two thousand years ago affect a kid going through adolescent challenges and adjustments today?

Whether we acknowledge it or not, one of the questions that junior highers bring to our Sunday school sessions and our youth group meetings is "What difference does Jesus make to *me* and *my* world?"

These studies are designed to help group members see that Jesus is someone who identifies with them in their daily struggles and temptations. As you lead these sessions, however, it is important to keep several issues in mind.

Don't Assume Your Kids Know Much about Jesus

Surveys reveal that many of our young people are quite illiterate with respect to the Bible and Christian history. Many do not know if Jesus lived five hundred years ago or two thousand years ago. Some think that Abraham and Moses were some of the twelve disciples. Was it Jesus who built that ark? How did Jesus kill Goliath?

To find out what group members believe, start by asking questions about Jesus. Their answers may reveal a lack of understanding about basic Christian facts. Responses may indicate certain stereotypes about Jesus' character and piety. Some will think of Jesus as an ethereal spirit-being who knew little about human living. Others may indicate that they wonder if Jesus ever really lived. A few may think He was a religious wimp.

Even if group members know the facts, ask some more questions about the qualities of Jesus. Perhaps the topics in this series can provide the basis for these questions. You may find that your group members do not associate Jesus with courage—after all, some of the pictures of Him seem to indicate a pale, weak individual. Jesus and humor? If He was God, He never laughed, right? What about love? If He never married, how could He know love?

Investigating group members' opinions or thoughts about Jesus will show you the challenges you face as you start this series.

Make Sure You Believe That Jesus Is Relevant Today

Junior highers come with built-in "hypocrisy detectors." They can observe their leaders and discern the difference between the people who know the facts and the people who *apply* the facts to their lives.

As a result, the issues of this series should cause us to ask, "Do I know the real Jesus in my own life? Do I know the Jesus who feels my pain, loves me in my weaknesses, inspires me to courage? Before I try to assure group members of Jesus' love and forgiveness, am I sure of it in my own life?"

Perhaps we should review the topics ahead of time and pray, "Lord Jesus, help me to know You better through this series." As leaders, we need to be walking in the direction we are instructing our group members to walk.

Present the Real Jesus, Not a "Problem Free" Jesus

The temptation we all face is to promise that following Jesus will come without cost or inconvenience. In our efforts to relate Jesus' life to our lives, we might be tempted to make the Christian life seem easier than it is.

In the weeks that follow, you will be faced with keeping two truths in balance. On one hand, understanding Jesus' love or friendship will cause you to encourage group members to follow Him with an increased sense that "Christian faith will work for you."

On the other hand, you want to remind group members that we follow Jesus because He is the truth—not just because "it works."

To achieve this balance, focus on the life of Jesus. Walk group members through a passage like Philippians 2:5-11, in which we learn that Jesus made tough decisions—even though it meant short-term pain. Help group members understand that life is not easy for anybody—even Jesus. Show them that Jesus followed God not just because it worked in the short-run but because He was committed to the eternal truth. As a result, He sometimes chose the more difficult path, a fact that all of us will face as we follow Jesus.

Be Alert

In an effort to make Jesus real to your group members, you may find yourself prone to overstate certain truths or oversimplify the faith. Consider three possible temptations which you should be aware of as you enter into this study series.

Temptation #1: To present Jesus' humanity at the expense of His divinity. This problem has faced Christianity through the ages. We want so much to know that "Jesus knows our every weakness" that we forget He was the incarnate Son of God. In an effort to be assured that Jesus identifies with us in our hardships, we remember He was "tempted in every way, just as we are"; but we forget the rest—"yet was without sin" (Hebrews 4:15).

To maintain a balance here, incorporate worship into the sessions on the real Jesus. Remind group members that the Jesus they are learning about is also the Jesus they worship, pray to, and sing praises about. This real Jesus of the Scriptures is alive today and longs to empower us with the qualities of love, courage, and compassion that He exemplified through His life.

Temptation #2: To make Jesus a twentieth-century guy, rather than someone who lived 2,000 years ago. In an effort to make Jesus more real to junior highers, you may be tempted to put extra words in His mouth. But no matter how you present the *humor* of Jesus, for example, you must understand that He never would have been invited to do an HBO Comedy Special. And the way that Jesus expressed His feelings in the first century might not be the way that we express our feelings today.

A useful exercise here could involve asking group members questions like, "How do you think Jesus would have demonstrated courage in the world today?" or "In what ways might Jesus have demonstrated love in today's society?"

As we present the eternally relevant Jesus, we can present Him as a person who had all of the qualities descibed in the sessions that follow. But we should make it clear that these qualities were expressed in a way that would be understood in His times and in His culture—demonstrating to us that we must, in the same way, seek to express the qualities of Christ in ways understandable to our times and our culture.

Temptation #3: To present Jesus as being removed from the junior-high context. How do we present a Jesus for junior highers when we know so little about the junior-high Jesus? I have always wished that the Bible told us more about Jesus' adolescent years. What was He like at age thirteen? How did He meet the challenges of maturing? Luke 2:52 indicates the complete nature of His growth, but there is little else written about these years.

This biblical silence can lead us to present a Jesus who was a faithful adult, but who had little to say to junior highers. If junior highers are saying, "But what difference does this make to me?" we want to give them answers.

To do so, look at these sessions through the eyes of your group members. Before each session, ask the questions, "What would I like my group members to learn about this quality of Jesus?" and "How will this quality apply directly to their lives?" Asking such questions will enable you to present a Jesus that junior highers can identify with and follow.

Paul Borthwick is minister of missions at Grace Chapel in Lexington, Massachusetts. A former youth pastor and frequent speaker to youth workers, he is the author of several books, including Organizing Your Youth Ministry *(Zondervan).*

Publicity Clip Art

The images on these two pages are designed to help you promote this course within your church and community. Feel free to photocopy anything here and adapt it to fit your publicity needs. The stuff on this page could be used as a flier that you send or hand out to kids—or as a bulletin insert. The stuff on the next page could be used to add visual interest to newsletters, calendars, bulletin boards, or other promotions. Be creative and have fun!

Who Is Jesus?

Ever wonder what Jesus is really like?
Does He have a sense of humor?
How tough is He?
Does He really care about you?

We'll find answers to these and other questions in our new series called *Face to Face with Jesus*. You might be in for a surprise.

Who:

When:

Where:

Questions? Call:

Unit Two: Face to Face with Jesus

Why are these people smiling?
Come and find out for yourself!

What's so funny?
Come and see!

Join the adventure!

Be there—or else!

SESSION 1

Does He Feel the Way I Do?

YOUR GOALS FOR THIS SESSION:
Choose one or more

☐ To help kids see that Jesus has strong, human feelings, just as they do.

☐ To help kids understand that they can approach Jesus because He is a real person with warmth and emotion, not an unfeeling historical figure.

☐ To help kids identify feelings they and Jesus have had in common, and to encourage them to draw closer to Him as a result.

☐ Other:_____

Your Bible Base:

Matthew 23:13-17;
  26:36-46
John 13:33—14:4

STEP 1

Attack of the Androids

(Needed: Electric drill or mixer [optional]; prizes)

Start your meeting with an "android contest." Make sure kids understand that androids are futuristic machines that look human but don't have emotions (as in the *Terminator* movies and *Star Trek: The Next Generation*).

Give volunteers a chance to do their best android impressions in front of the group. Explain that you'll be awarding prizes for the most expressionless face and voice, and the most mechanical movements. To get things going, you may want to assign android contestants to describe your last social event or explain how to get the attention of the opposite sex.

For more fun, add sound effects. As each "android" moves, stand at the back of the room and briefly press the button on an electric drill or mixer to simulate the whine of the android's motors.

After applauding all your androids and awarding prizes, discuss:

What's the difference between an android and a real person? (Androids have no feelings; they don't get sick and don't need food; they don't move as smoothly as we do; they don't have souls; they aren't human.)

Would you want an android as your friend? As your mom or dad? As your son or daughter? Why or why not?

As needed, point out how hard it would be to have a relationship with someone who didn't have feelings—someone who didn't understand our emotions or didn't care for us.

UNIT TWO

STEP 2

The Messiah's Mask

(Needed: Copies of Repro Resource 1; scissors [optional]; tape)

Before the session, make enough copies of "The Mask" (Repro Resource 1) so that half your group members will have one. Cut out the holes for eyes, nose, and mouth—or bring scissors and let kids cut out the holes themselves.

At this point in the meeting, form pairs. Give one person in each pair a mask and a two-foot of yarn taped to the mask to loop around the back of his or her head and fasten the mask in place. Explain that the mask is supposed to represent Jesus, even though we don't know exactly what He looked like.

Then say: **For the next five minutes, those of you with masks are going to play the part of Jesus. Everything you say and do should be the kind of thing you think He'd say and do. You and your partner should make conversation about any subjects you like. Just remember to act like Jesus if you have the mask on; if you don't have a mask, treat your partner as if he or she were Jesus.**

Kids will probably be uncomfortable at first, and may have questions about what to do. But try not to give further guidance. Just watch what they do.

After about five minutes, have kids remove the masks and discuss the experience, using questions like these:

How did it feel to play the part of Jesus? Why?

How did it feel to pretend to talk with Jesus? Why?

In what ways did you change the way you usually act? Why?

For those who wore masks: **Did you show much emotion when you played the role of Jesus? If so, what feelings did you express? If not, why didn't you?**

For those who didn't wear masks: **How did "Jesus" seem to feel about you? Do you think the real Jesus feels that way? Why or why not?**

Chances are that those who played the part of Jesus tried not to laugh or show "negative" emotions or be undignified. Kids who didn't wear masks may have thought their partners were nice enough, but found it hard to relate to them.

Say something like: **You've probably heard that each of us needs a personal relationship with Jesus. But how do you have a relationship with someone who's so different from you? For instance, does Jesus have normal, human feelings like we do? Or is He like an android, perfect but without emotions? If He is, we'll never get very close to Him. So let's find out what He's really like.**

Heart in Emotion

(Needed: Bibles; pencils; copies of Repro Resource 2)

Distribute copies of "What Did He Do?" (Repro Resource 2). Give kids a few minutes to fill them out individually.

When time is up, reveal that "c" is the answer to every question. Then go over the quiz, asking kids to tell what they know about each of the incidents described. Share as much of the following information as you want to, following up with some of the questions provided. Unless you have extra time, avoid asking kids to look up and read the passages.

(1) Mark 11:15-18 tells how Jesus threw out the people who were turning His Father's house into "a den of robbers." The verses don't say "Jesus was angry," but He obviously was. His reaction was controlled, considering what He *could* have done.

Ask: **Does the idea of Jesus angrily knocking over tables and chasing crooks fit the way you usually think of Him? Why or why not?**

You may want to explain that Jesus' action here doesn't mean that we can go around trashing things we don't like. Unlike us, Jesus is over all human authorities because He is God's Son.

(2) John 11:35 ("Jesus wept") shows Jesus crying over the death of His friend Lazarus and the pain of His friends Mary and Martha. He cried enough that bystanders said, "See how he loved him!" (vs. 36).

Ask: **Do you think Jesus really understands when you feel like crying? Why or why not?**

(3) In Luke 10:21, Jesus is full of joy. So are His disciples, who have just returned from doing miracles in His name. They all feel great, and Jesus responds by praising God.

Ask: **Do you think of Jesus as a happy person? Do you think He's ever happy about you? Why or why not?**

UNIT TWO

(4) Jesus was angry with the Pharisees, who were more interested in their rules than in stopping a disabled man's suffering (Mark 3:1-5).

Ask: **Do you ever feel Jesus might be angry with you? If so, when?**

(5) Jesus was angry at the religious leaders, but had tender feelings toward their followers. He even compared Himself to a mother hen wanting to gather its babies to protect them (Matt. 23:37-39).

Ask: **Have you ever wanted to be close to someone, but found that that person didn't want to be close to you? How did you feel? Do you think Jesus ever feels that way about you?**

(6) Matthew 4:2 shows that Jesus felt hungry. He was God, but He was human, too. He didn't use His hunger as an excuse to give in to the devil's temptation (vss. 3-4), but His stomach really must have been growling.

Ask: **If Jesus understands what it's like to feel hungry, what other feelings might He understand, too?** (Probably other appetites—thirst, the need to be touched, sexual feelings, wanting to be loved, etc.)

(7) Jesus was "in anguish" (intense pain, sorrow, or distress) and sweating heavily as He prayed in the garden of Gethsemane the night before His arrest (Luke 22:39-46). His prayers included "loud cries and tears" (Heb. 5:7). He was willing to do what God wanted, but knew it was going to be incredibly painful.

Ask: **If you were going through a hard time, would you rather be comforted by someone who had suffered, or someone who had never felt real pain? Which kind of person do you think Jesus is?**

(8) Jesus felt deserted when He was dying on the cross (Matthew 27:32-50). His disciples had run away. His heavenly Father seemed to have turned His back. Shortly before Jesus died, things got so bad that He cried out, "My God, my God, why have you forsaken me?" (vs. 46).

Ask: **Do you think this was the first time Jesus had felt lonely? Why or why not?** (He probably had felt lonely many times—growing up and being "different," being tempted in the desert, being misunderstood by friends and family, etc.)

After discussing the quiz, try the following exercise. Have volunteers read aloud each of the following passages—first without emotion, then with emotions that seem to fit the words:

- Matthew 23:13-17 (Jesus' anger at the Pharisees);
- Matthew 26:36-46 (sadness, loneliness, and pain in Gethsemane);
- John 13:33–14:4 (tenderness toward the disciples).

Then ask: **What does this tell you about Jesus' feelings?** (They must have been strong and real, because what Jesus said doesn't make much sense when you say it without emotion.)

Stop the Action!

Have kids pair up as they did in Step 2. Explain that you're going to describe a situation and that all pairs will act it out until you say, "Stop!" Then read the following:

Your brother or sister has been driving you crazy for a week. Your mom has warned both of you that if she catches you fighting again, you'll both be grounded. Sure enough, your brother or sister tries to start another fight by coming into your room and dropping chocolate chips into your aquarium. Act out what happens.

After about 20 seconds, say, **Stop!** Then discuss:

How does the person you're playing feel right now?
Do you think Jesus ever felt that way? Why or why not?
How do you think He feels about you when you feel that way?

You may want to point out that Jesus grew up with brothers who didn't believe in Him (John 7:5). He knew what it was like to be picked on and treated unfairly, and He knew what it was like to be angry. But He never sinned. So, if He was angry at His brothers, He must have found ways to express it without fighting. When we feel angry, He knows how we feel—but He's probably displeased when we give in to the temptation to fight.

Here's another situation. You're supposed to have a really hard science test today. You and your friend have studied, but you just can't seem to memorize all those chemicals and stuff. The teacher walks into the classroom. Suddenly he announces that he's changed his mind—it's going to be an open-book test, and you can even take it home and work on it together! Act out what happens.

After about 10 seconds, say, **Stop!** Then discuss: **How does the person you're playing feel right now?**
Do you think Jesus ever felt that way? Why or why not?
What do you think Jesus wants you to do when you feel that way?

You may want to explain that Jesus knew what it was like to be happily surprised. When a Gentile soldier showed great faith that Jesus could heal his servant from a distance, Jesus was "astonished" (Matt. 8:10) and pleased. Jesus probably wants us to celebrate pleasant surprises and thank God for them.

UNIT TWO

Here's one more situation. You're baby-sitting your two-year-old cousin, who's really cute. The two of you are playing with blocks together. Your little cousin is trying hard to build a tall tower, but the blocks keep falling down. Act out what happens.

After about 15 seconds, say, **Stop!** Then discuss:

As the baby-sitter, how do you feel right now?

Do you think Jesus ever felt that way? Why or why not?

How might this situation be like your relationship with Jesus?

You might note that the baby-sitter probably feels a mix of emotions—tiredness over trying to teach the same thing again and again, but feelings of love for the child who's trying so hard. Jesus felt love for a rich man who was trying hard to keep all the commandments and who wanted to know how to have eternal life (Mark 10:21), even though the man wasn't willing to give up his money. It's good to know that Jesus feels love for us when we try to learn from Him and do His will, even when we fail.

To wrap up this step, ask: **If Jesus understands the way you feel and has feelings for you, how could it affect the way you talk to Him?** (You might be less formal, more honest, less scared and guilty about approaching Him, more open about the way you feel, etc.)

How could it affect the way you feel about obeying Him? (You might feel better about obeying a person who cares about you even when you fail.)

How could it affect the way you treat other people? (You might be more careful about others' feelings and more open about your own.)

Meltdown!

(Needed: Heart-shaped object frozen in ice; two buckets; cup; hot water)

Before the meeting, find a small, heart-shaped object (an empty picture frame, plastic locket or jewelry box, etc.). Freeze it in a block of ice. (Suspend it from a string in an empty milk carton; fill the carton with water; and freeze it). Or simply cover the object with ice cubes.

To wrap up the session, display your frozen heart shape in a bucket. Have another bucket filled with hot water nearby. Encourage kids to come by one at a time and pour a cupful of hot water on the block of ice.

As they do, say something like: **Maybe you came to this group thinking that Jesus is pretty cold-hearted—not the kind of person you could relate to. As you pour hot water on the ice, you'll be helping to thaw out the heart shape that's frozen inside. I hope the things we've talked about help to thaw out your image of Jesus, too.**

As long as the heart is surrounded by ice, you can't get to it. But the more you melt the ice, the closer you can get to the heart. It's the same way in your relationship with Jesus. The more you see that He's a real person with real feelings, the closer you can get to Him.

When the ice is finally melted, pass the heart shape around the group. Each person who touches the heart should name a feeling that he or she felt recently—and that Jesus has felt too. When the heart gets back to you, close in prayer.

NOTES

FACE TO FACE WITH JESUS REPRO RESOURCE 2

What Did He Do?

How did Jesus react in each of the following situations? Circle the letter that's next to each answer you choose.

1. When Jesus saw that merchants were buying, selling, and cheating in His Father's temple, He . . .
   (a) shrugged His shoulders and said, "What can I do?"
   (b) told them they would be judged in heaven for their actions.
   (c) knocked over tables and benches, chased out the merchants, and stopped anyone who tried to carry merchandise through the temple courts.
   (d) snapped His fingers and burned the merchants to a crisp with a bolt of lightning.

2. After Jesus' friend Lazarus died, Jesus . . .
   (a) said, "That's OK. I'll see him in heaven."
   (b) went to the funeral and comforted everyone with Scripture.
   (c) cried.
   (d) threatened to kill Himself.

3. When His followers returned happily from a successful assignment, Jesus . . .
   (a) said, "Wipe those smiles off your faces!"
   (b) said, "Be not joyful, for therein lies the sin of happiness."
   (c) was full of joy Himself.
   (d) went out drinking with them.

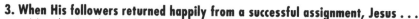

4. When some religious leaders didn't want Jesus to heal a man's deformed hand on the Sabbath, Jesus . . .
   (a) told the man to stop whining and use his other hand.
   (b) blessed the man and told him to "Come back tomorrow."
   (c) got angry and healed the hand anyway.
   (d) gave the religious leaders deformed feet.

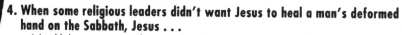

5. When He looked at Jerusalem, whose people had killed prophets His Father had sent, Jesus . . .
   (a) called down fire and brimstone, burning the city to the ground.
   (b) predicted the fall of the Jerusalem government.
   (c) longed to care for the people as tenderly as a hen protects its chicks, if only they would let Him.
   (d) felt nothing at all.

6. After going without food for forty days and forty nights in the desert, Jesus . . .
   (a) was ready for forty more.
   (b) did forty push-ups and forty jumping jacks.
   (c) was hungry.
   (d) grabbed a little boy's lunch of loaves and fish and ate it.

7. When Jesus faced being arrested and executed, He prayed . . .
   (a) "Thank You that I am about to be crucified."
   (b) peacefully and then "slumbered deeply."
   (c) with loud cries, tears, and sweat.
   (d) that the Roman soldiers would all be struck blind.

8. When Jesus hung on the cross, dying, He . . .
   (a) looked happily toward heaven.
   (b) never said a word.
   (c) cried out loudly, asking why God had abandoned Him.
   (d) spat on the people who were laughing at Him.

OPTIONS
SESSION ONE

STEP 1
Assign the "android" contestants situations that require movement or action: hitting a home run to win a World Series game, robbing a bank, doing a stand-up comedy routine, walking through a haunted house, etc. Emphasize that the contestants should remain as emotionless and mechanical as possible. Putting emotionless characters into emotionally charged situations should result in some funny presentations.

STEP 3
Designate each corner of the room "a," "b," "c," or "d" for each question on the quiz. Rather than having kids circle their responses on the quiz, instruct them to go to the appropriate corner. Once kids have chosen a corner, ask them how sure they are of their answer. If they're positive that their answer is correct, they should stand on their tiptoes and stretch both hands above their head. If they're somewhat sure, they should bend over and put their hands on their knees. If they're not sure at all, they should squat down.

STEP 2
Depending on how small your group is, you might want to have one person wear the Jesus mask and let the other group members attempt conversations with him or her. Make sure that the person you choose to wear the mask feels comfortable in front of an audience. So that no one feels awkward about talking to "Jesus" in front of everyone else, you might want to hold group conversations, in which "Jesus" fields questions from and/or talks to two or three people at once.

STEP 4
Rather than having kids pair up, ask for two volunteers to come to the front of the room and act out each situation. When you "stop the action," ask group members in the audience how each person in the roleplay is probably feeling at that moment. Then discuss whether or not Jesus ever experienced similar feelings. Depending on the number of volunteers you have, you can either switch acting pairs for each roleplay or have the same pair perform all three.

STEP 1
Rather than having one person at a time perform his or her android impression in front of the whole group, assign situations that require three or four group members to perform together. Among the situations you might suggest: watching a sporting event (cheering, yelling at the refs, taunting opponents, etc.), moving a piano or some other heavy object, being cheerleaders at a football game, etc. Give each group a minute or two to prepare its presentation.

STEP 3
After group members have completed Repro Resource 2, have them divide into three or four teams. As you go over the answers to the quiz, ask the accompanying questions and have the members of each team discuss their responses among themselves. Then have a spokesperson from each team summarize his or her team's responses for the rest of the group.

OPTIONS
SESSION ONE

HEARD IT ALL BEFORE

STEP 2

Jaded kids may be particularly susceptible to seeing Jesus as an ultra-serious, emotionless kind of guy who can only be communicated with through reverent, "prayer-like" speech. Emphasize to those who are wearing masks that they should act in the way that they've always been taught Jesus acts. Emphasize to those who aren't wearing masks that they should talk to Jesus in the way that they've always been taught they should speak to Jesus. Afterward, ask volunteers to explain what teachings have affected their view of Jesus and how they communicate with Him.

STEP 3

Sometimes teachers who are afraid of presenting Jesus in a negative light attempt to explain away His expressions of emotion (particularly in Mark 11:15-18) as being unfathomable, divine actions that have very little similarity to the emotions we experience. It's important in this activity that group members understand that— while Jesus never allowed His emotions to lead to sin—the feelings of anger, grief, and joy He experienced were very much like the emotions we experience today. After discussing each question on the quiz, ask group members to put themselves in Jesus' place and describe how they would have reacted in each situation.

LITTLE BIBLE BACKGROUND

STEP 2

If members of your group don't have a clear concept of who Jesus is and what He's like, the mask activity probably won't work well. In its place, you might want to have a group discussion of Jesus' personality. Ask group members to call out words that describe Jesus—particularly those that describe His personality. Emphasize that you're looking for personal opinions here; there are no "right" or "wrong" answers. You might want to question kids regarding their responses, but make sure you don't put anyone on the spot. List group members' suggestions on the board as they are named. Then talk about what it might be like to hang around with someone who exhibited these personality traits. Would it be boring, because He's always serious and talking about spiritual things? Would it be intimidating, because He's perfect? Would it be awkward, because you have nothing in common with Him?

STEP 3

Help kids find Matthew and John in their Bibles. Be prepared to assist the readers in pronouncing words like "Pharisees," "hypocrites," "Gethsemane," and "Zebedee."

FELLOWSHIP & WORSHIP

STEP 1

Have kids pair up. Instruct group members to share with their partners one thing that makes them happy, one thing that makes them sad, and one thing that makes them angry. When both members of a pair have shared, they should compare notes on their responses. Chances are, group members will find common ground in the things that affect them emotionally. Once group members have begun to identify with each other's feelings, you can introduce the idea of Jesus' being able to identify with our feelings.

STEP 5

Celebrate the fact that Jesus can identify with our feelings. Have kids form a circle. Ask each group member to say a short prayer (one or two sentences), praising Jesus for His ability to identify with one specific, emotion-provoking situation. The situations may or may not be personal experiences, but they should be experiences common to most junior highers. For instance, someone might say, "I praise You, Jesus, because You understand our anger when a friend talks about us behind our backs." Someone else might say, "I praise You, Jesus, because You can share in our joy when we get an 'A' on a test."

OPTIONS
SESSION ONE

MOSTLY GIRLS

STEP 2
Since it may be difficult for some girls to understand Jesus as relating to all human beings, and not just the guys, encourage them to talk about their questions. After the partners have finished their conversations and the masks have been removed, talk about Jesus, the Son of our Creator, who was fully human and fully God. Say: **It is difficult to understand, but do you think Jesus has the same feelings as all human beings? When you were wearing the mask, did you think you couldn't respond as Jesus would because you are a girl?**

STEP 3
After discussing the quiz, ask the girls to form groups of two or three. Have the members of each group choose from Repro Resource 2 the event or emotion that surprised them the most (such as crying or expressing anger) and explain why they were surprised that Jesus would express that feeling.

If group members don't seem surprised by any of the events, try something else. Have the groups choose one event that would most surprise kids who don't know much about Jesus. Then have each group develop a storyboard of that scene, showing several frames of stick figures. Ask: **If this scene were made into a movie, who do you think should play the part of each character? Why?**

MOSTLY GUYS

STEP 2
If your guys would be uncomfortable wearing masks and pretending to talk to Jesus, skip the activity. Instead, have group members respond to the following questions: **If Jesus walked into this room right now, how would you act? Would you treat Him like "one of the guys" or would you act differently toward Him? Would you try to talk to Him? If so, what would you talk about? What kinds of things would you avoid talking about? How would talking to Jesus be different from talking to your best friend?** If possible, try to focus discussion on whether Jesus has feelings and emotions similar to ours.

STEP 4
Rather than having your group members act out the scenarios, read the situations aloud and ask group members to imagine themselves in each scenario. What feelings would they experience? Do they think Jesus ever experienced similar feelings? How do they think Jesus would feel about them in that situation?

EXTRA FUN

STEP 1
If you have time for an additional opener, have group members compete in an emotion expression contest. One at a time, have volunteers come to the front of the room and express an emotion (anger, joy, sadness, etc.)—without speaking. Volunteers may use facial expressions, gestures, and body language, but they may not make any sounds. The rest of the group should then vote on which person best displayed each emotion.

STEP 3
Have everyone stand up for "A Run through the Emotional Spectrum." Explain that you'll be reading a list of emotional situations. When you read a situation, group members will immediately respond to it in an appropriate way. For instance, if you read a sad situation, group members should frown and pretend to cry; if you read a happy situation, they should smile and laugh; if you read an angry situation, they should scowl and snarl.

Here are some situations you could use:

- **Your pet goldfish just died.**
- **Your teacher just falsely accused you of cheating in front of the whole class.**
- **You just made the varsity basketball team.**
- **Your pet hamster climbed into the washing machine and went through the spin cycle...but he's OK.**
- **Your best friend told you he or she didn't want to go to a movie with you ... because he or she just got tickets for both of you to see your favorite band in concert.**
- **You just won first prize in a store giveaway—a year's supply of laundry detergent.**

OPTIONS
SESSION ONE

MEDIA

STEP 3
Before the session, record some clips of movies and TV shows that present emotion-provoking situations. For instance, you might record an emotional deathbed scene, a scene of a sports team celebrating after a victory, a scene in which bullies are picking on a helpless victim, a scene in which someone is being stalked, etc. Play each scene, and then discuss how Jesus might respond if He faced a similar situation. Emphasize that He would probably experience the same emotions that the characters in the scenes experienced, but that He would never allow those emotions to cause Him to respond in a sinful manner.

STEP 5
As your group members melt the block of ice, play a recording of Bryan Duncan's song "You're Never Alone." Ask: **Recognizing that Jesus experienced every emotion you experience, how might that affect the way you respond the next time you get angry? Sad? Fearful? Lonely? Happy?**

SHORT MEETING TIME

STEP 1
Rather than allowing everyone to participate in the android contest, simply choose three contestants from the group. (Make sure that the people you choose feel comfortable in front of a group.) Give the contestants one minute to consult with other group members about their routines, and thirty seconds to perform. Afterward, explain to the group the differences between an android and a real person. Then follow up by asking: **Would you want an android as a friend or family member? Why or why not?**

STEP 3
Rather than distributing copies of the quiz and giving kids time to fill it out, simply read the questions aloud and have group members respond by raising their hands. Be succinct in explaining each of the eight numbered points. After the session, offer to give copies of the quiz, as well as the accompanying Scripture passages, to anyone interested in further study. For each of the discussion questions, try to limit responses to two or three. (Make sure, however, that you seek out responses from different people for each question.)

URBAN

STEP 1
The urban equivalent of an android is a crack addict. Improvise by having your teens pretend to act with the lifelessness that comes with being on drugs. In essence, they must become as zombies or the "living dead." If the resources provide, play a spooky tape or record to accentuate the emotionless and inane existence of those who choose drugs over sanity. Shortly thereafter, remind the group that drug addicts often begin their habits to escape their deepest emotional hurts, and that Jesus Christ is a *friend* who will help them overcome those hurts.

STEP 2
To add a cultural edge to this activity, have your group members begin by coloring the masks with any number of colors they want. Be sure there is a diversity of colorings among the masks. Then explain that the masks are to represent Jesus. Of course, you will hear, "Jesus wasn't yellow, black, red" or whatever colors they have, but continue the game anyway. When it is completed, include a question on what it was like talking to a colorful Jesus. The responses will be varied, but make this point: Jesus loves the diversity of cultures found in the city and radiates from them all. He died for everyone—red, brown, yellow, black, and white. So to be in His presence means to see Him in others (who may look different), and feel and express the emotion of love Christ has for us all.

OPTIONS
SESSION ONE

STEP 2
As much as possible, try to pair up a junior higher and a high schooler for this activity. High schoolers probably will be more thoughtful and reverent in the role of Jesus than junior highers will, so try to distribute the masks to high schoolers. Also, junior highers probably will act differently (showing more respect) to "Jesus" if the role is played by a high schooler than they would if it were played by another junior higher.

STEP 4
Junior highers may be reluctant to demonstrate their true feelings in the roleplay (for fear of being thought of as childish) if they're paired with a high schooler. As much as possible, try to pair junior highers with other junior highers and high schoolers with high schoolers. Also, with the discussion questions that follow each roleplay, don't ask group members to share their responses with the *whole* group. Instead, have the members of each pair share their responses with each other.

STEP 3
Sixth graders may have some difficulty identifying specific feelings from the descriptions. Instead of having group members do Repro Resource 2 individually, have them work in groups of three or four, marking the correct answers and talking together about the feelings expressed. Then as each item is discussed, ask them to name the emotion or feeling and tell whether they also have that feeling.

STEP 4
Since it is difficult for some sixth graders to identify with the feelings of the other person, talk about how Jesus may have felt if He were a part of the situations in Step 4. Focus on the first two situations and eliminate the third situation about baby-sitting. For the first situation, add questions such as these: **Do you think Jesus would tease His brothers? Why or why not? Is teasing always hurtful?** For the second situation, ask: **How do you think Jesus would express happiness and excitement?**

DATE USED:
Approx. Time

STEP 1: *Attack of the Androids* _____
❑ Extra Action
❑ Large Group
❑ Fellowship & Worship
❑ Extra Fun
❑ Short Meeting Time
❑ Urban
Things needed:

STEP 2: *The Messiah's Mask* _____
❑ Small Group
❑ Heard It All Before
❑ Little Bible Background
❑ Mostly Girls
❑ Mostly Guys
❑ Urban
❑ Combined Junior High/High School
Things needed:

STEP 3: *Heart in Emotion* _____
❑ Extra Action
❑ Large Group
❑ Heard It All Before
❑ Little Bible Background
❑ Mostly Girls
❑ Extra Fun
❑ Media
❑ Short Meeting Time
❑ Sixth Grade
Things needed:

STEP 4: *Stop the Action!* _____
❑ Small Group
❑ Mostly Guys
❑ Combined Junior High/High School
❑ Sixth Grade
Things needed:

STEP 5: *Meltdown!* _____
❑ Fellowship & Worship
❑ Media
Things needed:

SESSION 2
Does He Have a Sense of Humor?

YOUR GOALS FOR THIS SESSION:
Choose one or more

☐ To help kids see that while Jesus isn't a comedian, He did show a sense of humor when He was on earth.

☐ To help kids understand that they can feel comfortable with Jesus because He understands the value of laughter and fun as well as seriousness.

☐ To help kids evaluate their use of humor, in order to follow Jesus' example of using humor to glorify God.

☐ Other:_____

Your Bible Base:

Luke 6:20-26, 41-42; 7:31-35; 12:16-21

Laughing Gas

(Needed: Aerosol can of air freshener with homemade "Laughing Gas" label; team prize)

OPTIONS

Before the meeting, get an aerosol can of air freshener. Make a new label that says "Laughing Gas" and tape it on the can.

As each person enters your meeting place, spray a little air freshener in his or her direction. Explain that it's "laughing gas," to help people get in the mood for this session.

Start the meeting with a laughing contest. Form two teams and give each an extra spray with your "laughing gas." Explain that you're going to read a list of hilarious words and phrases, and that kids are supposed to laugh after each one. The team that laughs loudest and most sincerely at a word or phrase (you'll be the judge) will win that round. Help kids along with more "gas" as needed.

Here's the list. Insert appropriate words or phrases as directed in brackets.

(1) **Asparagus**
(2) [Name of a school represented in your group]
(3) **Ant farm**
(4) [Name of a group member who's a good sport]
(5) **Hyperbolic paraboloid**
(6) **Mucus**
(7) [Your name]

Give a prize to the team winning the most rounds. Then discuss:

Did your laughter prove that you have a good sense of humor? Why or why not? (No, because it was faked.)

How do you think most of your teachers would have done in this contest? Why?

If you had to choose between a teacher who had a good sense of humor and one who didn't, which would you pick? Why?

Answers will vary, but a sense of humor is valued highly by most kids. They prefer teachers as well as friends who can kid around and take a joke—in other words, who can create an atmosphere in which kids can make mistakes and survive with their self-esteem intact.

UNIT TWO

Express Yourself

Explain: **I'm going to read a list of well-known people. Let's say that each of these people is going to come and speak to our group. When I mention each one, tell me whether you think he or she has a good sense of humor. But don't tell me out loud. If you think the person's got a great sense of humor, show me a grin. If you think he or she has a so-so sense of humor, frown. If you think the person has no sense of humor at all, put your hands over your face.**

Here's the list. Insert appropriate names as directed in brackets.
(1) [A comedian who's popular with your group]
(2) **The principal of your school**
(3) [An older comedian that kids' parents might like]
(4) [A cartoon character]
(5) **The President of the United States**
(6) **Jesus**

After getting responses, ask kids to explain their reactions to the last name you read. Most kids probably don't think of Jesus as having a great sense of humor, though they may be reluctant to say that. They may say He had a lot of serious work to do and didn't have time to joke around.

Hmm. Haven't we got a problem here? Most of us like our teachers to have a sense of humor. But we're not sure Jesus rates too highly in that department. If Jesus has no sense of humor, how can we get along with Him?

Some kids may suggest that we need to go to Jesus only with serious or important things, and that we can get humor from our friends. If so, ask kids how they feel about teachers who have no sense of humor. Is that the kind of relationship they want with Jesus?

STEP 3

Humorous or Humorless?

(Needed: Copies of Repro Resource 3 cut in half; pencils; Bibles)

Before the session, make copies of "Clash over Comedy" (Repro Resource 3). Cut the sheets in half as indicated.

At this point in the meeting, get kids back into their teams from Step 1. Give the "Debate Team A" half-sheets to one team, and the "Debate Team B" half-sheets to the other.

Say: **Does Jesus have a sense of humor? Team A says no; Team B says yes. See whether you can convince the other team that you're right. Elect a captain for your team, study the Bible verses listed on your sheet, and read the arguments there. Then add any other arguments you can think of that might help you make your point.**

Give teams five to ten minutes to prepare their arguments. Answer questions about procedure if you like, but try to let kids come up with their own arguments. Then have teams make their cases—first Team A, then Team B—for up to three minutes each. Finally, give each team a chance to reply to the other for up to two minutes each.

Let kids comment on whether they personally agreed with their teams' positions, and on whether they were convinced by the other team. Then add the following information as needed:

Team A:
Luke 6:20-26—The world is a sad place when you see all the suffering in it. But Jesus' point in verse 25 isn't that laughing (or being well fed) is bad; it's that those who suffer now will someday have a reason to laugh when they're rewarded in heaven. Many who have it easy now will find they have nothing in the next life (vss. 24-26).

Luke 12:16-21—This story is about those who get lots of stuff for themselves but don't care what God wants (vs. 21). Being "merry," like eating and drinking (vs. 19), isn't wrong unless you take it for granted, fail to thank God for it, overdo it, or neglect other things God wants you to do.

We should concentrate on the important work God has for us, as Jesus did. And a lot of people do use humor as a time-waster. But that doesn't mean Jesus is against laughing. His Word says there's a time to cry and a time to laugh (Ecclesiastes 3:4), and "a cheerful heart is good medicine" (Proviso 17:22).

UNIT TWO

Team B:

Luke 6:41, 42—This may not seem very funny to us. But Jesus didn't come to earth to be a comedian; He came to be our Savior. He used humor to teach some very serious things. It may be hard to believe that God could have a sense of humor, but the Bible says He knows how to laugh (Psalm 2:1-4).

Luke 7:31-35—If Jesus had no sense of humor, why did people invite Him to parties? Why didn't He hang around with the religious leaders (who took themselves very seriously) instead of with average people?

Maybe the best proof that God—and therefore Jesus—has a sense of humor is that He created us in His image (Genesis 1:27), **and we have a sense of humor.**

Wrap up the debate discussion by asking: **How could knowing that Jesus has a sense of humor affect your relationship with Him?** (You might look forward more to reading His teachings in the Bible; you might feel friendlier toward Him and less afraid to be yourself when you pray; you might feel more forgiven and less condemned; etc.)

It All Fits Together

(Needed: Puzzle pieces copied and cut from Repro Resource 4; envelopes)

Before the meeting, copy and cut enough sets of puzzle pieces from "Making It Fit" (Repro Resource 4) so that you have one set of pieces for every two to four kids. Put each set of pieces in a separate envelope.

At this point in the session, form teams of two to four kids; give each team an envelope of puzzle pieces. Announce that the first team to put its puzzle together will be the winner.

After a few minutes, kids will discover that not all of the pieces fit together. Call a halt to the contest and say: **Let's see why not all of these pieces fit together. Take a look at what's written on them. Put all the Bible verses in a pile on the left, and all the rest in a pile on the right.**

Now look at the pile on the right. What do these questions and comments have in common? (They're all about things that are supposed to be funny.)

What kinds of "funny" things are mentioned on these pieces? (A put-down; a joke based on making fun of a person's religion,

disabilities, and race; comedy that uses a lot of swearing; a cruel prank; and a dirty cartoon.)

Why don't these kinds of humor fit with the ideas in the Bible verses? (You can't love your neighbor as yourself and put that person down or be cruel to him or her. If you're stereotyping a whole race, religion, or other group, you're judging. You can't love and obey God and seek His kingdom first while you're doing things—like lusting and using His name in vain—that offend Him.)

Can you imagine Jesus using or liking these kinds of humor? If not, why do some of us get involved with them?

As needed, point out that a lot of us try to put "funny stuff" and "spiritual stuff" in separate piles. We forget that everything in our lives is supposed to fit together. Jesus made sure that His life fit together. He didn't try to hide part of it from God. He used humor to help people get closer to His Father; if it didn't fit that goal, He didn't use it. We should do the same, making sure our use of humor fits God's goals for us.

A Funny Thing Happened . . .

(Needed: Pens or pencils)

Pass out pens or pencils. Ask each group member to take two pieces of the puzzle from Step 4.

Ask: **Remember those "funny" things that didn't fit with the Bible verses? If you need God's help to quit using humor to put people down, or to stop listening to certain kinds of jokes, write on the back of your first puzzle piece a word or phrase about that problem. Use it to help you remember to pray about that problem this week.**

Give kids a moment to do this. Then continue:

If Jesus has a sense of humor, why not share your sense of humor with Him? It may be hard to believe that He'd be interested, but He cares about every part of your life. On the back of your second puzzle piece, write a word or phrase that will remind you to talk to Him this week when something funny happens to you. He'd probably like to hear from you.

Encourage kids to take the puzzle pieces with them. Close in prayer, thanking God for creating humor and for being interested in every part of our lives.

FACE TO FACE WITH JESUS

REPRO RESOURCE 3

Clash over Comedy

Debate Team A

Your Position: Jesus was totally serious—and we should be, too!
Please read the following verses:
Luke 6:20-26
Luke 12:16-21

Just look at these verses! In Luke 6:20-22 Jesus says the world is a really sad place, and that it's best to cry now, not laugh. He says we're doing well when people hate and insult us. What's funny about that? In verse 25, Jesus comes right out and says, "Woe to you who laugh now." Obviously He's against laughing, so what's the point of telling jokes?

In Luke 12:16-21 Jesus tells a pretty scary story about a man who thought life was all about being "merry" (vs. 19). What happened to him? God called him a fool and killed him. That sums up God's attitude toward humor: It's a waste of time, because we should be concentrating on serious things that will last.

People today think humor is so important, but they're only kidding themselves. They want to escape the real world. Christians shouldn't do that.

We might want to pretend that Jesus was funny so that people today will like Him. But the truth is that Jesus was one of the most serious people who ever lived.

Other arguments you could use:

Debate Team B

Your Position: Jesus showed His sense of humor—and wasn't against having fun!
Please read the following verses:
Luke 6:41, 42
Luke 7:31-35

People in Jesus' day had a sense of humor. But they didn't always express it in the words we'd use. Take Luke 6:41, 42, for instance. This may not sound like a joke you'd hear on TV, but it's funny when you think about it. It's like a cartoon—a guy walking around with a big board sticking out of his eye, all bothered about a speck of sawdust in somebody else's eye.

If Jesus had been against telling jokes and having fun, He wouldn't have gone to all those dinner parties with "sinners" (Luke 7:34). Luke 7:31-35 is all about how some people had criticized John the Baptist for being too serious—and then criticized Jesus for not being serious enough.

Jesus had serious work to do, and He wasn't a comedian. But He used humor in his teaching, and He spent time with people who also had a sense of humor. Besides that, Jesus is God—and God created humor when He created everything else!

Other arguments you could use:

NOTES

FACE TO FACE WITH JESUS

REPRO RESOURCE 4

MAKING IT FIT

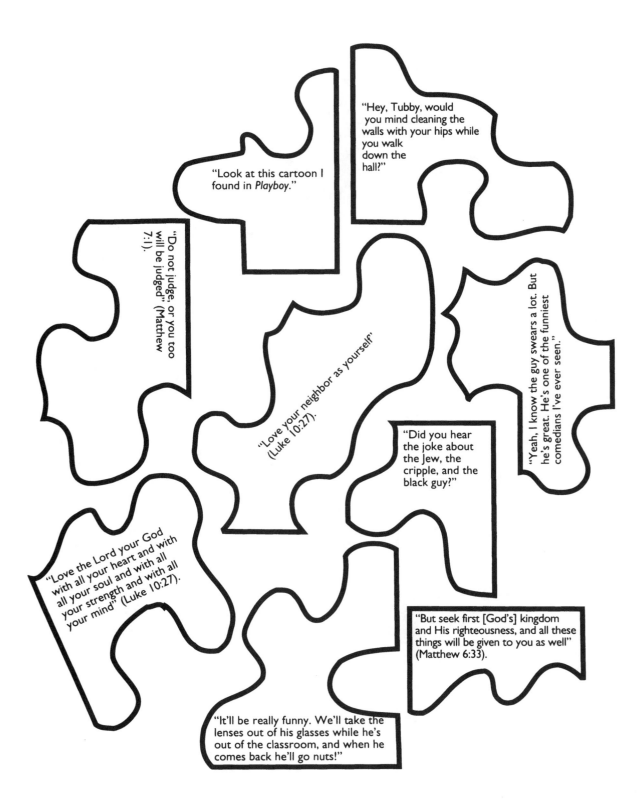

NOTES

OPTIONS
SESSION TWO

STEP 1

Rather than using just laughter to respond to the list of words, encourage the teams to do *whatever* they can think of to demonstrate hilarity. Some team members may double up from laughter; others may fall out of their seats; and still others may laugh themselves to tears. Award the prize to the team with the most convincing overall display of hilarity.

If you don't think your group members will be able to pull this off, try the opposite. Pair up group members. Have the members of each pair look at each other. Each one should say a word (any word, as long as it's in good taste). The two should continue saying words until one of them smiles or laughs. The first one to smile or laugh loses. Have the winners of each contest pair up and "do battle" again.

STEP 4

Add some action to the activity by making it a relay race. Place the envelopes at one end of the room and have the teams line up at the other end. When you say, **Go,** the first member of each team will run across the room, grab one puzzle piece, and bring it back. Then the second person will do the same thing. The teammates continue alternating until all the puzzle pieces have been retrieved. Then they can attempt to put the puzzle together.

STEP 1

Choose two or three people who don't mind acting foolishly in front of others and have them compete in a "laugh-off." Read each word on the list, and then give the contestants fifteen seconds to laugh. The rest of the group will then vote on which person laughed the loudest or most hysterically. Award a point to the person who laughs loudest/most hysterically at each word. The person with the most points after all the words have been read is the winner.

STEP 3

If your debate teams have only two or three people on them, they may not have enough input to come up with additional arguments to make their points. In that case, you might want to consider sitting in briefly with both teams as they brainstorm, offering suggestions as necessary. But don't just list arguments for the teams to use. Instead, lead them briefly in studying their assigned passages. Ask leading questions to illuminate relevant points. For instance, in Luke 7:31-35, you might ask: **What kind of people usually get invited to parties—boring, stuffy people, or people who know how to have a good time?**

STEP 2

Have kids divide into groups of five. When you read each name aloud, the members of each group will smile if they think that person has a good sense of humor, or frown if they think the person doesn't have a good sense of humor. If three or more members in a group are smiling, the group must form a smile on the floor by sitting or lying down. If three or more group members are frowning, the group must form a frown on the floor. Have a spokesperson from each group explain his or her group's reasoning.

STEP 3

Depending on the size of your group, choose six to eight people (three or four per team) to conduct the debate. Give them five to ten minutes to prepare. While they do, distribute Repro Resource 3 to the rest of the group. Instruct the other group members to read through the sheet, look up the passages, and come up with questions to ask if the debaters fail to address certain points. The object for the rest of the group is to stump the debaters, if possible.

OPTIONS
SESSION TWO

STEP 3

Kids who've "heard it all before" may not think of Jesus as having any sense of humor at all. Too often He's portrayed in church solely as the no-nonsense suffering servant who communicated only through dire warnings and complicated parables. If you have a couple of kids in your group who've heard it all before, try to assign them to Team B for the debate. This will give them an opportunity to study Jesus' lifestyle and words in a different light, and may help them recognize that Jesus did indeed have a sense of humor.

STEP 4

Have group members look up some other phrases used by Jesus that might demonstrate His sense of humor. Try to find phrases that your group members have probably heard a lot, but never recognized as being "humorous." For instance, you might have them look at Luke 18:24, 25 (try to picture a camel squeezing through the eye of a needle) and Matthew 23:23-24 (try to picture someone swallowing a camel).

If you don't mind a few groans, you might "announce" that scholars uncovered the following joke in the Dead Sea scrolls.

Jesus: Knock, knock.

Zacchaeus: Who's there?

Jesus: Israel.

Zacchaeus: Israel who?

Jesus: Israel nice to meet you. Now get out of that tree.

STEP 2

If some of your group members don't have much Bible background, they may not have an opinion one way or another about Jesus' sense of humor. Take a few minutes to talk with them about their impressions of Jesus. When they think of Him, what kind of person do they picture? An otherworldly being in human form who spoke and thought only of serious, heavenly things? A "regular guy" who went to a lot of parties and feasts with people that the religious leaders of the day considered to be sinners? A combination of the two?

Bring in some pictures of Jesus from Sunday school curriculum and/or picture Bibles. Have group members determine what emotions Jesus seems to be experiencing in each picture. Ask: **Do you think this is an accurate picture? Why or why not?**

STEP 3

For those group members who are unfamiliar with Jesus' use of hyperbole, you may want to explain what Jesus meant by His "speck of sawdust/plank in the eye" comparison. He was emphasizing how foolish and hypocritical it is for us to criticize someone for a fault while remaining blind to our own considerable faults.

STEP 2

Have kids pair up and share with their partners how important (on a scale of 1 to 10) humor is to them, and why. When they look for friends, do they look for people who are funny? When they watch TV or movies, do they prefer comedies over other genres? When they're down, would they prefer that someone make them laugh or try to comfort them?

STEP 5

Have group members form a circle for closing prayer. Ask each group member to say a short sentence prayer, thanking God for some aspect of humor. For instance, someone might say, "Thank You for giving me friends who make me laugh when I'm down." Someone else might say, "Thank You for giving me a sense of humor, because life would be pretty boring if I had to be serious all the time."

OPTIONS
SESSION TWO

MOSTLY GIRLS

STEP 4
After the puzzle pieces have been separated into two piles, have group members form five teams. Distribute one of the "funny" puzzle pieces to each team. Have the members of each team change their comment or joke to reflect what they would say if Jesus were a part of the team, or to reflect what they think Jesus might say. After each team presents its change, talk about how humor fits in with all the other parts of our lives.

STEP 5
Talk with your group members about how to respond when humor is used incorrectly or for the wrong reasons. Before they write on their puzzle pieces, have them form teams of three or four and act out one of the "funny" things mentioned on one of the pieces. Ask them to decide how they would respond if someone said to them something similar to what is written.

MOSTLY GUYS

STEP 1
Most junior high guys love to tell jokes. So instead of reading the list of words for the teams to laugh at, ask a couple of volunteers to stand up and tell jokes. Emphasize that the jokes must be clean and non-offensive. (If possible, preview the jokes yourself before the volunteers tell them in front of the whole group.) You may want to bring in a good joke book as a resource for your volunteers.

STEP 4
For the most part, guys probably are more likely than girls to enjoy—and use—inappropriate humor. Whether it's morning radio "shock jocks," stand-up comedians who do racially and/or sexually inappropriate material, teenage-sex comedies at the movies, or locker-room jokes, most teenage guys are exposed to some kind of offensive humor almost every day. Give your group members an opportunity to explain why this type of humor is popular, and to defend it if it's the type of humor they enjoy. If you can create a non-judgmental atmosphere in which kids feel free to share honestly, you'll be better able to have a dialogue with them about appropriate and inappropriate humor.

EXTRA FUN

STEP 1
Before the meeting, prepare with one of your funnier group members a presentation on how *not* to be funny. Open the session by having the person come to the front of the room and tell three jokes. On the first joke, the person should mess up the punchline. On the second joke, the person should laugh at himself or herself as he or she tells the joke. On the third joke, the person should stammer, pause, and start over as he or she tells the joke. When the person is finished, lead the group in a standing ovation. Then discuss what it means to have a good sense of humor.

STEP 3
Have group members form pairs. Distribute paper and pencils. Give each pair three minutes to write down as many *humorous* ways as it can think of to complete Jesus' statement in Luke 18:25: "It is easier for a _____ to _____ than for a rich man to enter the kingdom of God." For instance, someone might write down "It is easier for (the name of a short girl in your group) to beat Michael Jordan in a game of one-on-one than for . . ." After three minutes, have each pair read its responses. The rest of the group will determine whether a response is humorous or not. Award a prize to the pair with the longest list of humorous responses.

OPTIONS
SESSION TWO

MEDIA

STEP 1
Rather than reading the list of words for kids to laugh at, use video clips. Before the session, record seven or eight video scenes. These scenes could include obviously humorous things (i.e., a baby doing something cute) as well as unfunny things (i.e., a traffic light changing colors). No matter what the scene is, however, group members must laugh at it as though it were the funniest thing they've ever seen.

STEP 4
Record 30-second clips of several TV situation comedies. Make sure that each clip includes some kind of punchline or one-liner. (But make sure that you don't record any sexually suggestive or risque scenes.) Play the clips for your group members and have them determine whether or not each example of humor is something Jesus would say or do. Use this activity to lead into a discussion of what type of humor we should laugh at and encourage.

SHORT MEETING TIME

STEP 1
As group members arrive, divide them into two teams. Then, to start the session, give the teams one minute to laugh (and/or demonstrate hilarity in some other way) as hard as they can. After a minute is up, declare a winner.

STEP 3
Rather than dividing into teams for the debate, read aloud each position on Repro Resource 3 and have group members vote on which position they agree with. Ask several of them to explain their reasoning. Be prepared to play devil's advocate for each position, to force group members to defend their opinions.

URBAN

STEP 1
For an alternative knock out in laughter, give the teams a chair, a can of "laughing gas" (some kind of aerosol can), and a book. Line the teams up in pairs for a race. Explain that when they see the "gas," they are to laugh. When you say, **Go,** the first pair must run to its chair. One person will center the can of "laughing gas" on the chair and put the book squarely on top of it. The second person will then sit lightly on the book, causing the "gas" to be released from the aerosol can. That pair will then make way for the next pair. The first team finished wins.

STEP 4
Another puzzle to consider is one that will help group members learn to laugh at themselves and not be so serious that they cannot experience the humor of being human. This is often important for an urban youth whose image is everything and will fight not to lose his or her "rep"[utation] in the streets. Give each group member a puzzle piece. Instruct group members to write down one thing they take too seriously. In the weeks that follow, post group members' pieces to symbolize our brokenness and the need to help each other find humor in life.

OPTIONS
SESSION TWO

STEP 2
Chances are, your high schoolers and junior highers will have different ideas about what constitutes a great sense of humor. If you think that your junior highers might be reluctant to respond to this activity for fear of being made fun of by the high schoolers, separate the two groups. You may need to think of two different names for #1 and #4—one name appropriate for junior highers and one appropriate for high schoolers.

STEP 3
There are two ways to approach the debate with a mixed group. One would be to make sure that each team has an equal number of high schoolers on it. Your high schoolers probably will have more mature, logical opinions to express (or, at the very least, will be more willing to express their opinions). By splitting up your high schoolers, you're assuring relatively even teams. The danger of this approach, however, is that the high schoolers will monopolize the activity. Junior highers may be reluctant to share their opinions in such a setting. The other option would be to have your junior highers debate your high schoolers. If you chose this approach, you probably would want to help the junior highers prepare their presentation.

STEP 2
Before reading the list of names, ask your sixth graders to define the term *sense of humor*. Have them talk about people who try to make others laugh no matter who or what is hurt in the process, and contrast that with people who are able to see the funny side of things, without hurting others. After the list of names has been read and group members have responded, ask them to identify some people they know who are serious about important things and who also have a sense of humor.

STEP 3
Instead of separate debate teams, have the entire group discuss each position and then use a secret ballot vote. Let your sixth graders know that after the discussion they are to vote yes or no about Jesus' sense of humor. Lead the group through the Bible verses on the top half of Repro Resource 3 "Debate Team A" and then do the notes for "Debate Team B." Ask group members to talk about any other events in Jesus' life that would contribute to either position. Have the group members vote on paper; then collect and count the ballots. Present the results and ask for volunteers to explain why they think that position received more votes.

DATE USED:
Approx. Time

STEP 1: *Laughing Gas* _____
❏ Extra Action
❏ Small Group
❏ Mostly Guys
❏ Extra Fun
❏ Media
❏ Short Meeting Time
❏ Urban
Things needed:

STEP 2: *Express Yourself* _____
❏ Large Group
❏ Little Bible Background
❏ Fellowship & Worship
❏ Combined Junior High/High School
❏ Sixth Grade
Things needed:

STEP 3: *Humorous or Humorless?* _____
❏ Small Group
❏ Large Group
❏ Heard It All Before
❏ Little Bible Background
❏ Extra Fun
❏ Short Meeting Time
❏ Combined Junior High/High School
❏ Sixth Grade
Things needed:

STEP 4: *It All Fits Together* _____
❏ Extra Action
❏ Heard It All Before
❏ Mostly Girls
❏ Mostly Guys
❏ Media
❏ Urban
Things needed:

STEP 5: *A Funny Thing Happened ...* _____
❏ Mostly Girls
❏ Fellowship & Worship
Things needed:

SESSION 3
What Kind of Friend Is He?

YOUR GOALS FOR THIS SESSION:
Choose one or more

☐ To help kids see that Jesus was a loyal, caring, down-to-earth friend to His disciples.

☐ To help kids understand that friendship with Jesus starts with obeying Him and grows from there.

☐ To help kids name ways in which they need Jesus to be a friend to them, and to start that friendship by obeying Him.

☐ Other:_____

Your Bible Base:

John 15:4-17; 20—21

Magnetic Personalities

(Needed: Index cards; pens or pencils; team prize)

Give each group member an index card and a pen or pencil. He or she should tear the card in half and write a plus sign on one half and a minus sign on the other. Each person should hide half the card in one hand and half in the other so that no one else can see which hand is "plus" and which is "minus."

Form two teams. Each team's members should stand side by side, about arm's length apart. Make sure kids are still hiding their index cards.

Explain: **We're going to play a game called "Magnetic Personalities." You probably know that a magnet has a positive (plus) end and a negative (minus) end. If you put two magnets together, the plus and minus ends will attract each other and stick together. But if you put the plus ends next to each other, they repel—they push each other apart. Same with the minus ends. Opposites attract; likes repel.**

Each of you is now a magnet. You have a plus side and a minus side, based on the cards in your hands. When I say "Attract!" touch your hands to the hands of the people next to you. Then open your hands to see whether you attracted or repelled—based on whether you touched opposites or likes. If you attracted, hold hands. If you repelled, move apart. Ready? Attract!

The team that ends up with the longest unbroken chain of people wins that round. In case of a tie, the team with the most kids holding hands wins that round.

Play a few more rounds, each time giving kids a chance between rounds to switch their plus and minus hands (still hiding the cards) if they wish. Let kids trade places in their lines between rounds if they want to. When the game's over, give a prize to the team that won the most rounds. Then ask:

What do people usually mean when they say that someone has a "magnetic personality"?

Do you think it takes a magnetic personality to attract friends? Why or why not?

What kind of person attracts you as a friend?

UNIT TWO

On the Road Again

(Needed: Backpack and various objects to put in it [see instructions])

Here's a riddle. Based on the clues, who am I talking about?

Clue #1: People in church sometimes sing about what a great *friend* He is.

Clue #2: He was followed around by twelve people He called *friends*.

Clue #3: His enemies called Him a *friend* of sinners.

Group members probably will guess quickly that you're talking about Jesus.

So, tell me about this great friend of yours named Jesus. When was the last time you saw Him?

When you go to McDonald's with Him, what does He usually order?

Does He talk to you on the phone a lot? What did He give you for your last birthday? Do you play catch or Nintendo with Him?

Hey, what kind of friend *is* Jesus, anyway?

Kids probably won't have many answers to the preceding questions. They may even start to wonder whether Jesus is much of a friend after all. That's good, because it's the central issue of this session.

We hear a lot about how Jesus is supposed to be our friend. But what does that mean? What kind of friend can He be to us?

To start with, most of our friends are human beings. We do human-type stuff together. Jesus didn't do that, did He?

Take out a backpack and several items that you've collected before the session. Items should include a fingernail clipper, a bag of chips or some other snack, a harmonica or other small musical instrument, and a towel.

Let's say this is the backpack that Jesus is going to wear on His next hike with the disciples. Which of these things will He need?

Hold up each item and let kids vote on whether to put it in the backpack. Ask them to explain their reasons. As needed, add the following information.

WHAT KIND OF FRIEND IS HE?

Fingernail clipper—Sure, why not? Jesus had a human body like ours. His fingernails grew, His hair got longer, His feet got sore.

Bag of chips—They may not have had this snack in Jesus' day, but He ate plenty of other food. He got hungry, just as we do. He ate grilled fish on the beach and bread at the Last Supper. He was always going to dinner at people's houses, and shared a lot of meals with His disciples.

Harmonica—Jesus could have gotten some use from a musical instrument. Singing was one of the things He and His disciples did together (Matt. 26:30).

Towel—Maybe Jesus didn't need one of these for swimming, since He could walk on water (Matt. 14:25). But He used one to clean His disciples' feet after a long, dusty walk (John 13:5).

After putting the items in the backpack, say: **Jesus and His friends shared a lot of the same things we share with our friends—conversation, food, music, work. But is He the kind of friend we would want? Let's find out what it was like to be a friend of Jesus when He was on earth.**

STEP 3

OPTIONS

Yearbook Memories

(Needed: Bibles; copies of Repro Resource 5; pens or pencils)

Ask: **Does your school have a yearbook? What kinds of messages do kids write to each other in yearbooks?** (They say how they feel about each other; remind each other of big events they shared; give advice; look forward to seeing each other again; etc.)

What if Jesus had a yearbook with pictures of His friends and the times they spent together? Maybe it would look something like this.

Pass out copies of "Yearbook" (Repro Resource 5) and pens or pencils. Have kids follow the instructions on the sheet. If possible, form four teams—each representing either Peter, Thomas, Mary, or John. Each team should scan the Scripture passage for information about the person it represents, then write messages from that person on the sheets held by members of the other teams.

Before kids scan the chapters, you may want to explain that the disciple described as the one "Jesus loved" (20:2; 21:7, 20) was John, who apparently was especially close to Jesus. You may also want to remind kids that before the events of these chapters, Peter had three times denied knowing Jesus.

UNIT TWO

Allow kids plenty of time to look over the chapters. Then have volunteers share and explain the messages they came up with. As needed, add information like the following.

Peter—Peter's message might recall the amazement he felt over Jesus' resurrection and the incredible haul of fish he got after taking Jesus' advice. Peter probably would apologize for denying Jesus, thank Him for His forgiveness, and promise to "feed [His] sheep" (21:17) (take care of the other disciples and help make new ones).

Thomas—Thomas might also recall the fishing episode. He might express embarrassment over not believing at first that Jesus had been raised from the dead. Probably he would thank Jesus for helping him to believe, and might address Jesus as "My Lord and my God" (20:28) again.

Mary—Mary might mention how sad she felt when it seemed Jesus was gone, and how glad she was to see Him—even how much she'd wanted to hug Him.

John—John probably would have expressed his love for Jesus, the excitement he'd felt when he discovered the empty tomb, and his joy at seeing Jesus again. John probably would have had a lot to write, because he remembered so many events from Jesus' life (21:25).

After discussing the yearbook messages, ask: **Based on what you just read, what words would you use to describe what it was like to be Jesus' friend when He was on earth?** (Some possibilities: exciting, surprising, amazing, strange, hard to believe, busy, etc.)

Jesus' friendships were real. They were full of strong feelings—the kind of feelings that made Mary cry when she couldn't find Jesus (20:11), and that made Peter jump into the water to get to Jesus (21:7). But what about us today? What kind of friendships can we have with Jesus, since He's no longer walking around on earth?

Fishers of Friends

(Needed: Magnet on a string; mixture of paper clips and pennies)

Have kids stand in their teams from Step 1. Explain that you're going to read a passage about how to be friends with Jesus and with each other. Every time you read the words "remain," "love," "loved," and "friends," kids should clasp hands for one second with those next to them. Every time you say the word "apart," they should move apart.

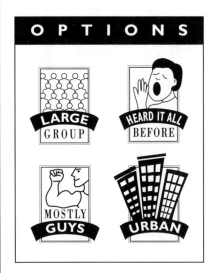

Before reading, note that Jesus said these things to His disciples, before He was crucified, to prepare them for the time when He would no longer be on earth. So most of the passage applies to us too.

Read John 15:4-17 aloud. Pause when you get to the five aforementioned words so that kids can clasp hands or move apart. As you read, they should clasp hands at least twenty-two times and move apart once.

After reading the passage, discuss the following questions. You may want to have kids look up the passage and refer to it.

Based on these verses, would you say Jesus wants to be close to you or apart from you? (Close, judging from the number of times we clasped hands.)

What does it mean to "remain" in Jesus? (Stay connected to, as a branch needs to stay connected to a vine.)

How do you stay connected with your friends? (Communicate with each other; spend time together; don't let disagreements get in the way; etc.)

How could you stay connected with Jesus? (Pray; read His teachings in the Bible; remember that He's with you wherever you go; ask forgiveness when you do something that would offend Him; etc.)

According to these verses, what's the greatest thing one friend can do for another? (Lay down [give] his or her life [vs. 13].)

Why do you think Jesus mentioned that? (He was about to do that for us.)

What are some things you've given up for your friends?

Say: **So far, friendship with Jesus sounds a lot like friendship with people we know—staying connected, giving things up for their sake. But things change in verse 14.**

Who does Jesus say His friends are? (Those who obey Him.)

Is that what you require of your friends—that they obey you? (Probably not.)

What gives Jesus the right to say that His friends have to obey Him? (He's the Son of God; He knows what's best for us.)

Jesus had started out thinking of His disciples as servants, but ended up thinking of them as friends (vs. 15). **Why?** (They didn't know much about His business until He taught them.)

Do you have to teach people a lot before they can be your friends? (Usually not.)

What kinds of things might we need to learn before becoming friends of Jesus? (This is a continuing process, but we'd need to learn who He is, what He's done, what He wants of us, how to stay connected with Him, etc.)

Isn't Jesus being a little picky about who can be His friends? Shouldn't He just be friends with everybody?

Let kids respond. If you have time, try the following object lesson to illustrate an answer.

UNIT TWO

Dump a mixture of paper clips and pennies on a table. Ask a volunteer to come to the front of the room; give him or her a magnet suspended from a string. Ask the person to "go fishing" for paper clips and pennies.

When some paper clips have stuck to the magnet, say: **Hey, have you got something against pennies? Why didn't you pick any up?** (The pennies aren't made of a metal that's attracted to the magnet.)

Thank your volunteer. Then explain to your group members: **The magnet offers the same attraction to everything, but only things that are open to its attraction are picked up. In the same way, Jesus was and is friendly to all kinds of people. But only those who are willing to obey Him will become His friends. Whether you'll be a paper clip or a penny is up to you.**

What, a Friend?

(Needed: Copies of Repro Resource 6; pens or pencils; hymnals and guitar or other accompaniment [optional])

Pass out copies of "Hymn and You" (Repro Resource 6). Encourage kids to fill it out individually. Then let volunteers share what they've written (but don't press).

If your group enjoys singing, supply hymnals and sing all the verses of "What a Friend We Have in Jesus."

Then wrap up the session: **Jesus told His friends, "If you remain in me and my words remain in you, ask whatever you wish, and it will be given you"** (John 15:7). **Are there any things on this handout that you'd like to ask the Lord for? Pick one or two and talk to Him about it now.**

Allow about half a minute for silent prayer. Then close, thanking Jesus for the opportunity to become His friends. If possible, offer to talk later with any group members who want to know more about starting a relationship with Jesus, or who need help with problems they mentioned on their sheets.

132

FACE TO FACE WITH JESUS

REPRO RESOURCE 5

Yearbook

If Jesus had a yearbook full of memories from His days on earth, what messages might His friends have written in it? After looking at John 20–21, write some notes to Jesus from His friends Peter, Thomas, Mary, and John.

Matthew poses with Future Tax Collectors of Judea Club.

Andrew (3,756th from right) serves loaves and fishes at Annual Feeding of the 5,000 Banquet

PETER

MARY

JOHN

THOMAS

Jesus—
I was up a tree until I met you.
Let's do dinner again.
—Zacchaeus

Jesus—
I'd be dead if it weren't for you. Thanks for everything!
—Lazarus

NOTES

Hymn and You

Here's a song about Jesus' friendship. Maybe you've sung it in church. But have you ever thought about the words?

What a Friend We Have in Jesus
by Joseph Scriven and Charles C. Converse

HYMN   ## YOU

What a friend we have in Jesus,

Jesus said, "You are my friends if you do what I command" (John 15:14). On a scale of 1 to 10 (with 10 being highest), how good a friend were you to Jesus last week?

_____

All our sins and griefs to bear;

Jesus paid for your sins on the cross. But what's one sin you need Jesus to help you stay away from this week?

_____

What's one "grief" (one thing you feel sad about) that you wish Jesus would help you with this week?

_____

What a privilege to carry Everything to God in prayer.

Are you really so glad about being able to pray that you do it every chance you get? Why or why not?

_____
_____

Oh, what peace we often forfeit;

When you "forfeit" peace, you give it up or lose it (like forfeiting a softball game because you didn't have enough players). One thing that takes away peace is worrying. What's one thing you're worried about this week that you could talk to Jesus about?

Oh, what needless pain we bear;

What problem bothers you the most right now?

_____

Have you prayed about it?

_____

All because we do not carry Everything to God in prayer.

How would you most like Jesus to be a friend to you this week?

_____

NOTES

OPTIONS
SESSION THREE

STEP 1
Explain that magnetic pull and magnetic repulsion are *constant* energies—they never stop. Your group members must demonstrate this in their actions. If a person "attracts" to another person, the two of them must move back and forth in unison, staying in constant motion. If a person "repels" with another person, he or she must continue bumping into that person and then "repelling" away. Once two or more people are "attracted" together, they will work in unison repelling against others.

STEP 3
Rather than having kids *write* their yearbook entries, encourage volunteers to stand up and *speak* them as though they were one of the characters. Don't put anybody on the spot by forcing him or her to stand and share, but encourage most of your group members to participate. Encourage volunteers to "ham it up" by using accents, mannerisms, or any props they can think of.

STEP 1
Before the session prepare two halves of an index card for each group member, one half with a plus sign on it and one half with a minus sign. Shuffle the cards well and put them in a pile. When group members arrive, have them draw two cards. (Unlike in the original game, a person may draw two plus cards or two minus cards.) Group members must hold one card in each hand—and they may not show their cards to each other. The object of the game is for group members to align themselves so that at least four people in a row "attract." After each round, collect the cards, shuffle them, and redistribute them. If group members can line up four "attracts" in a row within five rounds, they win a prize.

STEP 5
Group members may be reluctant to sing without a lot of others around to "drown them out." If that's the case with your group, bring in a recorded version of "What a Friend We Have in Jesus" and play it while group members work on Repro Resource 6. Encourage kids to meditate on the meaning of the lyrics as they're sung.

STEP 1
This activity could serve as an icebreaker for a large group. As group members enter, assign them to a team. Depending on the size of your group, you'll need to have four to six teams. As much as possible, try teaming up kids who don't know each other very well. Give the team members a moment to work together in creating a "strategy" (by arranging themselves according to how they *think* their cards will play). The more you encourage team spirit and unity, the better the "icebreaking" results will be. The winning team in each round gets to stay together. Everyone else must switch teams.

STEP 4
If your group members switched teams in the opening activity, form teams for this activity simply by having group members number off one through four (or six, depending on the size of your group). After group members have done the clasping hands-moving apart activity, have them remain in their small groups to discuss the following questions: **What does it mean to "remain" in Jesus? How do you stay connected with your friends? How do you stay connected with Jesus?** Appoint a spokesperson for each team to share his or her group's responses with everyone else.

OPTIONS
SESSION THREE

HEARD IT ALL BEFORE

LITTLE BIBLE BACKGROUND

FELLOWSHIP & WORSHIP

STEP 3

Expand the assignment for Repro Resource 5. Rather than having group members write messages from the four followers based on the events in John 20 and 21, have them write messages that mention at least two specific, personal experiences each character had with Jesus. For instance, Mary might write something like "Thanks again for driving those seven demons out of me. You really know how to change a person's life!" Or Thomas might write something like "Remember when Lazarus died and You and I were the only ones willing to go back to Judea? Those were exciting times." Kids who are familiar with the Bible probably have heard the various accounts at different times, but they may not have a sense of the friendships that were formed with Jesus on the basis of these events.

STEP 4

Young people who've been exposed to biblical teaching for most of their lives have probably heard or read this passage several times before. And yet, many of them probably still don't understand what it's saying. To help group members focus on what's actually being taught in the passage, read each verse aloud and then have group members rewrite that verse in their own words. After you've gone through all the verses in the passage, ask volunteers to read what they've written.

STEP 3

You may want to provide some additional information about the four followers before group members work on Repro Resource 5. For instance, you might want to explain that Peter, Thomas, and John were Jesus' disciples and that they'd committed the past three years of their lives to following Him. You might briefly discuss Peter's denial of Jesus shortly before Jesus' crucifixion, John's status as "the one Jesus loved," and Mary Magdalene's support of Jesus throughout His ministry (see Luke 8:1-3).

STEP 5

Before group members fill out Repro Resource 6, go through the sheet with them, making sure they understand the topics discussed. For instance, do your group members know how Jesus "paid for [their] sins on the cross" and why He had to? Do they know how to "carry everything to God in prayer"? Don't *assume* anything here. If your group members don't have a good grasp of Christian "basics," this activity won't be very effective for them.

STEP 1

After each round, give group members one minute for a quick fellowship activity. If two people attracted, they must share with each other one attribute that attracts them to someone else as a friend. If two people repelled, they must share one attribute that might prevent them from starting a friendship with someone else. Each person will have 15 seconds to share. Group members will share with the person on their right first, and then with the person on their left. (The people at each end of the line will share with each other as necessary.)

STEP 5

After having sung "What a Friend We Have in Jesus," give kids an opportunity to share their feelings about their friend in a way that's probably familiar to them. Have them pull out Repro Resource 5 again and write their own "yearbook message" to Jesus, praising Him for the things He's done and the effect He's had on their lives. Afterward, give group members an opportunity to share their messages if they want to. (Don't force anyone to share.)

OPTIONS
SESSION THREE

STEP 3

Have group members form two additional teams. Explain that these teams will represent two more of Jesus' friends, Martha, and her sister Mary. Instruct these teams to scan John 11 before they write their yearbook messages.

STEP 5

Before using Repro Resource 6, ask your group members to talk about their friendship and obedience to Jesus. Ask: **Do you think there are things you cannot or should not discuss with Jesus as a friend because you are a girl? Why or why not? Is obedience to Jesus different for guys than it is for girls? In John 15:4-17, was Jesus just talking to His guy friends or did He mean all people?**

STEP 1

Your guys will probably be wary of physical contact with each other. Do not ask them to hold hands for this activity. Instead, you might want to have them put their hands on each other's shoulders. Or you may want to have them just move close to each other, or have them touch feet. Whatever you do, make sure that you don't make your group members feel uncomfortable.

STEP 4

As in Step 1, you're going to want to be careful about asking guys to hold hands. Some guys are extremely uncomfortable about physical contact with other guys. Asking them to hold hands with one of their friends or with someone they don't know very well would probably spoil the activity for them and inhibit their learning. So instead of asking them to clasp hands, you should probably have them put their hands on each other's shoulders. Or you may want to have them stand back to back.

STEP 2

Bring in several objects—some of them odd, some of them common—and ask volunteers to explain/demonstrate how Jesus might have used them. For instance, He could have used comfortable *athletic shoes* because He and His disciples did a lot of walking. He could have used a *portable grill* because He and His disciples did a lot of outdoor cooking. He could have used a *desk lamp* because He spent a lot of time studying Scripture.

STEP 3

Bring in some of your old high school yearbooks for your kids to look at. Spend some time joking about outdated clothing styles, hairstyles, etc. If you think it would be appropriate, let your group members read some of the messages people wrote to you. Use this as a lead-in to the activity on Repro Resource 5.

OPTIONS
SESSION THREE

STEP 1
After the game's over, play a recording of Michael W. Smith's classic song, "Friends." Then ask questions like the following: **Do you have a friend who will probably be your friend forever? What do you like about him or her? What does the singer mean when he says, "A friend will not say never, 'cause the welcome will not end"?** Once kids have identified qualities of a "forever friend," you can begin to discuss how Jesus demonstrates those same qualities.

STEP 5
Bring in an instrumental recording of "What a Friend We Have in Jesus" as an accompaniment for your group members. Play it a couple of times before your group members sing so that anyone who is unfamiliar with the hymn can learn the tune.

STEP 3
Rather than having kids divide into teams to work on Repro Resource 5, work on it together as a group. Briefly summarize the events in John 20–21. Then have group members call out suggestions as to what the four followers might have written in Jesus' "yearbook." You may want to be prepared with a few suggestions of your own to give group members an idea of what you're looking for and to speed up the brainstorming process. For instance, Mary might have written "I can't believe I mistook You for a gardener!" Or Peter might have written "Thanks for the fishing tip. From now on, I'll only fish on the *right* side of the boat."

STEP 5
Rather than having kids complete Repro Resource 6 during the session, assign it as "homework." Wrap up the session by reading aloud John 15:7. Then give group members half a minute for silent prayer before you close by praying aloud. As group members leave, hand them a copy of the repro resource and have them fill it out at home—or perhaps before church on Sunday morning (where they could refer to the entire song in a church hymnal).

STEP 2
To modify the contents of the backpack in order to be more urbocentrically correct, try some of these items: a Walkman radio, an "X" cap, stone washed jeans, a bus pass, a gold chain, a fashion walking cane, food stamps, and government milk and cheese.

STEP 4
If you have an energetic group that loves to dance, bring in a radio with a "stand up and clap" gospel song (or perhaps MC Hammer's renditions of "Do Not Pass Me By" and "Pray"). Instead of having group members clasp hands when they hear the words "remain," "love," "loved," or "friends" in the Scripture passage, you will turn on the music for five seconds and group members will jump, dance, or clap their hands with joy. Include in your discussion afterward the joy and high praise that Jesus imparts into our personal friendships with others and in our spiritual relationship with Him.

OPTIONS
SESSION THREE

STEP 1
Since this is a contest that doesn't require skill or knowledge to win, you might want to have your junior highers compete against your high schoolers. Make a big deal about it if your junior highers win. Chances are, they probably usually come up short when they compete with high schoolers. Being able to win even the "Magnetic Personalities" game might give them a needed ego boost.

STEP 3
Your junior highers may be unfamiliar with the practice of signing yearbooks. If you suspect that to be the case, ask a couple of your high schoolers to bring in their yearbooks for the junior highers to examine. (You may want to check the yearbooks ahead of time to make sure that the messages are appropriate to be read.)

STEP 3
If your sixth graders are not familiar with a yearbook, show them one with handwritten messages in it. Before asking group members to write their own messages, simplify the project by talking about possible ideas of what to write and by identifying specific Bible verses for each group (Thomas—John 20:24-29; Mary—John 20:1-2, 10-18; John [the "other disciple"]—John 20:2-5, 8-9; 21:1-14; Peter—John 20:2-7; 21:1-19).

STEP 5
Instead of having your sixth graders complete all of Repro Resource 6, ask them to choose three of the "You" questions to respond to. Go over the phrases in the hymn, rewording each one so it is easier to understand. Then talk about the meaning of the words not already described (bear, privilege, needless, carry).

DATE USED: Approx. Time

STEP 1: *Magnetic Personalities* _____
❏ Extra Action
❏ Small Group
❏ Large Group
❏ Fellowship & Worship
❏ Mostly Guys
❏ Media
❏ Combined Junior High/High School
Things needed:

STEP 2: *On the Road Again* _____
❏ Extra Fun
❏ Urban
Things needed:

STEP 3: *Yearbook Memories* _____
❏ Extra Action
❏ Heard It All Before
❏ Little Bible Background
❏ Mostly Girls
❏ Extra Fun
❏ Short Meeting Time
❏ Combined Junior High/High School
❏ Sixth Grade
Things needed:

STEP 4: *Fishers of Friends* _____
❏ Large Group
❏ Heard It All Before
❏ Mostly Guys
❏ Urban
Things needed:

STEP 5: *What, a Friend?* _____
❏ Small Group
❏ Little Bible Background
❏ Fellowship & Worship
❏ Mostly Girls
❏ Media
❏ Short Meeting Time
❏ Sixth Grade
Things needed:

SESSION 4
Is He Tough Enough?

YOUR GOALS FOR THIS SESSION:
Choose one or more

- [ ] To help kids see that Jesus took real risks and suffered real pain in standing for the truth and sacrificing His life for us.

- [ ] To help kids understand that it takes courage to be the people God wants us to be, and that Jesus is our greatest example of courage in action.

- [ ] To help kids face a specific, threatening situation as Jesus did—by looking beyond the threat to the rewards God has in store.

- [ ] Other:_____
  _____

Your Bible Base:

Matthew 26:36—27:50
John 16:31-33
Hebrews 12:2-3

Indy and Cindy

(Needed: Two copies of Repro Resource 7; felt hat and leather jacket [optional])

Get two volunteers, preferably a guy and a girl, to act out the "Young Indiana James" skit on Repro Resource 7. If possible, loan your Indy a felt hat and leather jacket to wear. The rest of the group can provide sound effects during the skit—water dripping, rats squeaking, snakes hissing, bats flapping, etc.

After the skit, applaud your actors. Then introduce the subject of courage with questions like these:

Who do you think was the bigger coward—Indy or Cindy? Why?

Have you ever been in a really scary situation? What did you do?

What do you think the word *courage* means? (Possible definition: The strength to try something, keep going, or stand up to danger, fear, or difficulty.)

Courage Counters

(Needed: Index cards; pens or pencils; chalkboard and chalk, or newsprint and marker)

Before the session, write the following on a chalkboard or piece of newsprint.

1. Making a 20-minute campaign speech to the whole student body
2. Telling your best non-Christian friend how to become a Christian
3. Running into a burning building to rescue a neighbor's child

At this point in the session, distribute index cards and pens or pencils. Say: **Let's say that each of you has been given ten units of courage to get these three tasks done. The harder a task** would be for you, the more courage units you would need. Write down how you would divide your ten courage units to complete the tasks. For instance, if making a speech and running into a burning building would be fairly easy for you, you might need only two courage units for each task. That would leave you with six courage units for telling your best friend about Christ.

Give group members a few minutes to write down on their index cards how they would divide their ten courage units. They must use all ten units, and may not use more than ten.

Then instruct group members to form teams of three, using the following guidelines.
- Each person on a team will be responsible for one of the three tasks. That task should be circled on the person's card.
- The courage units for each team's three circled tasks should add up to ten.

For instance, let's say someone would need five courage units to make a speech. That person might then look for someone who would need three courage units to tell his or her best friend about Christ and someone who would need two courage units to run into a burning building. Together, their courage units add up to ten.

Explain: **The goal for each team is to make sure that all three tasks are covered and that your total courage units needed add up to ten. Go!**

Give kids a few minutes to try to work this out. Chances are, not everyone will be able to form teams of three. When time is up, regather the group and discuss what happened.

How did you do?

Which of the three tasks seemed hardest for most people?

Which seemed easiest?

In real life, courage doesn't come in units. Where do you get courage when you need it?

If Jesus were playing this game with us, how many courage units do you think He'd need to do each of the three tasks? Why?

Some kids may suggest that Jesus would use superhuman powers to perform the tasks, so He wouldn't need courage. Try not to judge answers at this point.

Do you think Jesus needed courage to do anything He did while He was on earth? Why or why not?

Answers may vary, which is fine. The point is to get kids thinking about what kind of person Jesus is—and whether the hard things He did on earth might have been hard for Him.

IS HE TOUGH ENOUGH?

Profile in Courage

(Needed: Bibles; slips cut from a copy of Repro Resource 8; pens or pencils)

I'm going to read a list of statements about Jesus. If you agree with a statement, stay seated. If you disagree, stand up.
- It was easy for Jesus to be brave because He could do anything.
- Jesus wasn't tough—He was gentle and meek.
- Jesus didn't have to be brave because He didn't feel pain like we do.
- It's harder for me to be brave than it was for Jesus, because unlike Him I don't know how things will turn out.
- It takes courage to do things like sharing my faith and standing up for what I believe.

Ask volunteers to explain their reactions to the statements. Then say something like: **A lot of us may figure that Jesus did good things, but that they weren't really *courageous* because He could make things turn out the way He wanted. If that's true, we may wonder whether it's fair for the Lord to ask us to do brave things. After all, those things are hard for us! So let's find out the real story about Jesus and courage.**

Pass out the slips you've cut from "Guts and Glory" (Repro Resource 8). Depending on the size of your group, you could give one or more slips to each person, or one slip to each of ten small groups.

Give kids a few minutes to read their passages and to complete the statements. Then bring the group back together and discuss results. Add the following information as needed.

Matthew 26:36-44—Choice to avoid danger or pain: Asking God to cancel the crucifixion, period. Notice that Jesus was so overcome by sadness that He felt like He was already dying (vs. 38). He had the same physical and emotional reactions that most of us would have had. It took courage to keep going, especially when He had no help from His friends. *The choice He made:* Letting God have His way, even if it meant being tortured and killed.

Matthew 26:45-50—Choice to avoid danger or pain: Escaping those who came to arrest Him, maybe hiding out for awhile. *The choice He made:* Going to meet His betrayer and the armed mob.

Matthew 26:50-52—Choice to avoid danger or pain: Trying to fight back, as one disciple (Peter) did. *The choice He made:* To go voluntarily, not using any of His power.

Matthew 26:53-56—Choice to avoid danger or pain: Asking God to rescue Him, and getting help from twelve legions of angels (that's 72,000). He could have chosen to do that at any time, but He didn't. Maybe that was His most courageous act of all. Notice the choice His disciples made—to desert Him. *The choice He made:* To suffer, so that the Bible's predictions about the Messiah would come true.

Matthew 26:57-75—Choice to avoid danger or pain: Giving in to the religious leaders and saying the whole thing had been a misunderstanding. Notice Peter's choice—to pretend he'd never even met Jesus. *The choice He made:* To say the truth, even though it had already gotten Him in trouble—the truth that He is the Messiah, the Son of God. The result was that He was punched, slapped, and spit on.

Matthew 27:1-10—Choice to avoid danger or pain: Escaping the death sentence by getting away from His captors. *The choice He made:* To let Himself be taken away, even though He had just been sentenced to die. Notice the choice Judas made to escape his guilt: suicide.

Matthew 27:11-26—Choice to avoid danger or pain: Explaining to Pilate that the charges against Him were phony, and possibly winning His freedom. *The choice He made:* Not to say anything in His defense. The result: Jesus was flogged, a kind of beating so terrible that victims sometimes died before they could be crucified.

Matthew 27:27-31—Choice to avoid danger or pain: Using His power to keep the soldiers away. *The choice He made:* To let them strip Him, make fun of Him, hit Him, and otherwise abuse Him. Since Jesus had a human body like ours, He felt every bit of it.

Matthew 27:32-44—Choice to avoid danger or pain: Drinking the wine and gall, a painkiller; coming down from the cross to answer the insults of the crowd and the robbers. *The choice He made:* To refuse the drugs; to stay on the cross, suffering incredible pain when He could have come down at any moment.

Matthew 27:45-50—Choice to avoid danger or pain: Coming down from the cross or going directly to heaven to be with His Father, who He felt had abandoned Him. *The choice He made:* To stay on the cross until His sacrifice for us was finished, even though the pain was intense.

If time allows, wrap up this step as follows:

Remember those statements we reacted to by standing up and sitting down? I'm going to read three of them again. How would you reply to them now?

- **It was easy for Jesus to be brave because He could do anything.** (But He chose not to use His power to escape pain and death—so it was far from easy.)

- **Jesus wasn't tough—He was gentle and sort of wimpy.** (He was gentle in a way, but it would take a tough person to stand up to the abuse Jesus took.)
- **Jesus didn't have to be brave because He didn't feel pain like we do.** (He felt it all—plus the pain of carrying the world's sins.)

Eyes on the Prize

(Needed: Worthless prize)

Ask: **Why do you think Jesus was willing to go through all that pain? Where did His courage come from?**

Listen to responses if there are any. Then say: **We'll look again at that question in a minute. But first let's play a quick game.**

Have kids line up in two teams. Then give the following directions as quickly as you can: **Do twenty pushups. Run fifty laps around the room. Form a human pyramid until you reach the ceiling. Then do one hundred more push-ups, but use only one hand.**

Take a worthless prize (a candy wrapper, chewed piece of gum, etc.) out of your pocket and display it. **And by the way, this is the prize you get if you do everything I just said.**

Chances are that no one will want to play the "game" because the prize isn't worth it.

Would you have tried to play the game if I'd offered you a million dollars? (Probably.)

Jesus was willing to suffer because He knew what the prize would be. Look at Hebrews 12:2 and tell me what the prize was. (The "joy set before Him"—saving us from our sins and taking His place of honor next to His Father.)

Look at verse 3. What are we supposed to do? (Remember Jesus' example, and keep going for the prize that awaits us.)

What prize is waiting for us? (Eternal rewards, congratulations from God, etc.)

Doing the brave thing is sometimes rewarded in this life, too. Remember the three tasks we needed "courage units" to do? Refer to the list of tasks on the board from Step 2. **What "prizes" could we get for doing these things?**

UNIT TWO

(1) Making a 20-minute campaign speech to the whole student body—
Possibly winning the election; learning to speak in public; making new friends; feeling more confident around strangers.

(2) Telling your best non-Christian friend how to become a Christian—
Learning how to share your faith; having a more honest relationship with your friend; feeling at peace around your friend instead of nervous about witnessing to him or her; maybe helping your friend become a Christian; possibly having the friend with you in heaven.

(3) Running into a burning building to rescue a neighbor's child—
Knowing you saved someone's life; learning to trust God; being more confident in scary situations; showing others that being a Christian isn't all talk and no action.

Breaking Down the Door

(Needed: Sheets of cardboard; markers; tape; refreshments)

Before the session, put an assortment of kids' favorite refreshments in a nearby room. Cover the room's doorway by taping sheets of cardboard over it. Make sure kids can't see the refreshments.

At this point in the session, bring kids to the doorway. Give each person a marker or pen.

On these sheets of cardboard, draw a symbol or write a word that stands for a scary or difficult situation you're facing—something you need courage to get through. Just as you don't know what might be on the other side of this door, you don't know what might happen in this situation.

Allow a minute or so for kids to draw or write. Then read aloud John 16:31-33—in which Jesus assures His disciples that He has overcome the world.

Jesus overcame the world because He had the courage to obey God. He was able to do that because He looked forward to the reward that was waiting for Him. What prize might be waiting for you on the other side of the situation you face? Learning something? Accomplishing something? Getting closer to God? Knowing that He's pleased with you? Try keeping your "eyes on the prize" this week.

And remember that we can encourage each other—give each other courage—this week. So let's crash through this

doorway together and see what prize is waiting for us on the other side!

After breaking through the cardboard, enjoy your refreshments as a group.

(If you don't have a doorway to use, put the refreshments inside a box and have group members write on the outside of the box. Then, when everyone is finished, open the box and pass out the refreshments.)

NOTES

FACE TO FACE WITH JESUS

REPRO RESOURCE 7

Young Indiana James

Characters: *Young Indiana James, adventurer*
Cindy Brandywhine, pampered young heiress

CINDY: Oh, Indy! It's so dark in here! Where are we?

INDY: In the lowest level of the deepest depths of the innermost innards of the Temple of Gloom.

CINDY: Oh, Indy! How will we ever get out?

INDY: Maybe we won't. (*Points toward corner.*) Looks like they didn't.

CINDY: Eeeeek! Skeletons!

INDY: Who's afraid of skeletons? I've got one, and so have you.

CINDY: Oh, Indy! There's something moving around my feet!

INDY: Just some giant rats.

CINDY: Rats? Eeeeeeeeek!

INDY: What's wrong with rats? They make fine pets.

CINDY: Oooh, there's something on my neck!

INDY: Only a crawling heap of tropical fungus beetles.

CINDY: I can't stand bugs! Help!!

INDY: Calm down. They taste great with a little ketchup on them.

CINDY: My hair! Something's in my hair!

INDY: Just vampire bats, rattlesnakes, spiders, eels, pond scum, and broccoli.

CINDY: Noooo! Help!!

INDY: You're such a wimp. OK, I'll get them off you. I'll just light this torch, so I can see better.

CINDY (*Offhandedly*): Did you know you've got a zit on your nose?

INDY (*In a panic*): A zit!? Nooooo-oooo!

CINDY: What's wrong with you? I get zits all the time!

INDY: Why did it have to be a zit? I hate zits! I can't let anyone see me—I've got to get out of here! (*He runs out.*)

CINDY: Get back here, you coward! Some adventurer you are! Take these creepy things off me, or this will be your last crusade!!! (*She runs after him.*)

NOTES

Guts and Glory

Matthew 26:36-44
The choice Jesus could have made to avoid danger or pain:
The choice He made:

Matthew 26:45-50
The choice Jesus could have made to avoid danger or pain:
The choice He made:

Matthew 26:50-52
The choice Jesus could have made to avoid danger or pain:
The choice He made:

Matthew 26:53-56
The choice Jesus could have made to avoid danger or pain:
The choice He made:

Matthew 26:57-75
The choice Jesus could have made to avoid danger or pain:
The choice He made:

Matthew 27:1-10
The choice Jesus could have made to avoid danger or pain:
The choice He made:

Matthew 27:11-26
The choice Jesus could have made to avoid danger or pain:
The choice He made:

Matthew 27:27-31
The choice Jesus could have made to avoid danger or pain:
The choice He made:

Matthew 27:32-44
The choice Jesus could have made to avoid danger or pain:
The choice He made:

Matthew 27:45-50
The choice Jesus could have made to avoid danger or pain:
The choice He made:

NOTES

OPTIONS
SESSION FOUR

STEP 1

Depending on the size of your group, assign three or more people the roles of rat, snake, and bat. Be sure to choose people who aren't afraid to "ham it up" in front of others. Encourage these actors to add as much humor and unpredictability to the skit as possible. For instance, the "rats" might nibble at Indy's and Cindy's legs; the "snakes" might lash out at Indy and Cindy unexpectedly; the "bats" might swoop down on Indy and Cindy throughout the skit.

STEP 4

Rather than naming all of the nearly impossible tasks right away, have the teams complete some easier tasks first. For instance, you could instruct them to carry a team member to the far wall and back. Then you could have each team pool its loose change together to get exactly 41 cents. After the teams have completed a few "easy" tasks, explain all the other things they have to do to receive the prize.

STEP 3

If you have fewer than six people in your group, try to get everyone involved in discussing these statements. After you read each statement, go around the group and have each person (not just volunteers) explain his or her reaction. Because of your small group, you have time to explore your group members' feelings. To get your kids to open up, you might ask questions like: **What Bible incidents or portrayals of Jesus in the media give you the idea that Jesus was kind of wimpy? If you knew that you were facing a horrible death in the future, do you think it would be hard to live your life day to day?**

STEP 3

Rather than having group members work individually on the slips, work on them together as a group. For each slip, have one person read the assigned passage; have another person complete the first statement; and have another person complete the second statement. Then ask other group members if they have anything to add. Alternate assignments for each slip until you've completed all ten.

STEP 1

Stage an elaborate production for the opening skit. Provide costumes for the two lead characters—a felt hat and leather jacket for Indy and an expensive-looking outfit for Cindy. Put a little makeup on the actors to make it look as though they've been through a rough adventure. Rather than having group members provide sound effects, try to find an appropriate sound-effects tape. Use rubber snakes, spiders, bats, rats, and bugs as props. (For extra effect, have the props attached to strings so that they can be maneuvered during skit.) If possible, the stage area should be dark enough to suggest a dangerous place, but light enough so that the audience can see what's going on. And, of course, no parody of Indiana Jones would be complete without the *Raiders of the Lost Ark* theme playing in the background.

STEP 2

The larger your group, the better chance your group members will have of finding teammates. Set a time limit—perhaps two minutes—and award prizes to the teams that complete the assignment on time.

OPTIONS
SESSION FOUR

STEP 2

To further explore your group members' opinions of Jesus, draw on some passages that they've probably heard many, many times in their lives. Have volunteers read aloud Matthew 5:5 and Matthew 5:39. Ask: **When you read of Jesus saying, "Blessed are the meek" and telling people to turn the other cheek to those who hurt them, how does that affect your opinion of Him? Why?**

STEP 3

It might be helpful for your "jaded" group members to put themselves into each scene described in the passages on the slips. They've probably heard and read these passages dozens of times; so, as a change of pace, encourage them to *live* the passages. Have them imagine that they're with Jesus (perhaps as His disciples) in each situation. How would they be feeling? What would they advise Jesus to do?

STEP 2

Task #2 assumes that most of your group members are Christians. If that's not the case, substitute the task with another situation that would require courage. For instance, you might use something like "Telling your father that you got an 'F' on your report card" or "Telling your mother that you broke her favorite lamp."

STEP 3

If your group members don't have much Bible background, you may need to give them the full picture of Jesus and His work on earth. You need to explain that He was fully God and fully human at the same time. As God, He knew what His mission on earth was: to save mankind by taking upon Himself the punishment for the world's sins—a punishment that included physical torture and one of the most painful forms of execution imaginable. Because He was human, His body would experience the same kind of pain that we would experience under similar circumstances. Throughout His life, He knew the agony He would face; yet He had the courage to go through with it.

STEP 2

Have group members pair up. Instruct them to talk with their partners about the scariest thing they've ever had to do. Have them explain why the situation was scary, how they felt at the time, and what happened. Then have them share how they managed to find the courage to face the situation. Be prepared to share a story of your own to get things started.

STEP 5

Wrap up the session with a time of silent prayer. Have group members refer back to the slip(s) they were given from Repro Resource 8. Have them thank Jesus for making the choice He made and for not choosing to avoid danger or pain. Then group members should pray that Jesus would give *them* courage to face their scary or difficult situations.

OPTIONS
SESSION FOUR

STEP 1

Instead of using Repro Resource 7 as a guy-girl skit, rename Indiana James as Young Wendy Fearless and have two girls play the roles. After the skit is concluded and the actors have been applauded, include these questions in the discussion. **Is courage easier for guys than for girls? Why or why not? Do you think courage has a different definition for girls? If so, what is it?**

STEP 2

Before the session, write only the first two statements listed and leave #3 blank. As you begin "Courage Counters," ask your group members to think of some things that would be very difficult for them and would take a great amount of courage. Then, as a group, vote on one suggestion to use. Substitute that suggestion for #3, and continue with the activity.

STEP 1

Rewrite the skit so that "Cindy" becomes "Lindy," Indy's younger brother. Lindy should act like a six year old throughout the skit. He should be scared of the various things in the temple, but rather than saying, "Eek!" and screaming, he should whine and say things like "I want my mommy." At the end of the skit, when Indy discovers his zit, Lindy should say, "What's wrong with having a zit? I thought all teenagers got zits!"

STEP 2

This activity may not work well if your guys aren't willing to share honestly with each other about what scares them. For instance, their competitive, macho natures may prevent them from admitting that someone else could do one of the tasks for fewer "courage units" than they could. To avoid this problem, you might want to list the three tasks (and any other tasks you can think of that would require courage) on the board, and then have group members rank them according to how scary they would be for *most people*. Guys may be more willing to share if they don't have to admit their personal fears. By putting the emphasis on "most people's" fears, you'll probably get a better response from your group members.

STEP 1

After the skit, play a game called "Guts." Bring in several different kinds of beverages—milk, cranberry juice, cola, coffee, egg nog, root beer, etc. Mix various combinations in a cup and then ask who has the "guts" to drink the concoction. For added effect, you might also want to bring in ketchup, mustard, mayonnaise, tabasco sauce, etc. to add to the mix. Use this activity to supplement your discussion of what it means to have courage (or "guts").

STEP 4

Turn this into an active exercise instead of a theoretical one. Explain that you will be giving group members four assignments to complete. The assignments will require work, but the first person to complete all four of them will get a prize. The assignments are as follows: do twenty push-ups; run to the far wall and back ten times; do twenty sit-ups; do thirty jumping jacks. (Adjust the assignments as necessary to fit your group.) When the first person finishes all four assignments, make a big deal out of awarding him or her the worthless prize.

OPTIONS
SESSION FOUR

Step 1
Record several action sequences from TV shows. Make sure you get some spectacular scenes in which the stunt people probably put themselves at risk. Try to get scenes that include someone jumping or falling off a tall building, someone hanging from a helicopter, someone in a high-speed car chase, someone battling a dangerous animal, etc. After you play each scene, have group members rate on a scale of one to ten how much courage it would take to do a stunt like that.

Step 3
Rent a couple of movies that deal with the life of Jesus (*The Greatest Story Ever Told, Jesus,* etc.). Show a couple of scenes from the movies in which Jesus is portrayed as being gentle, meek, or "wimpy." Then have group members talk about how accurate they think the portrayals are.

Step 2
Distribute index cards to your group members. Read each task aloud. (Add some of your own, if possible. For instance, you might suggest "Reporting an older student who's selling drugs in your school," "Singing a solo in front of the whole church," etc.) After you read a task, group members will rate that task on a scale of one to ten according to how much courage the task would require (one equals very little courage; ten equals a lot of courage). Group members will write their scores on their index cards and display them like judges at gymnastics or ice-skating competitions do.

Step 3
Rather than having kids work on Repro Resource 8 individually or in small groups, go through the sheet together as a group. Read each Scripture passage aloud. Then ask one person to name a choice Jesus had in that passage to avoid danger or pain; ask another person to name the choice Jesus actually made.

Step 1
Make the Temple of Gloom a scary "crack house" or "hotel" Indy and Cindy are trying to get out of. Instead of Cindy being afraid of skeletons, fungus beetles, rattlesnakes, and the like, have her fear the asphyxiating and intoxicating smoke, sewer rats, roaches, slipping on crack vials, someone propositioning them to get high, and a drug dealer with a gun. These images may resonate clearer for some city youngsters.

Step 2
Some urban examples of courage for this activity might include:

1. Going into an inner-city housing development at night.

2. Preaching at an Hispanic or African-American Sunday service without preparation.

3. Telling a drug dealer to stop his evil deeds.

4. Stopping a riot.

5. Protesting a Ku Klux Klan rally in a racist neighborhood.

6. Using the high school bathroom.

7. Telling your father to stop beating your mother.

OPTIONS
SESSION FOUR

STEP 2
Junior highers may be reluctant to honestly share in front of high schoolers how much courage it would take to do a certain task. If you think that might be the case with your group, skip playing the game. Simply collect the index cards and read (without revealing any identities) how group members divided the courage units.

STEP 5
Some of your junior highers may be reluctant to share some of their scary situations for fear that the high schoolers will think their fears are childish. To prevent this, recruit a couple of your high schoolers before the activity to help you. Ask them to recall their junior high days and think about what was scary to them at that time in their lives. Then, during this closing activity, these high schoolers can mention the situations they recalled. Not only will this help your junior highers feel more comfortable about sharing their fears, it may also help bridge the gap between the two age groups.

STEP 2
Change the list of challenges to be written before the session. Instead of using the campaign speech as #1, write, "Explaining at a school board meeting why your school should have more computers."

STEP 3
Instead of using all of the slips from Repro Resource 8, choose five or six and eliminate the others. Have group members work in small groups to find the information asked for on the slip. As the groups report what they've written, take a little extra time describing the event and the choice Jesus had to make. Help your sixth graders identify with each situation as if they were present and observing the alternatives.

DATE USED:

Approx. Time

STEP 1: *Indy and Cindy* _____
❑ Extra Action
❑ Large Group
❑ Mostly Girls
❑ Mostly Guys
❑ Extra Fun
❑ Media
❑ Urban
Things needed:

STEP 2: *Courage Counters* _____
❑ Large Group
❑ Heard It All Before
❑ Little Bible Background
❑ Fellowship & Worship
❑ Mostly Girls
❑ Mostly Guys
❑ Short Meeting Time
❑ Urban
❑ Combined Junior High/High School
❑ Sixth Grade
Things needed:

STEP 3: *Profile in Courage* _____
❑ Small Group (#1)
❑ Small Group (#2)
❑ Heard It All Before
❑ Little Bible Background
❑ Media
❑ Short Meeting Time
❑ Sixth Grade
Things needed:

STEP 4: *Eyes on the Prize* _____
❑ Extra Action
❑ Extra Fun
Things needed:

STEP 5: *Breaking Down the Door* _____
❑ Fellowship & Worship
❑ Combined Junior High/High School
Things needed:

SESSION 5

Does He Really Love Me?

YOUR GOALS FOR THIS SESSION:
Choose one or more

☐ To help kids see that Jesus felt and demonstrated real, personal love when He was on earth.

☐ To help kids understand that Jesus loves them in ways they can measure, even if they don't always feel His love.

☐ To help kids identify and work on removing one barrier that keeps them from feeling Jesus' love.

☐ Other:_____

Your Bible Base:

John 13—14
Romans 8:35-39
Ephesians 3:16-19

Love Scenes

OPTIONS

(Needed: Paper bags; bubble gum; hair dryer; prizes)

Get two pairs of volunteers—a guy and a girl in each pair. Seat the two pairs at the front of the room.

Explain that you're going to conduct a Hollywood screen test. The guy and girl in each pair will act out a romantic scene. To make it easy, these will be the only lines of dialogue:

GUY: "Oh, Priscilla."
GIRL: "Oh, Pemberton."

The actors should use the lines over and over, trying to sound as romantic as possible.

Then add: **Oh, there's one other thing. To find out whether you can work around all the noise of a Hollywood set, I may add a couple of minor distractions. But keep going. The couple that sounds the most romantic will win the prize. Go!**

After pairs have said the lines a couple of times, start jumping in with distractions. Add each of the following every 15 seconds or so.

(1) Get a breeze going on the actors with a hand-held hair dryer.
(2) Add another actor, whose job is to bother the pairs by yelling things like, "Peanuts! Popcorn! Get your peanuts right here!"
(3) Give all the actors bubble gum and tell them that they must blow at least one bubble each.
(4) Put paper bags over the actors' heads.

After your actors have suffered enough, let the rest of the group choose the winning pair. Award prizes.

Then ask: **Do you think the actors did a good job of communicating true love to each other? Why or why not?** (Probably not—since they weren't really in love, they couldn't use their own words, and too many other things were going on.)

In real life, how can you tell whether somebody loves you? (He or she says so; the person does thoughtful things for you and treats you as if you're special; the person wants to spend time with you; etc.)

UNIT TWO

Jesus Loves Me?

Have kids sit in a circle if possible. Announce that you're going to sing (or say) the words to the song, "Jesus Loves Me." But each person can say only one word; the first says, "Jesus," the second says, "loves," etc., all the way around the circle until you've finished the first verse and chorus. Anyone who doesn't know the words should feel free not to participate.

When you're done singing or saying the song in this way, ask:

What was that all about? What's the message of that song? (That Jesus loves us.)

But what does that mean? *How* **does He love us?** Answers will vary; you don't need to settle on one answer yet.

According to this song, how do we know Jesus loves us? (The Bible tells us so.)

Is that the only way to know? Or can you feel His love?

Let kids respond if they want to. Then say: **We hear a lot about how Jesus loves us and how we're supposed to love Him—but many of us aren't sure exactly what that means. Let's find out.**

Let Me Count the Ways

(Needed: Bibles; cut-up copies of Repro Resource 9; team prize)

Before the meeting, copy and cut enough sets of cards from "Out of Order" (Repro Resource 9) so that you have one set of cards for every three or four kids. Put each set in a separate envelope, and shake each envelope to thoroughly mix up the order of the cards.

At this point, form teams of three or four kids. Give each team an envelope of cards. Announce that the first team to put its cards in the right order will be the winner. All the quotes are from John 13–14.

162

Make sure each team has at least one New International Version of the Bible. Then say, **Go!**

Allow plenty of time for kids to scan the chapters and put their verses in order. Give a prize to the first team that puts its cards in the right order, or the team that gets the most done in seven minutes. (Note that the quotes appear in the correct order on the original Repro Resource 9.)

Then ask: **What do these quotes tell you about the kind of love Jesus has for people?**

As you work your way through the quotes, use the following information as needed.

"Having loved His own ..." (13:1)—Jesus loves specific people (here, His disciples), not just people in general. His love is also something He shows, not just something He feels.

"He poured water into a basin ..." (13:5)—His love makes Him willing to serve people, even doing the "low-down" jobs.

"One of them, the disciple whom Jesus loved ..." (13:23)—Again, Jesus loves specific people, has special feelings for them, and is willing to be close to them.

"As I have loved you ..." (13:34)—His love is an example of the way we should love each other.

"In my Father's house ..." (14:2)—Jesus' love makes Him interested in our futures, and He cares enough to prepare places in heaven for us.

"I will come back ..." (14:3)—Jesus loves us enough that He wants to have us with Him forever.

"You may ask me for anything ..." (14:14)—One way Jesus shows His love is by listening to our requests and answering them.

"I will ask the Father ..." (14:16, 17)—Jesus loves us enough to give us the guidance we need while He's away.

"I will not leave you as orphans ..." (14:18)—Because He loves us, He won't abandon us.

"Because I live ..." (14:19)—He loves us enough to give us eternal life. That's why He died on the cross for us.

"I am in my Father ..." (14:20)—He loves us enough to want to be part of us.

"He who loves me ..." (14:21)—He promises to love not just a few special friends, but anyone who loves and obeys Him.

"If anyone loves me ..." (14:23)—Jesus (and His Father) love us enough to live with and in us.

"Peace I leave with you ..." (14:27)—Jesus cares how we're feeling; He's interested in whether we are at peace or not.

"Do not let your hearts be troubled ..." (14:27)—He loves us enough to reassure and encourage us.

After discussing the quotes, ask: **Which of these quotes means the most to you? Why?**

UNIT TWO

STEP 4

Can You Feel It?

(Needed: Electric fan; crepe paper; tape)

Set up an electric fan at the front of the room. Kids should be far enough away from it that they won't feel the breeze. Turn on the fan.

Ask: **Is this fan off or on? How do you know?** (We saw you turn it on; we can hear it.)

Tape a few strips of crepe paper to the front of the fan, so that the breeze blows the strips. Ask: **Now how do you know whether the fan is on?** (We can see the paper moving.)

But you still can't feel it, can you? What would you have to do to feel whether the fan is on? (Get close to it.)

Choose one person to move closer to the fan until he or she can feel it. Then ask that person: **Is the fan off or on? How do you know?** (On; I can feel it.)

Now move closer to the fan until you can feel the breeze. Raise your hand as soon as you can feel it.

Wait until all the kids have raised their hands. **Now, when did the fan start blowing—when I turned it on, or when you raised your hand?** (When you turned it on.)

How might feeling the breeze from this fan be like feeling Jesus' love for us?

Listen to kids' responses. Then make the following points as needed.

(1) Just as the fan can be working even if we don't feel it, Jesus can be loving us even if we don't feel His love.

(2) We can tell from the Bible that Jesus loves us, just as we can tell from the blowing strips of paper that the fan is on—even if we don't feel it.

(3) We can listen to others who do feel Jesus' love, even when we can't.

(4) The closer we are to Jesus, the more we can feel His love—just as we felt the breeze as we got closer to the fan.

Have a volunteer read Ephesians 3:16-19. Then ask: **Do you think Paul, who wrote these verses, could feel Jesus' love?** (Yes; he seemed to know "how wide and long and high and deep" it is. Paul wanted his readers not only to know about Jesus' love, but to be full of His love in their hearts. Jesus' love is more than an intellectual thing—it surpasses knowledge.)

OPTIONS

LITTLE BIBLE BACKGROUND

MOSTLY GIRLS

URBAN

He was praying that all Christians would know that, too. What things did he think would help them do that? (Having power from God's Holy Spirit; believing that Christ lives in our hearts; being "rooted" in love—so that we know what love is in the first place.)

Something's Come between Us

(Needed: Paper plates; markers or pens)

Pass out paper plates, one for each group member. Kids should still be standing close enough to the fan that they can feel the breeze.

Have kids hold the paper plates in front of their faces. Ask: **Can you still feel the breeze on your face? Why not?** (No; the plate is in the way.)

What are some things that keep us from feeling Jesus' love for us, just as the plates keep us from feeling the breeze? (Feeling guilty about something we've done, too guilty to get close to Jesus; not communicating with Him in prayer; keeping busy with lots of other things; being mad at Him because we think our prayers weren't answered; having doubts that we don't get answers to; etc.)

Hand out markers or pens. **On your plate, write or draw letters or symbols that stand for something that keeps you from feeling the love of Jesus. Then decide what you want to do with the plate. If you don't want to do anything about the problem that keeps you from feeling Jesus' love, you might keep the plate. If you want to get rid of the problem, you might sail the plate into a corner or tear it up.**

After giving kids a few moments to decide what to do, ask them to face the fan so that they can feel the breeze again. As they do, read Romans 8:35-39.

Then say: **Jesus' love for us is stronger than anything else. No one can take it from us. But He won't force His love on us if we don't want it.** Give kids a chance to pray silently, telling the Lord how they feel about His love and asking for His help in removing anything that keeps them from feeling that love.

NOTES

FACE TO FACE TO JESUS REPRO RESOURCE 9

Out of Order

"Having loved His own who were in the world, He now showed them the full extent of His love."	"He poured water into a basin and began to wash His disciples' feet, drying them with the towel that was wrapped around Him."	"One of them, the disciple whom Jesus loved, was reclining next to Him."
"As I have loved you, so you must love one another."	"In My Father's house are many rooms. . . . I am going there to prepare a place for you."	"I will come back and take you to be with Me."
"You may ask Me for anything in My name, and I will do it."	"I will ask the Father, and He will give you another Counselor to be with you forever—the Spirit of truth."	"I will not leave you as orphans; I will come to you."
"Because I live, you also will live."	"I am in My Father, and you are in Me, and I am in you."	"He who loves Me will be loved by My Father, and I too will love him and show Myself to him."
"If anyone loves Me, he will obey My teaching. My Father will love him, and We will come to him and make Our home with him."	"Peace I leave with you; My peace I give you."	"Do not let your hearts be troubled and do not be afraid."

NOTES

OPTIONS
SESSION FIVE

STEP 3
For added excitement, turn this activity into a relay race. Give each team a roll of masking tape. Once team members have determined the order of the cards, they must take turns running the cards one at a time to the other end of the room and taping them to the wall. The first team to tape all fifteen cards to the wall in the correct order wins.

STEP 5
After group members have drawn their symbols on their plates, place a trash can in the middle of the room. Have group members try to toss their plates into the can. Explain that getting the plate in the trash can represents getting rid of the obstacle. If group members don't hit the trash can on their first shot, they should stand where their plates land and try again. Point out that getting rid of the obstacles that prevent us from feeling Jesus' love isn't easy. It may take several tries, over long periods of time. We may think we've gotten rid of an obstacle, only to have it pop up again later. Therefore, we should constantly be prepared to remove such obstacles.

STEP 1
If you have fewer than seven or eight people in your group, this would be a great activity in which to involve *all* of them. Use only one pair of actors for the activity. Then have the rest of your group members take turns trying to distract the pair. You may want to brainstorm some additional distractions for group members to use (such as plugging the actors' noses while they talk) or let your group members come up with their own.

STEP 3
Cut apart one copy of Repro Resource 9, and spread the cards on the floor in front of the group. Give group members six minutes to arrange the cards in order. If they complete the assignment in the allotted time, they get a prize; if not, they have to perform some kind of stunt (singing "The B-I-B-L-E" as loud as they can, making ugly faces in front of the entire group, etc.).

STEP 1
Stage an elaborate "production area" for your Hollywood screen test. Create a set—perhaps the living room of a house (with couches, tables, TV, etc.) or a street corner (with a lamppost, fire hydrant, etc.). Give your actors stage directions to follow as they recite their lines. You could also have props available for the actors to use. You might consider having romantic music playing in the background. Depending on how big your group is, use three or four pairs in your screen test. Encourage the people doing the distracting to use their creativity—and any props on hand—as they disrupt each scene. For instance, someone could turn up the volume of the background music so loud that the actors can't hear each other—or perhaps substitute a rap or heavy metal recording. If you use a living room set, someone else may come in, sit between the two actors, and pretend to watch TV.

STEP 2
Have your kids form groups of six or seven. Each group should sit in a circle. The object of the activity is to create a "round" in singing "Jesus Loves Me." Have one group begin the song (with the first person in the group singing "Jesus," the second singing "loves," etc.). When the first group gets to the word "know," point to a second group to begin the song. When the second group gets to the word "know," point to a third group, and so on. Each group should keep repeating the song (maintaining the proper pace) until you give the signal to stop.

OPTIONS
SESSION FIVE

STEP 3

Kids who've grown up in the church have heard expressions like "Jesus loves me" and "Jesus cares about me" so often that the words tend to lose their significance and meaning. Help these group members "redefine" these expressions by having them describe Jesus' feelings toward them—without using the words *love* or *care* (or any variation of the words).

One way to do this would be to have group members create valentines that Jesus might send to us—without using the words *love* or *care* on the valentines.

STEP 5

If no one mentions it, you may want to suggest that "overfamiliarity" may hinder us in experiencing Jesus' love. Kids who've been raised in the church and who've heard (over and over and over) powerful testimonies of what Jesus' love has done in the lives of others may tend to (a) experience His love vicariously through others rather than experiencing it firsthand, or (b) doubt the power of Jesus' love in their own lives because they haven't had any dramatic evidences of it.

STEP 3

Some of your group members may have a hard time truthfully stating, "Jesus loves me, this I know." They may *not* know that Jesus loves them. And "for the Bible tells me so" may not be enough to convince them. You may need to review with your group members Jesus' ultimate proof of His love—His willingness to take the punishment that we deserved for our sin and to give His life for us. You could introduce the topic by reading John 15:13, 14 and asking: **Can you think of a better way to prove your love for someone than by dying to save that person?**

STEP 4

For those group members unfamiliar with Scripture and Bible history, it might be interesting to hear the background of Paul, the writer of Ephesians—and the person testifying to the power of Jesus' love. Point out that Paul (then known as Saul) was feared by most early Christians because he was a leader in the movement to stamp out Christianity. (Christianity was illegal in the early part of the first century.) He was probably personally responsible for arresting, torturing, and killing many Christians. But after a powerful encounter with the risen Jesus, Paul's life turned completely around. He ended up writing most of the books in the New Testament and beginning several of the early churches. Emphasize that Jesus' life-changing love is still available today to *anyone*, regardless of his or her background.

STEP 2

Have group members pair up. Instruct them to share with their partners about a time in their lives when they experienced Jesus' love. They may share about something dramatic, like a recovery from a serious injury; or they may share about something less dramatic, like a comfort they received from a certain Bible verse or song. Then have group members share with their partners about a time in their lives when they doubted Jesus' love for them. They may share about the death of a loved one, about feeling lonely all the time, etc. Encourage group members to be honest and candid with their partners.

STEP 5

Close the session by singing "Jesus Loves Me" as a group again. However, in place of the phrase "for the Bible tells me so," have group members substitute a *specific* passage from the Bible (perhaps one of the verses from John 13–14) that reassures them of Jesus' love. For instance, someone might sing, "Jesus loves me, this I know, for *John 14:14* tells me so. . . ."

OPTIONS
SESSION FIVE

STEP 1

Instead of a guy-girl skit, have three volunteers each try to convince the rest of the group that she is loved the most. Have the three girls use one of these statements, repeating it over and over with exaggerated, dramatic expression. "I know Jerry loves me because he sent me flowers." "I can tell Zack loves me; he says flowers aren't important enough for our love." "I know how much Chuck loves me when I read the poetry he writes about me." Use the same distractions, and then see how many group members are convinced by these statements about love.

STEP 4

Have your group members talk about the frequent unreliability of human feelings. After using the fan as an illustration, have your group members divide into three teams. Give each team a set of the "Out of Order" slips. Give the teams two minutes to decide how many slips involve doing something to show love. Afterward, have someone read aloud II John 6 and John 15:9-14. Explain that Jesus' love for us is something that will never change.

STEP 1

Instead of using two guy-girl pairs, use two pairs of guys. Explain that the pairs will be acting out a dramatic scene in a love story. Assign one person in each pair this line of dialogue: "I love her with all of my heart." Assign the other person in each pair this line: "You can't love her— I love her!" Use the same distractions, and then award a prize to the winning pair. Afterward, ask: **Do you think the actors did a good job of communicating their love for the girl? Why or why not? In real life, how can you tell whether somebody loves you?**

STEP 5

Guys may be reluctant to write even letters or symbols on their plates for fear that someone else will see what they wrote and figure it out. So rather than having them write on their plates, have them *think* of something that prevents them from feeling Jesus' love. Then explain that the plate *represents* that obstacle.

STEP 1

Open the session with a game of "If You Love Me." Have group members form a circle. Choose one person to be "it." That person will kneel in front of someone of the opposite sex and say, "If you love me, _____, smile." In addressing the victim, the person who is "it" should think of some goofy pet name to call the person—"Squirrel Cheeks," "Chicken Lips," "Honey Bunch," etc. The victim must then respond, "_____ (his or her pet name) loves you, but I just can't smile"—without smiling. If the victim smiles, he or she becomes "it"; if not, the person who is it must find another victim.

STEP 2

After group members have recited the song normally, have a contest to see if they can recite it *backward*. Give them a minute to think of the lyrics. Then point to a person to begin. Going clockwise around the circle, group members will recite the words to the song in reverse order, one word at a time ("so," "me," "tells," "Bible," etc.). If a person says a wrong word or takes more than five seconds to think of the next word, he or she is out. Continue until only one person remains.

OPTIONS
SESSION FIVE

STEP 1

Before the session, record several clips from TV shows, movies, commercials, or popular songs in which the word *love* is mentioned. Look for several different uses of the word. For instance, someone in a commercial might say, "I love what you do for me, Toyota" or "Quaker Oats—you're gonna love it in an instant." Characters in TV shows or movies might use the word love to describe their feelings about everything from a person to a pet to a particular flavor of ice cream. Most popular songs deal with the topic of love (although you'll want to be careful about which songs you choose to record). After your group members have seen and listened to the various clips, have them come up with a definition of love that can be applied to every usage you just saw or heard. Then discuss how that general, vague definition compares to Jesus' feelings for us.

STEP 5

As your group members work, play a recording of "Silent Love" (from the album *Medals*) by Russ Taff. When kids finish their plates, encourage them to listen to the lyrics of the song. Have them think about *why* the Lord's love is "silent."

STEP 1

Rather than using volunteers to disrupt the skit, do it yourself. Use the bubble gum distraction and the paper bag distraction. Also, you might want to startle the actors a couple of times by yelling or jumping at them while they speak. Don't let the skit go on too long—60-90 seconds would be ideal.

STEP 3

If you're running short of time, don't distribute Repro Resource 9. Instead, call out the Scripture references one at a time. Group members will then race to look up each passage and read aloud the quote that talks about Jesus' love.

STEP 2

Expand the issue of love for your final question. Ask: **How do you know if Jesus loves the city?** Point out that people tend to look down on the city as a bad place to live. This false image has to be broken first among its inhabitants. Cause the group to wrestle with what godly things their city has to offer the kingdom of God. Some may recognize churches, the youth group, a quiet park or stream. Others may acknowledge the multiplicity of the city or elders in their communities as a blessing. Still another may notice the animals (squirrels and pigeons) that inhabit the city. Let group members know that Jesus loves the city, and can be found just as powerfully there if we search Him out.

STEP 4

Have a volunteer go to the other side of the room and put either cologne or perfume on—just enough so that it's obvious he or she has it on. Instruct this person to stand away from the fan. Ask the rest of the group members to determine whether he or she is wearing cologne or perfume. The group members should not be able to answer. Then have the person stand in front of the fan. Eventually, the group will be able to describe the aroma and identify if it's cologne or perfume. Have group members slowly move closer and notice how the fragrance pleasantly intensifies. Then discuss how the Holy Spirit (wind) moves from the Son (the volunteer) through the power of God (the fan) to alert the world of the "aroma" of Christ.

OPTIONS
SESSION FIVE

STEP 1

If possible, use two high schoolers for one pair of actors and two junior highers for the other pair. Then have a junior higher try to distract the high school pair and have a high schooler try to distract the junior high pair. The high schooler doing the distracting might say things like, "You two are too young to be in love! You're just little kids!" The junior higher doing the distracting might say things like, "If you're in love with him, why are you wearing _____'s letter jacket?" If you don't think the rest of the group can be objective in determining a winner, you may need to choose the winning pair yourself.

STEP 3

This activity would work well as a competition between junior highers and high schoolers. Split up the two age groups and give one set of cards to each team. The first team to arrange all fifteen cards in order wins. To "raise the stakes" in the competition, you may want to announce that the losing team has to sing "You Win and We Lose" (to the tune of "Happy Birthday to You") to the winning team.

STEP 1

Instead of using guy-girl pairs for a love scene, ask three or four volunteers to sit in front of the room and mime the facial expressions and actions they would use to show their love to someone (exaggerating as necessary). Use the distractions described in the session to interrupt your volunteer mimes. Afterward, take a vote to see who best expressed love.

STEP 3

Help your sixth graders be more specific in their discussion of how Jesus expressed His love. As you talk about the quotes from John 13—14, summarize on the board the key ideas from each quote. For example, you might write, "Jesus shows His love by loving individuals, doing everyday jobs, caring about our future, listening, etc."

DATE USED:

Approx. Time

STEP 1: *Love Scenes* _____
❏ Small Group
❏ Large Group
❏ Mostly Girls
❏ Mostly Guys
❏ Extra Fun
❏ Media
❏ Short Meeting Time
❏ Combined Junior High/High School
❏ Sixth Grade
Things needed:

STEP 2: *Jesus Loves Me?* _____
❏ Large Group
❏ Fellowship & Worship
❏ Extra Fun
❏ Urban
Things needed:

STEP 3: *Let Me Count the Ways* _____
❏ Extra Action
❏ Small Group
❏ Heard It All Before
❏ Little Bible Background
❏ Short Meeting Time
❏ Combined Junior High/High School
❏ Sixth Grade
Things needed:

STEP 4: *Can You Feel It?* _____
❏ Little Bible Background
❏ Mostly Girls
❏ Urban
Things needed:

STEP 5: *Something's Come between Us* _____
❏ Extra Action
❏ Heard It All Before
❏ Fellowship & Worship
❏ Mostly Guys
❏ Media
Things needed:

NOTES

Unit Three: Extreme Closeup

How You and God Can Stay Connected

by Paul Borthwick

Several years ago, my sister-in-law returned home after a meal out at a local restaurant. A few hours later, she was overcome with nausea. Her first thought? Food poisoning. She quickly grabbed the telephone directory, searching for the number for the "Poison Control Hotline."

By the time she found the number, she felt so sick that she thought she was going to die. She managed to dial the hotline number. The phone was busy. She tried again. And again. On the third attempt, she finally got through. A gracious sounding voice answered, "Poison control hotline, please hold." My sister-in-law was too shocked to speak. She thought she was dying of ptomaine poisoning, and they put her on hold. In her hour of great need, there was no one there to respond.

Is this how many of your young people feel about God? Do they think that He's too busy to care about them? That He doesn't really want to relate or talk to them? That He's aloof and uncaring about their deepest needs? As spiritual leaders, we want to communicate to kids that God both cares and desires to communicate with them. They can build a relationship with Him that lasts. They can stay connected with God and His purposes.

Identify the Condition of Your Group Members

How do your kids feel about their relationship with God? In most youth groups, kids' opinions vary widely. A few might feel that Jesus walks with them as their best friend, while others sense that their relationship with God either does not exist or has been put "on hold"—with no communication either way.

How do we find out what group members think so that we can make sure we address the real needs of our kids? A formal or informal survey serves as an excellent starting point. A survey or personal conversation helps us discover if kids ever read the Bible on their own, pray for others, or serve others in a way that is consciously connected with their faith (some participate in good deeds without really connecting it as an outflow of their relationship with God).

A printed survey (or one-on-one conversations with group members) might include questions like the following:

1. What have you read lately in the Bible?
2. Do you feel that God speaks to you through the Bible? Through prayer?
3. When do you feel most connected to God?
4. What do these terms mean to you: prayer, worship, fellowship?
5. What are some examples of service that you think a junior higher could attempt? Have you ever tried any of these?
6. What do you think are your greatest obstacles to reading the Bible? To prayer? To serving others?
7. Do you believe that God really loves you and wants to communicate with you?

The answers to these questions help us understand the spiritual perspectives of group members. This in turn equips us to adapt and utilize the sessions that follow in order to fit the needs we uncover.

Find Out What's Working and Build on It

Another step—perhaps again achieved through some formal research like a survey, although informal conversations usually yield better results—is to find out what positively affects kids regarding the Bible, prayer, fellowship, worship, and serving.

What aspects of worship seem to have the greatest impact on them? Why do some kids pray while others do not? Is there an effective way already in place that involves kids in Bible study? If kids are serving, what attracts them to service and how are they growing as a result?

Discovering the answers to these questions gives us concrete ideas to build on. We need not create new programs or devise new tactics if something already works in the lives of young people. As we encourage increased Scripture study, prayer, worship, fellowship, and service, we can build on models we observe in junior highers who exemplify what we want to stimulate in the whole group.

A young person involved in care for the handicapped or in outreach at a nursing home illustrates an example of service. Kids who already write in a journal as part of their prayer time and Bible study can share their experiences with the whole group. Group members who lead in prayer or worship demonstrate some of the growth possibilities for others in the group.

Steps toward Greater Effectiveness

Our goal is to help kids connect with God, to sense that He communicates with them and desires to be involved in their daily lives. As you use the sessions in this book, keep the following principles in mind.

- *Be realistic.* Try not to overload kids with unrealistic expectations about what spirituality looks like. Spiritual growth does not require pious language and sanctimonious behavior. We want to help kids grow as followers of Jesus Christ, not become thirteen-year-old Pharisees who use spiritual pretense to mask a judgmental spirit of others.

We once had a young person in the youth group who started getting very excited about his spiritual growth. Unfortunately, genuine spiritual growth started degenerating due to the influence of some well-meaning, pietistic adults. The young man started talking in King James English, praying with words like "Verily" and "multitudinous blessings" and using only "Thee," "Thou," and "Thy" in reference to God. The issue came to a head when he began "smiting sinners" at school with his enormous black leather Bible.

Highly influenceable young people respond to the expectations we thrust upon them, so let's make sure we dedicate ourselves to helping our kids "connect" with God in ways that positively affect their growth.

- *Meet them on their level.* Talk in terms kids understand. The writings of Richard Foster or the classical work of Bernard of Clairvaux may be changing your life spiritually, but make sure to translate what you're learning into language a teenager can understand.

- *Exemplify what you teach.* As we lead, we can feel free to make sure that kids understand our difficulties in "staying connected" with God. Young people do not expect us to be perfect, but they often think that being "spiritual" is easier for adults: "Of course you write in a journal; you're old!"

Kids need to know our struggles because sharing them helps the young people realize that their problems are normal. However, kids also need to know that we strive to do what we teach. Therefore, we should be writing in our journals and showing kids how we do it. I periodically ask kids to hold me accountable regarding prayer. When we lead the group in worship, we set the pact with our own worship. In group functions, we can demonstrate the difference between fellowship and simply having fun together. If we look for opportunities to serve, we imitate Jesus and Paul by leading with the imperative, "Follow me."

• *Adjust your schedule accordingly.* To implement these sessions, we need to allow time in the overall youth program. The activity-orientation of most youth groups often precludes any time allotment to help kids stay connected with God. Kids doubt the priority of worship, serving, or fellowship if there is no impact on the youth group schedule.

To encourage Bible study and prayer, we should allow time on a retreat for daily personal Bible study, writing in journals, and personal worship. We can factor corporate worship and fellowship time into weekly activities like Sunday school or mid-week Bible study. If we build service opportunities into the youth group calendar, kids are more likely to take action.

Two years ago, Jim cut back on his youth group "fun" activities because he saw that there were no opportunities for group members to engage in significant service to others, and the schedule was too full to add anything else. At first, kids (and some parents) complained because the monthly "fun" activities were reduced from four to three. Jim weathered the complaints and endured. After several months, kids (and some parents) began recommending more service opportunities because they could see the growth in their lives. But these results occurred because Jim wanted a schedule that reflected his real priorities for the group.

Francis Schaeffer wrote a book titled *God Is There and He Is Not Silent*. This is the message that we desire to communicate to young people. God does not put us on hold or neglect us in our moments of need. He desires to commune and communicate with us. We can stay connected with God because He desires to stay connected with us.

Paul Borthwick is minister of missions at Grace Chapel in Lexington, Massachusetts. A former youth pastor and frequent speaker to youth workers, he is author of several books including Organizing Your Youth Ministry *and* Feeding Your Forgotten Soul: Spiritual Growth for Youth Workers *(Zondervan).*

Publicity Clip Art

The images on these two pages are designed to help you promote this course within your church and community. Feel free to photocopy anything here and adapt it to fit your publicity needs. The stuff on this page could be used as a flier that you send or hand out to kids—or as a bulletin insert. The stuff on the next page could be used to add visual interest to newsletters, calendars, bulletin boards, or other promotions. Be creative and have fun!

How's Your Relationship with God?

Is reading the Bible a chore for you? Do you ever fall asleep in the middle of your prayer time? Does God seem a little more "distant" than you'd like Him to be?

In our new series *Extreme Closeup,* we'll explore some practical ways to improve your relationship with the Lord. If you'd like some helpful tips on reading the Bible, praying, and serving others, join us.

Who:

When:

Where:

Questions? Call:

Unit Three: Extreme Closeup

SESSION 1

Why Read the Bible?

YOUR GOALS FOR THIS SESSION:
Choose one or more

- [ ] To help kids discover that the Bible is an interesting book that can be enjoyable and beneficial to them.

- [ ] To help kids understand that the Bible is God's "love letter" to us.

- [ ] To help kids establish a daily time in the Bible that will strengthen their relationship with God.

- [ ] Other: _____

Your Bible Base:

Psalms 1; 119:97-105

STEP 1

Love Letters

OPTIONS: SMALL GROUP, FELLOWSHIP & WORSHIP, MOSTLY GUYS, SHORT MEETING TIME, URBAN

(Needed: Table, paper, pencils, envelopes, stamps, wastebasket, chalkboard and chalk or newsprint and marker, prizes)

Have kids form teams of three. Explain that they will be competing in a "love letter relay." Instruct the teams to stand at one end of the room in single-file lines. At the opposite end of the room, set up a long table. Place a piece of paper, a pencil, an envelope, and a stamp together in a pile on the table for each team. Explain that each team must write a love letter, fold it up, put it in the envelope, seal the envelope, address it, stamp it, and then drop it in the "mailbox" (a wastebasket that you've set up on the opposite end of the room from the table).

Each of the three team members will perform two steps of the process. After the first person from each team has finished his or her first assignment, he or she must run back to tag the next team member, who will then complete his or her assignment, and so on. Each team will go through the line twice.

The six steps of the process are as follows (write them on the board so that contestants will know exactly what to do):

1—Write "My Dearest [the name of a person in the group], I love you so much. I want you to love me, so let me tell you a little bit about myself."

2—Write "My favorite food is _____. My favorite TV show is _____. My favorite music group is _____."

3—Write "Would you like to get to know me better? Circle yes or no. Love, [your name]."

4—Fold the letter, put it in the envelope, and seal the envelope.

5—Address the envelope to [the name of a person in the group], [the name and address of your church]. Use your own address for the return address. Then put a stamp on the envelope.

6—Drop the letter off in the "mailbox," run back to your team, and sit down.

The first team to get its letter dropped off in the mailbox and then have everyone on the team sitting in a single-file line is the winner. Afterward, open the letter of the winning team to make sure that everything was done correctly. Then award prizes to the winning team members.

UNIT THREE

Unopened Mail

Say: **Wow, if I'd known that writing love letters was that much trouble, I never would have written the thousands I wrote when I was in junior high!**

After your kids stop hooting and hollering over your "slight exaggeration," ask: **How would you feel if someone sent you a love letter?** (Flattered, eager to read what it says, curious, overjoyed, embarrassed.)

If you came home from school one day and found a letter in the mail addressed to you, how long would you wait before opening it? Why? (Most kids probably wouldn't wait very long because receiving a letter is exciting.)

Point out that God has sent us a letter—a *love* letter, no less—called the Bible. In this letter, God tells us how much He loves us. He also tells us a lot about Himself—through actual events that happened in history, through parables, and especially through His Son, Jesus Christ.

Explain to your kids that for a variety of reasons, people often treat the Bible like an unopened piece of mail, never bothering to check what's inside. That's too bad, because they're missing out on some very interesting reading material.

Blockbuster Bible

(Needed: Bibles, copies of Repro Resource 1, pencils, prizes [optional])

Have kids form groups of three or four. Hand out copies of "Bible Epics" (Repro Resource 1) and pencils to each group. You might want to give the following references for the Bible stories listed on the sheet: *David and Bathsheba*—2 Samuel 11:1–12:25; *Jacob and Esau*—Genesis 25:21-34; 27:1–33:20; *Esther*—Esther 1–9; *the birth of Jesus*—Matthew 1:18–2:23; Luke 1:26–2:40. Give the groups a few minutes to fill out the sheet. When everyone is finished, have a spokesperson for each group

read what his or her group came up with for movie titles, actors and actresses to star in the movies, and movie categories. Vote to see which group came up with the most clever movie title and which group came up with the best casting for actors and actresses. Award prizes, if you like.

Afterward, say: **We've seen that the Bible is more than just genealogies in which someone "begat" somebody else or weird laws like prohibiting cutting the hair on the side of your head or clipping off the edges of your beard** (Leviticus 19:27). **The Bible also teaches us how God wants us to live and gives us answers on how we and God can become better connected. Let's take a look.**

STEP 4

What's in It for Me?

(Needed: Bibles, dictionary, stopwatch, blindfold)

Have kids turn in their Bibles to Psalm 1. Ask for a volunteer to read aloud the psalm. Afterward, ask: **What do you think it means to be blessed?** (Kids may offer such answers as "to receive some special favor" or "to be lucky.")

After a few kids have responded, pull out your trusty *Webster's New Collegiate Dictionary* and read what *blessed* really means—"of or enjoying happiness." Then ask: **Based on this meaning of *blessed*, what are some words that people today might substitute for "blessed" in Psalm 1:1?** (Rich, well-liked, popular, successful, etc.) Explain that even though it's tempting to enjoy material, worldly things in our lives, we shouldn't let them become our main focus because they won't make us blessed.

Have your volunteer read Psalm 1:2 again. Then say: **Verse 2 indicates that this "blessed" person whom the writer is talking about isn't focusing on some of those material things we've just mentioned. It says his delight is in the law of the Lord and that He meditates on that law day and night. What is the law of the Lord?** (His Word, the Bible.)

Your kids may not be too sold on the idea of being "in the Bible" for more than a few minutes, not to mention being in it "day and night." Ask them the following questions to lighten the mood: **What's the latest you've ever stayed up studying for a test or doing** homework? **Have you ever stayed up all night before? If so, when?** Get several responses.

Explain to your kids that Psalm 1:2 isn't talking about twenty-four-hour Bible vigils; it's talking about reading and studying God's Word enough so that its teachings constantly "shine through" in our everyday lives.

Highlight the benefits of delighting in God's Word by having kids find God's promises to us in verses 3 ("whatever he does prospers") and 6 ("the Lord watches over the way of the righteous").

Have your kids turn to Psalm 119. Ask for a volunteer to read aloud verses 97-105. Then ask: **How would you describe the attitude of this psalm's writer, based on verses 97-104?** (Confident, because he knows that meditating on God's laws makes him wiser than other people, particularly his enemies; happy, almost giddy, about God's law in verses 97 and 103.)

How would you describe your attitude when you think about God's law and what the Bible has to say? Explain that we should delight in reading God's Word, rather than approaching it negatively, assuming that the Bible simply tells us what we *can't* do.

Emphasize that God's Word can be a lamp to our feet and a light to our path. Then ask: **When might the Bible be a light in your life?** (When you feel lonely, when you're unsure about what to do, when you struggle with temptation, when you don't feel joy, despite the fact that you're a Christian.)

Ask two kids to leave the room. Have the rest of the group members set up a maze in your meeting room (using pathways of chairs, desks, etc.) that the two volunteers will have to maneuver through by crawling. When the maze is set up, have the volunteers come in one at a time. Blindfold one of them. Have each of them crawl through the maze, timing each one with a stopwatch to see who gets through the maze more quickly.

Afterward (assuming the blindfolded contestant lost the race), ask: **What might have helped** [name of blindfolded contestant] **get through the maze quicker? How might you compare reading and studying God's Word with the maze activity we just did?** (Studying God's Word makes navigating the "maze" of life a bit easier by giving us light for our path and a lamp for our feet.)

Take Hold of the Wheel!

(Needed: Two chairs)

Say: **For those of you who haven't driven before, how do you feel when you think about finally getting to drive?** (Scared, excited, nervous, pumped up, unsure, confident, etc.)

How would you feel if, during your entire driver's education class, you never once got to drive, not even around the parking lot? Explain that in case this unfortunate circumstance should ever happen to any of your group members, you're going to give them a simulated driving experience to see if they would be up to the test.

Ask for a volunteer to come to the front of the room. Set two chairs next to each other at the front of the room to serve as the driver's and passenger's seats of a driver's ed car. Announce that you will serve as the instructor.

Explain to your volunteer and to the other group members that the volunteer is to pretend that he or she is backing out of a driveway and then pulling away. Let your kids know that you have a list of the actual steps that must take place for this driving maneuver to be done successfully. Explain that whenever the volunteer misses a step or makes a mistake, you will say, **You forgot something** or **Are you sure you want to do that?** The volunteer must then figure out what he or she did wrong. If the volunteer can't figure it out, check to see if any of the other group members know.

The proper steps are as follows:
(1) Open the door.
(2) Sit in the driver's seat.
(3) Close the door.
(4) Fasten your seatbelt.
(5) Adjust mirrors.
(6) Lock doors.
(7) Put the key in the ignition to start the car.
(8) Place your hands on the steering wheel in the "10 and 2" position.
(9) Press down on the brake pedal and put the car in reverse.
(10) Press slightly on the brake pedal, with your left hand on the steering wheel and your right hand on the back of passenger seat as you turn to look behind you over your right shoulder.

UNIT THREE

(11) Let off the brake slightly to move down the driveway, but brake at the edge of driveway, checking both ways for cars.
(12) Press the gas pedal enough to back out into your lane of traffic, as you turn the steering wheel to get into your lane.
(13) Brake.
(14) Put the car into drive and turn the steering wheel back in the opposite direction to compensate for the turn you made to get into your lane.
(15) Press on the gas pedal to take off down the road.

Afterward, applaud the volunteer for his or her participation. Then ask: **How might we relate the example of being in driver's ed—but never driving—to studying God's Word?** (It doesn't matter much if you've just *heard* about what God's Word says without having any personal, "hands on" experience with it.)

Ask kids to reflect on these questions: **Do you need to "get behind the wheel of God's Word" yourself? If so, how can you go about it?**

Baby Steps

(Needed: Copies of Repro Resource 2, pencils)

Ask: **If you wanted to become a world-class runner, what might be some steps you would take to achieve that goal?** (Kids may mention things like training, running every day, getting good shoes, stretching, etc.)

If no one mentions it, ask: **How about learning to run?** Then ask what steps they would need to take to learn to run. If no one mentions it, ask: **How about learning to walk?** Kids should pick up on the pattern as you progress downwardly to standing, crawling, and learning balance.

The point you're trying to make is that we need to take "baby steps" to gradually progress to the point where we can begin to take bigger and bigger steps. The same principle holds true when it comes to studying God's Word.

Explain that you're not expecting group members to have the Old Testament read and outlined by next week's meeting. Instead, emphasize that setting *and meeting* small goals of consistently being in God's Word can help lay a strong foundation of being connected with God.

Don't restrict kids with a certain Bible-study format. Instead, encourage them to decide what steps they want to take in areas such as
- choosing a time to be in God's Word
- choosing a book or passage of the Bible to study
- choosing a translation of the Bible they're comfortable with
- choosing a devotional guide they enjoy
- choosing a setting in which they will have their study time.

Hand out copies of "Baby-Stepping through the Bible," (Repro Resource 2). After kids have read through the instructions, answer any questions they may have about the activity. After a few minutes, close the session in prayer, asking God to help the Bible come alive for your group members.

EXTREME CLOSEUP

REPRO RESOURCE

BIBLE EPICS

You're a film producer in Hollywood. After watching *The Ten Commandments* on TV, you decide that Hollywood should be making more movies based on Bible stories. Below is a list of some Bible stories that might have potential as movies. Your job is to come up with a title for each movie, decide who would play the major roles, and determine what type of movie (comedy, action-adventure, romance, etc.) you'll make from each Bible story. We've left one spot blank for you to come up with your own Bible story to film.

Bible Story	*Movie Title*	*Stars*	*Movie Category*
David and Bathsheba			
Jacob and Esau			
Esther			
The birth of Jesus			

EXTREME CLOSEUP

REPRO RESOURCE 2

Baby-Stepping through the Bible

Do you think you can set aside 10-15 minutes a day to read the Bible? Let's see. Write today's date in the upper left-hand box. Then write in the dates of the next 27 days following today, which will give you four full weeks. For each day that you spend at least 10-15 minutes reading the Bible, write in that square what passage(s) you read. If you don't have a Bible study time, draw an "X" through that day. After 28 days, bring in your calendar and be prepared to discuss any impact that the last four weeks have had in your relationship with God.

NOTES

OPTIONS
SESSION ONE

STEP 4
At the beginning of the step, make sure that each person has a Bible. Bring out an ample supply of string, masking tape, and bendable metal coat hangers. Challenge kids to use these materials to make "Bible holders" that keep their Bibles open and in front of them (without requiring the use of hands or tables) during this step. Then discuss where kids usually keep their Bibles. Ask: **How close at hand should our Bibles be? Why?**

STEP 6
Stage a bread-eating contest. One team gets a large, unsliced loaf of hard-crusted bread; the other team gets a plateful of cut-up, bite-sized pieces. Neither team may use its hands. After one minute, see how much progress each team has made. Discuss the fact that it's much easier to "eat" the Bible a bit at a time instead of diving in and trying to consume it in huge chunks.

STEP 1
With a small group, you might want to try a different opener. Have kids form two teams. Give each team a stack of magazines, scissors, paper, and tape or glue. Explain that the teams will be competing to see which can create a love note first by cutting out letters and words from the magazines and taping or gluing them on the sheet of paper (ransom-note style). The first team to create a complete love note is the winner.

STEP 6
In connection with the commitment requested from your group members on Repro Resource 2, let kids know that small groups have opportunities larger groups don't. For example, depending on your own willingness, you might say: **If you are doing individual Bible reading during the week and happen upon a particularly noteworthy or interesting passage, give me a call. If you think that what you've found is important, perhaps everyone else will too. We can try to study it as a group.** Naturally you won't be able to do this if everyone calls with a different passage. But as kids begin to connect what they're doing on their own with what they're doing at your weekly group meetings, they are likely to get a lot more meaning out of God's "love letter."

STEP 3
Give your group members an opportunity to use their creativity a little more by having them create sequels to the "movies" they described on Repro Resource 1. After the members of each group have shared their responses, ask them to choose one of the Bible stories to do a follow-up to. Instruct the groups to create a "trailer" (a preview) for their sequel. (For example, "First he lost his birthright. Then he lost his blessing. This time, Esau's going to win—at any cost. Coming this summer—*Birthright II: The Wrath of Esau*.") After a few minutes, have each group share what it came up with. Then lead in to Step 4.

STEP 6
As you wrap up the session, help your group members recognize that reading the Bible doesn't have to be a chore. Point out that there are some pretty interesting stories in God's Word. Have kids form groups. Instruct the members of each group to write headlines for Bible stories as they might appear on the front page of a supermarket tabloid. (For example, the headline for a story about Noah might read "Man Claiming End of World Is Near Builds Giant Floating Zoo.") Have each group choose two or three stories to work on. After a few minutes, have each group share its headlines. Emphasize that while not all Bible passages are exciting, your kids may be surprised at how interesting many portions are.

OPTIONS
SESSION ONE

STEP 2

Describing the Bible as a love letter isn't a new analogy—and if kids have heard it before, they may have had time to consider whether it really makes sense. What kind of love letter is thousands of pages long, spends much of its time on history and rules, comes from an invisible sender, and doesn't have the recipient's name on it? Don't count on this analogy to make kids eager to read the Bible; instead, include it as only one of several comparisons. Ask kids to come up with their own. For example, the Bible is also like a car owner's manual, a computer database, a cookbook, a time machine, a diary, and a novel. Yet it's like no other book—which is still another reason to read it.

STEP 6

If your kids are experienced churchgoers, they've probably heard repeated admonitions to read the Bible. Perhaps they've even tried it—and given up. Chances are that the Repro Resource 2 take-home activity will be ignored. Instead, consider one of these alternatives: (1) asking kids to try 1-5 minutes a day rather than 10-15, or three times a week instead of daily; (2) using part of your next meeting as a time for kids to practice individual Bible reading under your supervision; (3) pairing volunteers to have "telephone devotions" once or twice this week, taking turns reading a Bible passage to each other and then discussing it.

STEP 3

Group members who are not familiar with the Bible may not know all of the stories referred to on Repro Resource 1. So rather than handing out the sheet, you might want to talk kids through the exercise. (Besides, creative ideas usually flow better in a group setting, rather than an individual setting.) Depending on the knowledge of your group members, you might want to substitute "David and Goliath" for "David and Bathsheba," "Cain and Abel" for "Jacob and Esau," and "Jonah" for "Esther." Another option is to use actual movie titles and then try to think of Bible stories that they might describe. For instance, *The Lion King* could be about Daniel; *The River Wild* could be about the baby Moses; *The Nightmare before Christmas* could be about Herod's killing of the innocent children; and so forth.

STEP 4

In connection with your study of Psalm 1, bring in something to plant. (The easiest thing might be bulbs that come packaged with their own vases, available at most nature shops and elsewhere.) When you discuss "a tree planted by streams of water," pull out your plant and explain that you're going to plant it to see what happens. As the plant grows over the next few weeks and months, kids should be reminded of the importance of their own spiritual growth. (Just be sure to remove the plant in its prime, before it withers and dies.)

STEP 1

As kids arrive, hand them paper and pencils. To begin the session, instruct kids to complete the following statements:

- The best book I've ever read is . . .
- I really liked that book because . . .
- The reason I read it is . . .
- I would/would not recommend it to my friends because . . .

After a few minutes, have kids mill around the room, sharing their answers. Any who have chosen the same book should congregate together. After a few minutes of mingling, ask kids to share their answers. Point out that kids who chose the same book probably have different reasons for choosing it. If no one chose the Bible, ask why not. (Chances are pretty good that kids will say it's boring and that they don't understand it.) Explain that over the next few weeks, you'll be taking an extreme close-up look at the Bible. Suggest that your kids may discover that it's anything but boring, and that there are ways to help us understand it.

STEP 6

Bring in a recording of Amy Grant's song "Thy Word." Before playing it, however, make sure that each person has a sheet of paper and a pencil. As kids listen to the song, have them write down the ways that God's Word helps us, as mentioned in the song. After the song is over, encourage kids to share their lists. As they share, make a "master list" on the board that everyone can see. Then play the song again. While the song is playing this time, encourage kids to thank God for all He's given us through His Word.

OPTIONS
SESSION ONE

STEP 4

After talking about the fact that the Bible is a lamp to our feet, hand out paper and pencils. Explain that you want to help your group members see how the Bible can help them with the problems they face every day. Ask your girls to think about a problem they or someone they know is facing right now that might require an answer from the Bible. Have them write it down. Emphasize that they don't need to write their names on the sheet. Assure them that no problem is too large or too small for God's love and attention. Collect the papers and briefly read through them. If there are any problems that you can respond to with Scripture, do so immediately. If not, explain that you'll look the sheets over this week and bring them back to discuss the following week. As you're looking for answers, try to find references that are story examples or that are as close to the problem as possible. Kids know when they're getting general, "pat" answers. Bring their questions and your answers back next week. It's important to follow through on this activity.

STEP 6

If possible, take a few minutes to visit your church's nursery, encouraging your girls to notice all they can about the babies—the noises they make, their physical capabilities, their ability to do things for themselves, etc. After a few minutes, return to your own room to share your findings. Ask: **What would happen if a baby never grew?** You may or may not get responses to this question. Then say: **God designed us to start out small and then to grow. That's how He designed us spiritually as well. We may need to start by doing "baby" things, but He wants us to continue to grow. The way we do that is by reading His Word.** Go through Repro Resource 2 as instructed in the session.

STEP 1

Rework the relay exercise so that team members write portions of the letter for the last person on the team to read and follow to find an edible prize. For example, adapt the following instructions for your own church: "(1) Dear Group Member—Go down the stairs; (2) Turn left and go down the hall; (3) At the end of the hall, turn right and go to the second room on the left; (4) Enter the room and turn on the lights; (5) You'll find a special treat in the refrigerator. Love, Your Youth Leader." Make a copy of these instructions for each team. Place each numbered step in an individual envelope. The first person on each team should run across the room, pick up one of the envelopes marked "#1," open it, and begin a letter by writing (on stationery that you've provided) what's on the instructions. Then he should return to his team and tag the second person, who will run to open the second envelope and add to the letter. After the fifth person finishes, the sixth person should run to the letter, grab it, and follow the instructions.

STEP 2

Most guys like to get mail as much as girls do; but in many cases, girls seem to do a much better job of responding. Challenge your guys to acknowledge gifts from other people. When given gifts, they should write thank-you notes. When they get letters, they should write back. And when they realize that God's Word is like a personal letter for their own benefit and encouragement, they should not only read it, but respond to it as well. Ask: **How should you respond to a letter that God has written?** (Doing what it says shows respect. Praying is a way of "writing back" and letting God know *our* thoughts. Being decent to other people is equated to treating God well [see Matthew 25:31-46].)

STEP 4

If possible, meet in an extremely dark area to do the Bible study portion of the session. The ideal place will have just *barely* enough light to see to read. Or you might meet in a completely dark room with a penlight as your only source of light. As you study Psalm 1, no one will understand what's going on. But when your volunteer reader gets to Psalm 119:105, arrange for someone to hit the light switch. Flood the room with as much light as possible. Then spend a few minutes discussing how the Bible can make a similar change in the lives of your young people.

STEP 6

Hand out paper and pencils. Ask kids to write out a number of specific instructions using the following formula: "If you want to learn to _____, you need to _____." Use the driving instructions in Step 5 as an example. The instructions don't have to be quite that detailed, but they should be very specific. Instruct kids to write the "If you want to learn to" statement at the top of the sheet and the instructions at the bottom of the sheet. Kids may write down as many ideas as they wish (on separate sheets of paper). Examples might include how to tie your shoe, kiss somebody, siphon gas out of a car, kick a field goal, drink out of a straw, blow your nose, or whatever. After a few minutes, collect the sheets. Cut apart the top section of each sheet from the bottom one. Then look for unusual "matches" where the instructions make for a humorous conclusion to the opening statement. Use this activity to lead in to the "If you want to learn to run" discussion.

OPTIONS
SESSION ONE

STEP 3

Show scenes (after pre-screening them for appropriateness) from some of the following videos. Then discuss, using the questions provided. During discussion, note that the Bible contains a lot more than family trees and rules.

- *Ace Ventura, Pet Detective*. Play a scene in which Ace (Jim Carrey) acts especially goofy and out-of-control. Ask: **Can you think of someone in the Bible who acted crazy or weird?** (David pretended to be crazy [I Sam. 21]; Nebuchadnezzar went temporarily insane and acted like an animal [Dan. 4].)

- *Tombstone*. Play a scene from the showdown at the OK Corral. Ask: **What are some showdowns you remember from the Bible?** (David vs. Goliath [I Sam. 17]; Peter vs. the soldier in the Garden of Gethsemane [Matt. 26].)

- *The Adventures of Baron Munchausen*. Show one of the many scenes using impressive special effects. Ask: **What are some Bible events that would require special effects to show on the screen?** (Any of the miracles; most of the Book of Revelation.)

- *Jurassic Park*. Show a scene featuring one or more of the largest dinosaurs. Ask: **Can you think of any large or unusual creatures mentioned in the Bible?** (The great fish that swallowed Jonah [Jonah 1]; the creatures around God's throne in heaven [Rev. 4].)

STEP 4

Play and discuss one or more contemporary Christian songs that encourage Bible reading. Some examples might include "End of the Book" (Michael W. Smith), "Thy Word" (Amy Grant), "The More I Know of You" (Glad), and "He'll Shine His Light on You" (Michelle Pillar).

STEP 1

Replace Steps 1 and 2 with a shorter opener. Wrap three pocket New Testaments in gift wrap; tape a "#1" tag to each one. Also wrap three boxes of Milk Duds, Junior Mints, or other candy; tape a "#2" tag to each one. Have three volunteers come to the front of the room and choose between package #1 and package #2. Let volunteers unwrap their choices at the same time. Discuss who got the best "deals" and why.

STEP 3

In place of Repro Resource 1, have each group choose a Bible character (or assign one to each group). Instruct each group to come up with a hypothetical telephone answering machine message for that person. The message should include the character's name, two things he or she might be doing instead of answering the phone, and a unique "sound" after which the caller is to leave a message. (For example: "Hi. This is Daniel. I can't come to the phone right now because I'm eating my vegetables—or because I'm having a vision about a guy made out of different kinds of metal. Please leave a message after the lion's roar.") Have kids read (or tape and play) the results; then discuss the Bible stories referred to in the messages. In Step 4, skip the maze activity. Skip Step 5 too.

STEP 1

You'll need to bring in a stopwatch and sixty-six books of varying sizes and shapes. Stack the books at one end of your meeting area. To begin the session, have kids form two teams. Instruct the members of one team to line up at the opposite end of the room from the books. See how long it takes the team to transport (relay-style) the books from one end of the room to the other. The first person in line will run to other side of the room, grab a book, run back to his or her team, set the book down, and tag the next person in line. That person will then do the same thing. The team will continue until all sixty-six books have been moved. Write the first team's time on the board; then see if the second team can better it. After the game, see if your group members can guess the topic of the session based on the clue of "sixty-six books." (There are sixty-six books in the Bible.)

STEP 3

After you've gone through Repro Resource 1, help your group members see that the Bible contains stories that are relevant to kids today. Have kids read Genesis 16:1-16; 21:8-21, in which God provides for Hagar—a single mother—and her son Ishmael. Then ask: **Do you think God still takes care of single parents and their families today? If so, how?**

OPTIONS
SESSION ONE

STEP 3

For the Repro Resource 1 activity, divide kids into groups of three or four, making sure that you mix your junior highers and high schoolers. After kids have completed Repro Resource 1, give them the Scripture references for the stories listed on the sheet. Instruct the groups to look up the references and identify the principle (or principles) shown in each passage that God wants us to follow. Also ask the groups to identify ways shown in each passage that we and God can become better connected. After a few minutes, have each group share what it came up with.

STEP 4

Instead of asking only two kids to leave the room, dismiss all of your junior highers (with a lot of supervision, of course). Then have your high schoolers set up the maze that the junior highers will have to crawl through. As your high schoolers are setting up the maze, have them identify problems and obstacles they faced when they were in junior high and how a better knowledge of God's Word would have helped them. Then call in your junior highers to crawl through the maze, blindfolding some but not others. After all of them have gone through the maze, discuss the ways in which life is similar to the maze. Then call for high school volunteers to share the obstacles and dead-ends they hit when they were in junior high.

STEP 3

Briefly review each of the stories on Repro Resource 1. As you're reviewing each story, make some kind of a "mistake" in your retelling. See how many kids correct you. (For instance, you might say: **Esau sold his birthright to his brother Jacob for $500.**) In addition to being fun for your kids, this exercise should give you an idea of your group members' biblical literacy. If your group members don't catch one of your mistakes, be sure to correct it yourself. After all, the last thing you want to do is arm kids with false information about the Bible!

STEP 6

Describe—but don't let kids taste—a plateful of individually wrapped treats. Tie this into the need to "taste" Scripture for ourselves. Hand out Repro Resource 2 along with the wrapped treats, asking kids to save the treats until they've first "tasted" at least one Bible verse at home.

DATE USED:

Approx. Time

STEP 1: *Love Letters* _____
❏ Small Group
❏ Fellowship & Worship
❏ Mostly Guys
❏ Short Meeting Time
❏ Urban
Things needed:

STEP 2: *Unopened Mail* _____
❏ Heard It All Before
❏ Mostly Guys
Things needed:

STEP 3: *Blockbuster Bible* _____
❏ Large Group
❏ Little Bible Background
❏ Media
❏ Short Meeting Time
❏ Urban
❏ Combined Junior High/High School
❏ Sixth Grade
Things needed:

STEP 4: *What's in It for Me?* _____
❏ Extra Action
❏ Little Bible Background
❏ Mostly Girls
❏ Extra Fun
❏ Media
❏ Combined Junior High/High School
Things needed:

STEP 5: *Take Hold of the Wheel!* _____
Things needed:

STEP 6: *Baby Steps* _____
❏ Extra Action
❏ Small Group
❏ Large Group
❏ Heard It All Before
❏ Fellowship & Worship
❏ Mostly Girls
❏ Extra Fun
❏ Sixth Grade
Things needed:

SESSION 2

Why Pray?

YOUR GOALS FOR THIS SESSION:
Choose one or more

☐ To help kids recognize that God wants to communicate with us.

☐ To help kids understand that communicating with God involves both talking and listening.

☐ To encourage kids to develop the daily discipline of prayer in their own lives, perhaps using a written journal.

☐ Other: _____
_____

Your Bible Base:

2 Chronicles 7:14
Matthew 6:5-8; 7:7-11

WHY PRAY?

Let Me Finish!

(Needed: Copies of Repro Resource 3, pencils, prize)

Hand out copies of "Hitting the Cutoff Man" (Repro Resource 3) and pencils. If kids don't understand the instructions on the sheet, explain that this is a race to see who can connect all of the pairs of connected comments the quickest. When someone completes his or her sheet, he or she should hand it to you. Wait until everyone has finished the sheet before discussing the correct answers. Then check the paper of the person who finished first. If his or her answers are correct, give him or her a prize. If the sheet wasn't totally correct, go to the sheet of the person who finished second and grade that paper. Continue in this manner until a winner is found. The answers for Repro Resource 3 are as follows: 1—f; 2—d; 3—j; 4—b; 5—a; 6—g; 7—c; 8—h; 9—e; 10—i.

It's a Two-Way Street

(Needed: Copies of Repro Resource 4)

Say: **We've just worked through some examples in which people were cut off by others. Now it's time to give you a chance to experience it for yourself.**

Ask for a couple of volunteers. Hand each of them a copy of "Zip the Lip!" (Repro Resource 4). Give your volunteers a few minutes to read through the scenario before they act it out in front of the group.

After the presentation, ask your kids to describe a time in their lives when they were cut off or interrupted while talking to someone. Encourage them to describe how they felt when this happened.

Ask: **When people interrupt someone who is speaking to add their own comments, what might that say to the**

person who was cut off? (He or she is not being listened to. The other person thought of something important to say. The other person is rude.)

Say: **Let's think about prayer for a moment. What are some ways during prayer that we might make God feel like He is being "cut off"?** If no one mentions them, suggest things like not focusing on God during prayer and rattling off a list of things that we want from God without listening to what He might want to tell us through our consciences or thanking Him for all He's done for us.

Ask: **What are some other things that might keep us from having an effective prayer time with God?** Make a note of group members' responses so that you can address these problems later in the session.

Call-Waiting

(Needed: Bibles, chalkboard and chalk or newsprint and marker)

Ask: **How many of you have call-waiting on your telephone at home?** Ask some of the kids who have the service to share some reasons why they like it.

Then explain that call-waiting is similar to our "prayer line" to God. God has constant call-waiting. You can always get through to Him when you need to talk to Him; He's never busy.

Have someone read aloud 2 Chronicles 7:14. Then ask group members to think of a time when they prayed to God about something, but felt like God didn't answer their prayers.

Ask: **How did you feel when God didn't seem to be answering your prayers?** (Like He wasn't listening; like He doesn't care enough to pay attention.)

How might 2 Chronicles 7:14 change our thinking about God's answering people's prayers? If no one mentions it, point out that the verse doesn't say that if we just *pray*, God will hear us from heaven. It says that we are to be humble before God, seek Him, and turn from our wicked ways. In other words, we shouldn't pray to God for things while we are willingly living ungodly lives.

Write the following questions on the board for your kids to discuss:
- What is prayer?
- How should we pray?
- When and where are we supposed to pray?
- Is prayer better individually or in a group? Why?

After briefly discussing each of these questions, have volunteers read aloud Matthew 7:7-11 and Matthew 6:5-8. Then go through the questions on the board again, in light of these two passages.

Say: **Matthew 6:8 says that God knows what we need before we ask Him. So why should we pray when He already knows what we're going to say?** Let your kids wrestle with this question for a while. Then explain that God wants us to come to the realization that praying to Him can be a real power source in our lives. God knows the power He has and the blessings He wants to pour out on us when we pray to Him. And although we can be told by others that there's power in prayer, we won't *know* that until we experience it for ourselves.

Suggest that praying to God, who already knows what's on our hearts and minds, can be a bit unnerving at times. Ask: **Have you ever felt overwhelmed or in awe when you were praying to God? If so, explain. If not, why do you suppose that is?**

How do you think God feels when we have an attitude of awe toward Him? Explain.

Write It Down!

(Needed: Chalkboard and chalk or newsprint and marker, prizes)

Ask for several volunteers to come to the front of the room. When they do, explain that they've been selected for a Bible spelling bee. Choose a few easy words for your kids to spell first; then move on to tougher words like Nebuchadnezzar and Thessalonians. If your volunteers are struggling a little bit, you might want to help them out a little. Award prizes for the top three finishers.

Afterward, ask: **After seeing what a spelling bee is like, how many of you would rather take a written spelling test?** Get a show of hands; then ask some of the kids who raised their hands why they would rather take a written test. Answers might include being nervous about having to talk out loud and being distracted in a public setting.

Relate the concept of a spelling bee to the idea of praying out loud to God. Point out that some people get nervous and distracted when they pray out loud.

Say: **If the idea of praying out loud sometimes rattles your prayer life, you might want to consider journaling.** Explain that journaling is simply writing down what you want to say to God on a daily basis, as well as any insights and thoughts you have about areas of your life that you and God are working on.

Ask your kids to name some things that they think might make journaling hard for them. If no one mentions it, suggest that one concern might be writer's block (or, in this case, "journaling block")—not knowing what to write.

Explain that you've got a little formula that's a guaranteed cure for "journaling block"; it's called ACTS. Write the following four words on the board:

Adoration
Confession
Thanksgiving
Supplication

Explain that although these look like big words, they're simple in meaning, and can improve one's prayer life when used consistently. Discuss the four areas as a group, keeping in mind these four definitions:

Adoration—telling God how great He is
Confession—telling God things in your life that you're sorry for
Thanksgiving—telling God what you're thankful for
Supplication—telling God of any requests you might have

Personalizing Your Prayer Closet

Emphasize to your kids that journaling may not be for all of them. There are as many different styles of prayer as there are pray-ers. The point is that we shouldn't be worried if our spoken prayers don't rank up there with the polished prayers of pastors and evangelists. Read Matthew 6:5-8 again to remind your kids that God wants us to pray humbly before Him, not in a manner to impress others with our words.

As you wrap up the session, challenge kids to work on one specific area in their prayer lives that needs improvement. Maybe it's being "still before God" during prayer and listening more for what we might learn during that time. Or maybe it's getting in the habit of praying regularly to Him, or praying out loud in a group, or journaling our prayers to Him. Close the session by praying that your kids' prayer lives will be an area that brings them closer to God.

NOTES

EXTREME CLOSEUP

REPRO RESOURCE 3

HITTING THE CUTOFF MAN

Draw connecting lines from the conversation starters on the left to the statements that cut them off on the right. Some are obvious and some aren't. Finish as quickly as possible, sign your name to your sheet, and hand it in to your leader.

CONVERSATION STARTERS

1. Did you watch *The Simpsons* last night? My favorite part was . . .

2. When I stepped outside this morning, I couldn't believe how humid it . . .

3. I'm getting really hungry. I feel like I could eat a . . .

4. Did you hear about Sue? I heard that yesterday after school . . .

5. Have you seen *Schindler's List*? I hear that . . .

6. Do you think the White Sox can win the World . . .

7. My parents are taking me shopping so I can pick out a present for my . . .

8. I'm excited about tomorrow's big game against South High, I can hardly . . .

9. I can't wait for the new Whitney Houston album to come out. It's supposed to be . . .

10. I'm thinking about signing up for the youth group's mission trip to . . .

INTERRUPTIONS

a. There's no way I could sit still for over three hours. I'm pretty squeamish too.

b. Have you noticed that she has alcohol on her breath all the time? I heard she was pretty messed up at her old school before coming here.

c. Hey, there's a mall-wide sale this weekend! Can you believe it?

d. I had to wring my shirt out after third period because I was sweating so much!

e. I hated *The Bodyguard*.

f. Oh, that Ned Flanders is so weird! I'd go crazy if he were my neighbor.

g. Who cares? Everybody knows that the Cubbies are the city's favorite team.

h. They've got a really great program. Haven't they been conference champs for the last three years?

i. Well, I'm kind of getting tired of going on Thursday nights. Power Hour isn't fun anymore, and lately, Pastor Donny has been way too boring.

j. Speaking of food, did you hear about the freshman who found a toenail in the chicken and dumplings they served for lunch today?

NOTES

EXTREME CLOSEUP

REPRO RESOURCE 4

ZIP THE LIP!

Scene: Two teenagers are hanging out, shooting the breeze. The two have always been good friends, and haven't been able to talk to each other for a while. They are pretty excited about the opportunity to catch up on each other's lives.

FRIEND #1: Wow, it is so good to see you. We have—

FRIEND #2 *(cutting in)*: You know, we haven't talked in the longest time. It seems like forever. Oh, what were you saying?

FRIEND #1 *(laughing)*: Actually, I was just going to say the same thing, that we haven't talked in the longest time and that it seems like forever. Oh, I forgot to tell you that last weekend when you were out of town, a couple of friends and I went to see a movie. We saw—

FRIEND #2 *(excitedly interjecting)*: Oh, that reminds me—you've got to see the new movie *Betrayal of Friendship*! It was so suspenseful! I couldn't sleep at all the night I saw it! You'll love it! What did you see?

FRIEND #1 *(a bit deflated)*: Well, what I was *going* to tell you was that I saw the new movie *Betrayal of Friendship*, and that it was so suspenseful I couldn't sleep the night I saw it, and that I loved it.

FRIEND #2: Oh. Well, I guess we both loved it.

FRIEND #1: Yeah, I guess we did. *(Regaining excitement)* Anyway, do you have any plans this weekend? I thought we should maybe try out this new restaurant called—

FRIEND #2 *(nearly salivating while cutting in again)*: Oh, you'll die when you taste the food at this new restaurant I ate at. It's called "Straight from Heaven." Don't you just love the name? And the barbecued ribs there are soooo good! We've got to eat there. What's the place you want to eat at? I forgot what you said while I was thinking about those ribs!

FRIEND #1 *(a little peeved)*: I noticed. I guess it wouldn't be very exciting for you now. If you must know, I wanted to try out "Straight from Heaven." I just loved the name, and I heard that the barbecued ribs there were really good. But obviously, you just told me that.

FRIEND #2 *(half apologetically)*: I'm sorry. I just think of things that I want to say.

FRIEND #1 *(upset, yet composed)*: But you don't stop to think how rude it is to cut people off. It tells them that you're not really listening. Anyway, just work at it. Now, I've really got something to tell you. I was standing by my locker today when this really cute guy [or girl] walked up and—

FRIEND #2 *(absolutely ecstatic, cutting in)*: I almost forgot! Today during lunch, the cutest guy [or girl] came up to me and asked me out for Saturday night. He [or she] said I was the best-looking person in school. His [or her] name is Terry Taylor.

FRIEND #1 *(surprised)*: What? That's the same guy [or girl] that walked up to *me* at *my* locker today!

FRIEND #2: That can't be right! You're just jealous! What did he [or she] say to you?

FRIEND #1: Why should I tell you? I'm sure you know what I'm going to say anyway. Let's just say that you're not the only one with a date this weekend.

(Friend #2 storms out of the room.)

NOTES

OPTIONS
SESSION TWO

STEP 1

Have kids form teams. Give each team a bag containing three paper cups, a ten-foot length of kite string, a candle, a rubber band, a toothpick, and a flashlight battery. Say: **In this bag, you have the makings of a working, two-way communication device. See whether you can make that device, using exactly five of the items, in three minutes. Go!** See what happens. The solution is to rub the candle on the string to thoroughly wax the string. Then use the toothpick to poke a hole in the bottom of each of two cups. Put the string through the holes; tie a large knot in each end of the string so that the string stays connected to the cups. Stretch the string taut. Two kids can talk and listen to each other as if the cups were telephones. Award a prize to each successful team, if you like. Use this activity to introduce the idea of low-tech, two-way communication.

STEP 3

If you made paper-cup phones earlier (see the "Extra Action" option for Step 1), have partners try to read 2 Chronicles 7:14 to each other through their phones. Sound quality will be mediocre at best. Use this to lead into a discussion of what it feels like when our prayers don't seem to connect with God. In Step 4, bring four blocks of wood; write one of the four "ACTS" words on each block. Make the first letter of each word large and bold. Have kids form three teams. Give the first team fifteen seconds to stack the blocks so that the bold letters spell a word. Give the second team a chance to spell a different word; then give the third team a chance. (Possibilities include CATS, ACTS, and SCAT.) Discuss which arrangement of Adoration, Confession, Thanksgiving, and Supplication might make the best kind of prayer and why. Avoid insisting that kids follow the ACTS formula, however.

STEP 3

Any time members of a small group discuss prayer, they should probably be reminded of Jesus' promise in Matthew 18:19-20: "I tell you that if two of you on earth agree about anything you ask for, it will be done for you by my Father in heaven. For where two or three come together in my name, there am I with them." Emphasize that big numbers are not the secret to "big" prayer. The goal is for your group members to focus their thoughts and "come together." As they grow closer to Jesus as individuals, they will find themselves naturally pulling together as a group.

STEP 5

Suggest that a small group is the best place to learn to pray out loud. As you conclude the session, challenge everyone to pray aloud—even if it's just one sentence. To reduce awkwardness for new people or for those unaccustomed to praying, ask each person to think of something specific to pray about. (It can be from any of the areas of adoration, confession, thanksgiving, or supplication.) When one person expresses a prayer request, find another person willing to pray about it during the closing prayer. Have your group members "trade off," with each person responsible for someone else's specific request. That gives everyone something to say. Anyone who wants to pray for things in addition to that specific request should feel free to do so. You should close the prayer session, filling in any "gaps" and thanking God for the opportunities He gives us to communicate with Him.

STEP 1

Have kids form three teams. Give each team an Etch-a-Sketch. Before the session, you'll need to write a message (at least ten words long) on each team's Etch-a-Sketch; then cover each screen with a piece of paper so that no one else can see the message. Set up an obstacle course in your room. Explain that the teams will be competing in a relay race to complete the obstacle course. The catch is that each person must carry his or her team's Etch-a-Sketch while running the obstacle course. So after the first person on a team completes the course, he or she will hand the Etch-a-Sketch to the next person in line, who will then do the same thing, and so on. The first team to complete the course—without erasing the message on its Etch-a-Sketch—is the winner. If team members jostle the Etch-a-Sketch too much while running, they won't be able to read the message on the screen at the end of the game. Use this activity to lead in to a discussion of the things that prevent us from clearly receiving messages from God via prayer.

STEP 5

As you wrap up the session, set up a "mini-prayer vigil" for your kids. Designate a day in the coming week for your vigil. Prepare a schedule divided into five-minute increments. Ask each of your kids to commit to praying for five minutes on your designated day by signing up for one of the sections on the schedule. Make sure that all of the slots on the schedule are filled so that you have a continuous prayer link going for at least a couple of hours. Hand out copies of a list of requests for your kids to pray about during the vigil. Have kids write down the time they signed up for on their list of requests. At your next meeting, discuss how the prayer vigil went.

OPTIONS
SESSION TWO

HEARD IT ALL BEFORE

STEP 2
Kids may have heard prayer described as "two-way" communication, but find the idea confusing or frustrating—and ignore it as just another meaningless Christian cliché. How can prayer be "two-way" when God doesn't say anything? Take care not to imply that kids are supposed to hear God's side of the conversation. Point out that God can communicate with a voice if He wants to, but He hasn't promised to. Instead, He may help us remember something we've read in His Word. Or He might guide our thoughts in a certain direction. Instead of emphasizing the two-way idea, you may want to observe simply that when we focus only on ourselves and our needs when we pray, we aren't giving God first place.

STEP 4
If kids have heard of journaling, they probably associate it with super-saints or English class assignments. Your chances of convincing most kids to journal are remote, but you may be able to help them relate to the process. Give each person an index card and a pencil. Say: **On one side of your card, do either of the following: (1) Pretend you've been keeping a diary of the ups and downs of your friendships. Jot down three items you might have included last week. (2) Pretend you've been keeping a maintenance record on your family car—tracking repairs, oil changes, accidents. Jot down three items you might have included in the last six months.** When kids have completed that assignment, ask them to turn their cards over and either (1) do the same with notes on their friendship with God during the last week, or (2) do the same with notes on how well they've maintained their relationship with God during the last six months.

LITTLE BIBLE BACKGROUND

STEP 2
Hand out paper and pencils. Ask your group members to write down three questions about prayer. These may be general questions, personal inquiries, or things their friends may have asked. Collect the questions. Then have your group members try to answer each other's questions to the best of their ability. By working together as a group, with a little insight from you, kids may surprise themselves with how much they already know. And even if this isn't the case, they will at least find answers for their questions.

STEP 3
The session deals with portions of the Sermon on the Mount before and after the Lord's Prayer (Matthew 6:9-13). Yet it may be that the Lord's Prayer is essentially all some of your kids know about praying. If so, use it as a natural starting point for them. Point out that memorizing the specific words isn't what Jesus was suggesting. Rather, the Lord's Prayer makes an excellent *outline* for our own prayers. It starts by focusing on who God is and submitting to His will. It moves on to personal daily needs. It concludes with an emphasis on God's forgiveness and a reminder that we live in an evil world. Encourage your group members not just to memorize the prayer as a "quickie" prayer for emergencies, but rather to use it as a starting point for expressing all of the things on their mind.

FELLOWSHIP & WORSHIP

STEP 1
Begin the session by playing some worship music, the lyrics of which describe the power, might, and strength of God. (An excellent tape with songs on this theme is *Praise and Worship, Mighty God* from Hosanna! Music.) Songs you may want to play include "Lift Up Your Voices," "My Help Comes from the Lord," and "Mighty Is Our God." After playing (and singing, if your kids know the words) these songs, ask: **When you think of the strength and power of God, how do you feel?** (Some may find comfort in these things; others may find fear.) If no one mentions it, ask if anyone ever feels intimidated by God, especially when they think of praying to Him. Allow time for responses.

STEP 5
If your junior highers are somewhat mature, a great way to build fellowship among your group members is to set up prayer partner arrangements. There are a number of ways that you can do this. For instance, you might pair up kids (preferably ones who know each other well) to pray for the needs of their partner during the week. Or, rather than pairing individuals, you might set up prayer teams and instruct kids to pray for the members of their team during the week. Or you might set up a prayer chain. When a need arises, one person in the chain calls another to pass along a prayer need. That person will then call the next person in the chain, and so on. (However, you need to be careful to prevent the prayer chain from becoming a gossip chain.) Or you might let kids offer their ideas for a prayer partner arrangement. The options are endless.

OPTIONS
SESSION TWO

STEP 1

After you've discussed the answers to Repro Resource 3, refer back to the sheet. Say: **Now we're going to roleplay these situations to see what interrupting can lead to.** Ask for volunteers to roleplay each couple of lines, taking the conversation a few lines further. Encourage some of the pairs to keep interrupting each other. Encourage others to realize what they've done and apologize. Try to get a variety of responses. Afterward, discuss as a group the different reactions and how the people may have felt in each scenario.

STEP 4

Ask: **What do you do when you have something you need to share, but have no one to share it with?** If no one mentions it, suggest writing in a diary. If you wish, read a few lines from *Anne Frank: The Diary of a Young Girl.* Say: **Keeping a diary is one way many people choose to "get out" thoughts and feelings that they have no one else to tell.** Ask if any of your girls keep a diary. Then explain that there's a way we can keep a diary of our prayers; it's called journaling. Keeping a journal is a lot like keeping a diary. Explain the ACTS model and continue Step 4 as written.

STEP 2

If you have an athletic group of guys, many of them are probably familiar with the important role a coach can play in their lives. If so, eliminate Repro Resource 4 and spend time instead trying to help kids see that God acts as the best coach they could ever want. Ask: **In what ways is listening to God sort of like listening to a coach?** (We need to know the "playbook"—the Bible—which tells us what to do in many specific situations we will encounter. The coach sees things shaping up long before most of the players do. The coach speaks from experience that players don't have. A good coach not only wants to win, but also wants his players to be the best possible individuals they can be. A coach is a teacher, motivator, counselor, and friend.) Explain that prayer is how we keep in contact with our Coach. Bible reading is certainly important, but it's the personal communication of prayer that keeps us strong.

STEP 4

Keeping a journal may sound like "writing in a diary" to some guys—something that's "for girls." If you think this might be true of your guys, prepare to confront this attitude by going to a library before the session and collecting several examples of literature from the journals of famous men. You can find writings of historical figures, well-known writers, church fathers, contemporary Christians, and much more. For example, Jim Eliot kept a journal before being killed by the Auca Indians. C. S. Lewis kept a journal as well. Many of the world's great men kept up their journals throughout their lifetimes. Show your guys that maintaining a journal doesn't guarantee fame, but it certainly doesn't hurt, either.

STEP 1

Have kids form pairs and take them outside. Instruct the members of each pair to put as much distance between themselves as possible. Ideally, partners should be out of hearing range of each other. Give one person in each pair a message to try to communicate to the other. (Assign different messages to each pair.) With the partners extremely far apart, have each person try to communicate his or her message. No one should be able to do so at first, so move the listeners a little closer and have the speakers try again. Keep moving the listeners a few steps closer until someone is finally able to hear what is being said. (The listener must be able to repeat the message word for word.) Use this activity to demonstrate the fact that sometimes God may be wanting to communicate with us, but if we've wandered too far away, we miss what He's trying to say. Sometimes we recognize that He's there, but we're not close enough to hear clearly what He is saying. The purpose of prayer is to get close enough to God to communicate clearly with Him.

STEP 4

If you don't think kids will keep up with individual journals, try a group journal. Starting this week, give kids an opportunity to jot down their feelings, thoughts, frustrations, desires, or whatever they wish. A "prayer journal" sounds a bit somber, so use the concept of a "group journal" even though you might want to keep up with prayer requests as well. If a few kids volunteer to write a few sentences each week, they may be surprised at how quickly they create a written history of the group. The journal will be an excellent resource to recall good memories, to find comfort during future hard times, and to see how God works on a regular basis.

OPTIONS
SESSION TWO

STEP 1

Show one or more "dysfunctional conversation" scenes from the following videos (after pre-screening them for appropriateness):

• *Wayne's World 2*. In an early scene, Wayne, Garth, and friends pull up to a fast-food drive-through and place an order, leaving out key words in an effort to drive the order-taker crazy—but the latter still gets it right. Ask: **What tends to get left out of your prayers? Do you think God understands our prayers even if we don't pray them "right"? Why or why not?**

• *Ghost*. Play a scene in which fake medium Whoopi Goldberg has a hard time communicating with the deceased Patrick Swayze, whom she can hear but not see. Ask: **Is this like prayer? How is it different? Why do you suppose God usually doesn't communicate with us in a voice that we can hear?**

• *Indiana Jones and the Last Crusade*. Show the scene in which Indy (Harrison Ford) is trying to have a rare, meaningful conversation with his father (Sean Connery), who acts as if there's no need to talk. Ask: **When you pray, do you find God to be this kind of father? Or is God more interested in having a good talk with you than you are in having one with Him? Why?**

STEP 3

During the week before the session, record the touch-tone "beeps" made when you telephone the home of each group member. On paper, keep track of which sounds go with each person's phone. To start the step, play the tape of the tones. See whether kids can guess which sounds match their home phones. Award a prize for each correct guess. Then ask: **When it comes to prayer, do you think God knows your personal number? Is He interested in hearing from you, or just from humans in general? Why?**

STEP 1

Stage a "Knees and Elbows Race" (preferably on a lawn or carpeted floor). Have kids line up side by side. Give each person four pieces of uncooked elbow macaroni. At your signal, each person must put one piece behind each of his or her knees and one in the crook of each of his or her elbows—and get to the finish line across the room or lawn. The first to reach the finish line with all four pieces wins. Kids will soon discover that they must walk on their knees and keep their arms bent to make this work. After awarding a prize, ask: **Did you have a good prayer time during this race?** (No.) **But you were on your knees. Isn't that what prayer is all about?** Discuss the difference between "going through the motions" of prayer and making prayer a way to grow closer to God.

STEP 3

Replace Steps 3, 4, and 5 with the following activity. Have volunteers read aloud Psalm 102:1-17. Then discuss: **When have you felt most like the writer of this psalm? Have you ever prayed a prayer like this? Why or why not? What kind of relationship does the person seem to have with God? What do you think happened before the person asked God for help? What does the person want God to do? What does the person talk about, other than making requests?** If possible, play a contemporary Christian "psalm" that addresses God. Possibilities include "Sincerely Yours" (Gary Chapman), "Here I Am" (Russ Taff), "Do I Trust You" (Twila Paris), "A Way" (Michael W. Smith), and "Sparrow Watcher" (Pam Mark Hall). Close the session by having kids write brief psalm-prayers that (1) thank God for something He's done and (2) ask Him to do something in the future.

STEP 3

Bring in an old record player and three non-valuable records. Remove the needle from the record player. Announce that you've got some songs you want your kids to hear. Explain that a friend of yours told you that the songs were excellent. Put the first record on the turntable. Say: **Now, listen closely.** Nothing should happen. Lift the record arm and place it down further on the record. When nothing happens, act frustrated. Say: **I can't believe this! My friend said this song was great. There must be something wrong with this record!** Angrily lift the record from the turntable and smash it. Repeat this process with the other two records, growing increasingly angry and claiming that you will never trust your friend again. Then calmly stop your act. Say: **What do you think? Was there really anything wrong with the records? Maybe the problem was with the record player itself. You know what? Sometimes we do the same thing to our relationship with God. We don't feel close to God so we "trash" the relationship. Maybe the problem is not with God. Maybe it's something in our life—something like a lack of prayer—that creates a barrier, just like the broken needle.**

STEP 5

As a group, brainstorm some prayer requests that stem from living in an urban environment. Perhaps one of your kids is worried about gang infiltration in his or her neighborhood. Perhaps another person is concerned about not having a safe place to play after school. Whatever the requests, help your group members recognize that God is concerned with every one of their requests, no matter how minor or trivial it may seem. Close the session with a time of prayer in which you take your kids' requests before the Lord.

OPTIONS
SESSION TWO

STEP 4

After explaining the ACTS model of prayer, hand out paper and pencils. Give kids an opportunity to do some journaling, using ACTS as a model. Be sure to explain that no matter what method we use to pray, there's no right or wrong way to do it. Some people may feel very comfortable using ACTS as a guide. Some may wish to write poetry. Some may need to "dump out" their feelings to God. Whatever the method, assure your group members that their prayers are personal communication between them and God.

STEP 5

Offer your group members—especially your high schoolers—an opportunity for some accountability in the changes they've said they need to make. It's very easy to say that we need to change something and even promise that we will. It's much more difficult, however, to stick to it and actually do it. Set up a partner program to allow your group members to share with each other what they've identified to work on. Encourage them to be specific. Then, at your next meeting, allow time for your accountability partners to share with each other how their weeks went. Encourage them to continue their relationship as the year goes on.

STEP 1

Instead of using Repro Resource 3, try another opening activity. Before the session, write the words to the children's prayer "Now I Lay Me Down to Sleep" on index cards, one word per card. Prepare three sets of cards. To begin the session, have kids form three teams. Give each team one set of cards, making sure that the cards in each set are well-scrambled. See which team can arrange its cards in the proper order first. Award prizes to the winning team. Afterward, ask: **How many of you have prayed this prayer before? What other kinds of things do you pray to God about? How often do you pray? What keeps you from praying more?**

STEP 4

Rather than using the spelling bee activity with your sixth graders, simply ask: **Is there anything that you would rather write to someone in a note than say to them out loud? If so, what? Why is writing sometimes easier than talking?** Use group members' responses to lead in to a discussion of journaling.

DATE USED:

Approx. Time

STEP 1: *Let Me Finish!* _____
❏ Extra Action
❏ Large Group
❏ Fellowship & Worship
❏ Mostly Girls
❏ Extra Fun
❏ Media
❏ Short Meeting Time
❏ Sixth Grade
Things needed:

STEP 2: *It's a Two-Way Street* _____
❏ Heard It All Before
❏ Little Bible Background
❏ Mostly Guys
Things needed:

STEP 3: *Call-Waiting* _____
❏ Extra Action
❏ Small Group
❏ Little Bible Background
❏ Media
❏ Short Meeting Time
❏ Urban
Things needed:

STEP 4: *Write It Down!* _____
❏ Heard It All Before
❏ Mostly Girls
❏ Mostly Guys
❏ Extra Fun
❏ Combined Junior High/High School
❏ Sixth Grade
Things needed:

STEP 5: *Personalizing Your Prayer Closet* _____
❏ Small Group
❏ Large Group
❏ Fellowship & Worship
❏ Urban
❏ Combined Junior High/High School
Things needed:

SESSION 3
Why Praise God?

YOUR GOALS FOR THIS SESSION:
Choose one or more

☐ To help kids recognize that God is worthy of praise.

☐ To help kids understand why Christians are called to praise God.

☐ To help kids begin to praise God—both in corporate worship settings and in the way they live their lives.

☐ Other:_____

Your Bible Base:

Psalms 149:1-6; 150
Matthew 18:20
Romans 12:1-2
Revelation 3:15-16

WHY PRAISE GOD?

Tell 'em How Great They Are

(Needed: Chairs)

Have kids arrange their chairs in a circle in order to play the "Compliment Game." Have someone stand in the middle of the circle. Explain that group members must, one at a time, compliment the person standing in the middle. Have those in the circle keep a fairly steady rhythm with their compliments (either by feet-stomping or hand-clapping). If a person doesn't pay a compliment in time or gives a previously-stated compliment, that person must bow down to the person in the middle and chant "I'm not worthy" three times. Then resume the compliments until everyone has given one. Continue until everyone has had a chance to stand in the middle of the circle.

Afterward, ask: **What are some different ways that people react to being praised or complimented? How did it feel for you to be praised and complimented?** Get several responses.

Then say: **Let's take a look at someone else who is often praised and complimented. The funny thing is that this person doesn't need others' praise. And it probably does more good for those who do the praising than it does for Him.**

Brush with Greatness

(Needed: Small paintbrushes, watercolor paints, glasses of water, newsprint or butcher paper, prize)

Hand out paintbrushes (the small, skinny kind used in art classes). Have kids form pairs. Give each pair a large piece of newsprint or butcher paper, a set of watercolor paints, and a glass of water (for rinsing).

213

UNIT THREE

Explain that you want each person to paint one thing that he or she thinks is great about God. Emphasize that group members are free to paint anything they want, but that they should be prepared to explain how their picture describes God's greatness.

After kids have finished this assignment, instruct them to paint a picture that shows their favorite way to worship God. Point out that singing hymns in church isn't the only way to praise God. Things like playing an instrument, playing a sport, drawing, speaking, acting, and giving one's best effort in work and at school all can be forms of worship. When everyone is finished, have kids display and explain their masterpieces. Then let group members vote on their favorite portrait. Award a prize to the winning artist.

Afterward, say: **We've seen several different ways that people can worship God. It may be through singing—or it may not. God's probably glad that singing isn't the only form of worship, considering some of our voices. But it's not the method of worship He's concerned with, anyway. He desires to be worshiped by us because He knows that we'll be the ones who benefit. Let's find out how and why worship is important for us.**

Everything That Hath Breath

(Needed: Bibles, copies of Repro Resource 5, pencils, chalkboard and chalk or newsprint and marker, stopwatch, prizes)

Have kids pair up for a breath-holding contest. When you say, **Go** (and start a stopwatch), one person in each pair will hold his or her breath while his or her partner watches. When the person finally takes a breath, the partner must raise his or her hand. The last person whose partner hasn't raised his or her hand is the winner. Announce the person's time when he or she finally takes a breath. Then have partners switch roles. Award prizes to the winner of each round.

Then have kids turn to Psalm 150. Ask someone to read the psalm aloud, focusing specifically on verse 6. Afterward, say: **Obviously, since all of us seem to be breathing, we can't escape the Bible's call to worship God. Why do you think the psalmist placed such an emphasis on praising and worshiping God?** (Perhaps the

psalmist knew how it would benefit those who praised God. Perhaps the psalmist felt it was the duty of God's people.)

Have someone read aloud Matthew 18:20. Then ask: **What are some different instances in which people get together in God's name?** Emphasize the importance of corporate worship in drawing closer to God.

Have someone reread Psalm 150. Then read Psalm 149:1-6. Discuss as a group some of the different instruments these psalms mention as being part of praising God.

Hand out copies of "Strike Up the Band" (Repro Resource 5). After a few minutes, ask volunteers to share what they came up with. Then ask: **Do you think you could use your band to worship God? Why or why not?** Help your group members see that God can be praised in any musical style.

If you're not musically inclined, and not likely to start a band in the near future, what are some other creative ways that you could praise God with a group of your friends? Encourage kids to be as creative as possible in their suggestions. Write kids' ideas on the board as they're named. (You'll refer to them later in the session.)

STEP 4

Actions Speak Louder Than Words

(Needed: Bibles, copies of Repro Resource 6, pencils)

Have someone read aloud Romans 12:1-2. Then ask: **What do you think it means to offer our bodies as living sacrifices that are pleasing to God?** (Perhaps it means that we are to praise and worship God not merely through ritual activity, but also in the way we live, with all of our heart, mind, and will.)

What does being "transformed by the renewing of your mind" have to do with worship? (When we demonstrate by the way we live that we are different from the non-Christian world, in a sense, we are directing praise to God, the source of our transformation.)

As a group, brainstorm some specific examples of how the principles of Romans 12:1-2 might be demonstrated by Christians.

UNIT THREE

Examples might include things like keeping our minds and bodies sexually pure, keeping a check on any bad attitudes, watching our language and speech habits, and avoiding harmful substances like alcohol and drugs.

Ask: **How does it make you feel to know that you can worship God in the way you live? Explain.** Get responses from several group members.

Ask kids to call out the names of some things that are bad when they're lukewarm. Some examples might include hot chocolate, pizza, bath water, etc. Then have someone read aloud Revelation 3:15-16.

Ask: **How might this passage relate to our worship of God?** (God is not looking for half-hearted praise from us. He wants us to be "on fire" in our worship for Him. If we're not excited about worship, we shouldn't just go through the motions.)

Hand out copies of "What's That You Say?" (Repro Resource 6). Give group members a few minutes to complete the sheet. When everyone is finished, discuss as a group the importance of truly reflecting what's in our hearts when we worship God.

Refer back to the list of creative worship ideas you wrote on the board in Step 3. Encourage group members to choose one of the ideas on the board (or come up with one of their own) to put into practice in the coming week in order to "spark" their worship and praise of God.

Close the session with a group worship time. Let your kids request some of their favorite praise and worship choruses for the group to sing together. Take as many requests as time allows.

EXTREME CLOSEUP

REPRO RESOURCE 5

One Friday afternoon after school, the phone rings. It's for you.

"Is this _____?" asks a voice on the other end of the line.

"Yes, it is," you answer, a bit hesitantly.

"Well, you've been randomly chosen as the winner of the Tricky Ricky Records grand-prize drawing! Do you have any idea what you've just won?"

After a few seconds, you remember that you signed up at a local music store to win a record deal with one of the music industry's major companies.

"I've won a record deal?!" you scream into the phone.

"That's right," says Tricky Ricky. "An all-expense paid record deal for you and your band. Last year's winner, the Talking Donkeys, cut an album that went platinum."

All of a sudden, Tricky Ricky's words hit you: "you *and your band*." You don't *have* a band. Never did. You just said you did because you had to have one to be eligible to win.

Your head is buzzing, so Tricky Ricky's final words don't really register with you as you hang up the phone. You do remember him saying something about having you and your band at the record company Monday morning, prepared to play a couple of songs.

Your mind races. Who, among your friends, will be in your band? What instruments will they play? Who will sing? What will be the band's name? What style of music will you play? What will be the titles of your first two songs?

Don't worry if you or your friends don't play instruments or sing well. You've got the whole weekend to become accomplished musicians and singers. But first, you've got to get everything set up. Get going!

Name of the band:

Style of music you'll play:

Lead singer:

Instruments in the band:

Who will play what in the band:

Names of your band's first two songs:

NOTES

EXTREME CLOSEUP

REPRO RESOURCE 6

What's That You Say?

Do you ever wonder if sometimes, when mankind is singing and worshiping God, God ever asks, "What's that you say?" You know, when He hears one thing from us, but sees another? It's tough to always stay consistent both in our worship to God and in our daily living. But below are a few questions that may help. Answer them as honestly as possible. (Don't worry, your answers are just between you and God.)

The Bible states that we're all sinners (Romans 3:23), but it also states that if we confess our sins to God, He will forgive us for them (1 John 1:9). Are there some sins in your life that you know you haven't confessed to God? If so, what are some of the areas in your life that are holding you back from truly worshiping God?

Describe a time in your life when you felt close to God, when you know you truly worshiped Him.

NOTES

OPTIONS
SESSION THREE

STEP 2

Instead of using the painting activity, take the group to your church sanctuary (assuming that it's empty). Say: **Show me the best place to sit if you want to goof off during the service.** Let kids sit to show their opinions; ask a few to explain. Then say: **Show me the best place to sit if you want to pay close attention to the sermon.** Kids should rearrange themselves and explain. Say: **Now show me where to sit if you want to get the best sound from the music.** Kids should move and explain. Say: **Now show me where to sit if you want to feel close to God.** Let kids move and explain. Then say: **Now show me where to sit if you really want to worship God.** Let kids move and explain. Ask: **If the audience sits in the pews and the participants are on the platform, where should you sit if you want to worship God?** (On the platform, since God is the audience.) Sitting as a group on the platform, discuss the mistaken idea that during worship we are the audience and the "platform people" are the participants. Note that we can worship from any spot as long as we remember that we're the players, not the spectators.

STEP 4

Point out that some people say they don't need to go to church to worship; they can do that anywhere. Have kids form teams, assigning an adult helper to each team. Have each team walk to a different spot in your neighborhood (a park, a street corner, a church member's garage, etc.) and attempt to (a) sing a praise chorus, and (b) pray sentence prayers of praise. After a certain amount of time, regather the group and discuss what happened. Were some places better for worship than others? If singing and praying didn't work, what might have been better? What kinds of worship might work best at school? At home? At church?

STEP 1

In a small group, you can try a written variation of the "Compliment Game." This will give kids something to take home and keep for times when they need it. Give everyone a small paper bag, a pencil, and several sheets of paper. Kids should write their names on the bags, which should then be placed at a central location in the room. Group members should then write out compliments for each other. (Make it extremely clear that nothing but positive comments may be written on these sheets!) Everyone in the room should write something (or several things) to every other person. The writers need not identify themselves. When they finish, group members should deliver their compliment sheets to the respective paper bags. Give kids a few minutes to read what's been written about them. Then discuss how it feels to be praised and complimented.

STEP 2

Explain that another way to "compliment" each other is to work together. For example, one person's outgoing personality "complements" another's shyness. Within a small group, it is important for people to learn to "complement" each other as well as to "compliment" each other. With this in mind, have your group members work *together* on a poster of praise to God. One person might come up with a good theme; another might have an idea for a general design. One person might use artistic talent to draw everything in place; others might fill in the colors and add specifics. Make sure that everyone contributes something unique to the poster. Afterward, explain that God is less honored by a piece of cardboard and a little color than by the fact that part of His "body" worked together to accomplish something for Him.

STEP 1

Before the session, write the words to a well-known hymn or praise song on index cards, one word or phrase per card. As kids arrive, give each of them a card. Explain that group members must arrange themselves in the correct order, according to the lyrics of the song. When kids have what they think is the correct order, ask them to sing the song, with each person singing his or her word or phrase. (If kids don't know the tune, they should make one up.) Afterward, play a tape of the song so that kids can hear how it really goes. Use this activity to introduce the idea of singing praises to God.

STEP 4

Hand out copies of your church's bulletin. As a group, go over the components of your church's worship service one item at a time, deciding how each aspect lends (or doesn't lend) itself to worship. Then have kids form three groups. Instruct the members of each group to design their own worship service, incorporating components of your church's worship as well as other items that they come up with. To make the activity a little more challenging, you might have one group plan a service for younger children, one group plan a service for teens, and one group plan a service for residents of a nursing home. After a few minutes, have each group share its plan. Note the similarities and differences between worship plans.

OPTIONS

SESSION THREE

HEARD IT ALL BEFORE

LITTLE BIBLE BACKGROUND

FELLOWSHIP & WORSHIP

STEP 2

Kids may automatically paint pictures of mountains or sunsets without really thinking about the greatness of God. They may also paint "favorite" worship methods without really liking *any* kind of worship. Or they may paint whatever worship method is easiest to depict. So instead of using the painting activity, have kids form teams. Give each team a different kind of magazine (computers, sports, travel, entertainment, music, etc.). Instruct each team to tear pictures from its magazine, trying to find five that could somehow illustrate the greatness of God. To do this, teams will have to talk about why God is great; they'll also have to get creative as they explain their choices to the rest of the group. Instead of having kids paint pictures of favorite worship methods, ask whether kids *have* any favorites and why.

STEP 3

If your kids are likely to yawn over Psalm 150, try instead passages in which people worshiped God in unusual situations. For example, in 2 Samuel 6:14-16, 20-23, David dances in a "praise parade." In Acts 16:22-31, Paul and Silas sing hymns in jail. In Job 1:13-22, Job praises God despite great loss. Ask: **Why do you think these people went to such lengths to praise God? What things, big and little, tend to keep you from praising God?**

STEP 2

As soon as you begin to discuss the importance of praising God, ask your group members to work together to create a "top-ten list" of reasons to praise God. See what they come up with out of their limited knowledge of Scripture. It is somewhat unusual for people in our culture to praise someone else unless there are ulterior motives. See if this attitude is reflected in your group members' reasons to praise God. If it is, you can deal with it during the Bible study that follows. If not, you will still be better equipped to know where your kids stand spiritually as you present the rest of the session.

STEP 4

Romans 12:1-2 is not an easy passage for beginners. The Psalms references in the previous step are fairly self-explanatory, so be sure to save some time to discuss what it means to be a "living sacrifice" and to "renew one's mind." You will probably need to be prepared to do a quick review of the Old Testament system of sacrifices, of Jesus' sacrifice, and of related verses to make this passage relevant. Another option is to assign related passages and have kids read them during the following week. If your group members are new to the Bible, the best way to help them "catch up" is to challenge them to do so on their own. An hour a week in a group setting is a start, but kids need encouragement to establish a daily (or *almost* daily) Bible-reading regimen.

STEP 1

After kids have finished playing the "Compliment Game" with each other, explain that now you're going to put in the middle the one who deserves all of the compliments and praise that we can offer—God. Place a Bible in the middle of the circle to represent God. Then have kids play the "Compliment Game" in the same manner as before, offering praise to God. Afterward, ask: **How did it feel to say or to hear someone else saying "I'm not worthy" at the "feet" of God?** Explain briefly that none of us is worthy of God's love; however, because He offers His love so freely, our natural response and desire should be to praise Him.

STEP 4

Read Psalm 150 again; then do just what the psalm says. Praise God in His sanctuary. Praise Him in His mighty heavens by moving outside. Praise Him with the trumpet, with dancing, and with resounding cymbals. If you can't find a harp or lyre, you may need to improvise. Also, depending on the restrictions or limitations of your particular church, you may need to get creative. But remember, our God is a creative God, and He loves to hear His children's praise.

OPTIONS
SESSION THREE

Mostly Girls

STEP 2

If some of your girls have trouble coming up with their favorite way to worship God, ask them why. Some may say that worship is boring. Others may say that they can't relate to worship activities. As group members mention their reasons, make a list of them on the board. Then brainstorm as a group some ways for a person to enjoy worship more. Read Psalm 150. Then ask: **Does this sound like God wants us to be bored with worship?** (Obviously not!) **Looking at Psalm 150, what are some things you think we could do to liven up our worship?** If time permits, you may want to put some of your group members' suggestions into practice.

STEP 4

Hand out paper and drawing materials (colored pencils, markers, crayons, or whatever else you prefer). Instruct your group members to draw what they think of when they hear the word "hypocrite." After a few minutes, have your girls display and explain their drawings. Then read aloud the following definition from *Webster's Dictionary:* "one who affects virtues or qualities he does not have." Ask: **Do any of you know Christians who are hypocrites?** Do *not* let anyone name names here. **How could a Christian be a hypocrite?** (By not living out the beliefs she professes to hold.) Field any questions this discussion may foster; then have someone read Romans 12:1-2 and continue Step 4 as written.

Mostly Guys

STEP 1

Complimenting other guys may feel a little strange for some of your group members. So rather than playing the "Compliment Game" as written, "trick" your guys into complimenting each other. Ask: **Who are some of the men that you most admire?** Write down kids' responses on the board. Then ask: **In what ways is** [the name of one of your group members] **like** [the first name on the list]**?** It may take a while for the comparisons to come, but they will. For example, while your first guy might not have the muscles of his most-admired linebacker, perhaps others will observe that "He always puts 100 percent effort into whatever he's doing." Eventually guys should see that their adult heroes were once kids too—like your group members are now. What matters most at this point is effort and hope—and both of these things are made easier with a little praise and a few compliments from others.

STEP 4

Who says guys can't sing? Before the session, assemble a variety of praise music by all-male groups. Try to include a song by the Vienna Boys' Choir, an all-male gospel quartet number, a Gregorian chant, a bluegrass version of a hymn, a favorite male contemporary Christian group, and anything else that would show your guys that not all singing men sound alike. Then, as you sing some songs to conclude the session, explain to your guys that if they can't sing on key, they should at least sing loud. God appreciates the enthusiasm much more than He does the technical quality of the music.

Extra Fun

STEP 1

Begin the session by playing dodge ball, with one person in the center being pelted by those around him or her. If dodge ball is not feasible, try a similar kind of game that inflicts a low level of pain on someone who isn't quick enough or alert enough. Play for a while, goading group members into being competitive and aggressive. Then suddenly shift from that game to the "Compliment Game." Afterward, ask: **Was it easier for you to get smacked with a ball or to receive genuine praise from your peers?** Some people are likely to prefer the former to the latter. Discuss their reasons.

STEP 4

After group members complete Repro Resource 5, say: **Suppose we *as a group* were offered a recording contract. What should we do?** Go through the same issues that kids went through for Repro Resource 5—name of the band, music style, instrumentation, and so forth. But this time, kids must work *together* and agree on what to do. Afterward, you might actually do whatever kids suggest to the extent that you are able. The singers can sing. The musicians can play air guitar, air tuba, or whatever. The group roadies can set up the stage. Prepare at least two songs with your impromptu band. If you're successful, plan a road tour.

OPTIONS
SESSION THREE

STEP 2

Have kids form teams. Let the group watch TV or listen to the radio for at least three minutes. Have each team listen for "praise phrases" ("car of the year," "beautiful," "Baby, it's you," "world's largest," "supergroup," etc.) and write them down. The team that collects the most words and phrases wins. Afterward, ask: **Which of these phrases would apply to God? Why? Which aren't strong enough? What "praise phrases" would you add to describe God?**

STEP 3

Compare and contrast the styles of worship found in scenes from the following videos (after pre-screening the scenes yourself).

- *Say Amen, Somebody*. Play one or more scenes from this spirited documentary in which African-American pioneers of Gospel music sing individually, in groups, and in choirs.
- *Agnes of God*. Show a scene in which the nuns pray, sing, or otherwise worship.
- *Tender Mercies*. Play the scene in which Mac (Robert Duvall) is baptized in a small, rural church.

Ask: **Why do people worship God in different ways? How do you think He wants you to worship Him? Why?**

STEP 1

Replace Steps 1 and 2 with a shorter opener. Before the session, ask one of your church's better bakers to come up with homemade refreshments for the meeting. As you serve the refreshments, bring in the baker and announce that she or he provided the food. Ask your group: **Is there anything you'd like to say to this person?** See what kids come up with. Then ask: **Other than just saying "Thank you," can you think of ways in which we could show our appreciation?** Have kids form teams. Give each team a hypothetical amount of money (ranging from a nickel to $500) to spend on showing appreciation. After a couple of minutes, have each group share its ideas. Use this activity to introduce the concept of praising God in a variety of ways.

STEP 3

Skip Repro Resource 5. Also skip Step 4. Instead, read John 4:23, 24. Then ask: **What does it mean to worship in spirit?** (To worship with your heart, and not just go through the motions.) **What does it mean to worship in truth?** (To have the true God and His Son at the center of your worship.) If your church bulletins include an order of service, give each person a recent copy. After each item in the order of service, kids should draw one to five hearts (five being strongest) to show how involved their hearts usually are at each point in the worship. Kids should also draw one to five crosses after each item to show how well they tend to focus on God or Jesus at each point. (If your bulletins don't include an order of service, jot one down yourself and read it aloud as kids reply by drawing crosses and hearts on index cards.) Close with silent prayer in which kids can talk to God about how they've been worshiping Him.

STEP 1

If you think your kids would be uncomfortable complimenting each other, try a variation of the "Compliment Game." Have kids arrange their chairs in a circle. Ask them to imagine that Michael Jordan or some other sports or entertainment celebrity is standing in the middle of the circle. Explain that each person will have five seconds to think of a compliment to give to the celebrity. If a person can't think of one in five seconds (or if he or she gives a compliment that's already been used), he or she is out. Continue until only one person remains. Afterward, ask: **What if it had been God in the middle of the circle? How might your compliments have been different? Why?** After you've received several responses, move on to Step 2.

STEP 4

During your group worship time at the end of the session, give your kids an opportunity to praise God for things associated with living in an urban environment. Kids often hear about the pitfalls and drawbacks of living in an urban setting. But there are some advantages to city life. Ask your kids to consider some of these advantages as they praise God. Make the point that every day we have hundreds of things to praise God for—things that we often take for granted.

OPTIONS
SESSION THREE

STEP 1

For an added twist to the "Compliment Game," divide kids into two groups—a junior high group and a high school group. To begin the game, have your high schoolers sit in a circle; then have your junior highers enter one by one for their shower of compliments. After all of your junior highers have had a turn in the middle of the circle, switch the game around. Have your junior highers sit in a circle; then have your high schoolers enter the circle one by one for their compliments. Afterward, ask your junior highers: **How did it feel to be complimenting someone older and probably wiser than you?** See if any of them felt intimidated. Then ask your high schoolers: **How did it feel to receive so many compliments? Did it matter that the people offering them are younger than you?** Explain that some people may feel intimidated when they think of praising God, or may think that because He is all-powerful and all-knowing, He doesn't need or want our praise. The truth is that He wants us to praise and worship Him because He knows the benefits that we receive when we do.

STEP 3

Instead of using Repro Resource 5 after reading Psalm 150, divide your group into teams of four or five, making sure to combine junior highers and high schoolers on each team. Have kids refer back to Psalm 150. Explain that each team will create an act of worship based on one of the commands from the psalm. Teams may wish to move outside to worship. They may wish to create a dance of worship. Whatever strikes their fancy, they may choose. Allow the teams time to pull together their act of worship. After several minutes, have each team present its act of worship for all to enjoy (and join in, if possible).

STEP 1

If you think it might be difficult for your sixth graders to offer sincere compliments to each other, try another option. Have kids form pairs. Give the members of each pair five minutes to list as many different compliments as they can think of. When time is up, have each pair read its list. If a compliment was listed by more than one pair, each pair that listed the compliment must mark it out. The pair with the most remaining compliments on its list is the winner. Afterward, discuss as a group which compliments on the pairs' lists could apply to God. Lead in to Step 2.

STEP 4

Rather than asking your kids to name things that are bad when they're lukewarm, demonstrate your point using refreshments. Serve some "hot" chocolate made from barely warm tap water. If possible, you might also want to serve mildly warm pizza. When kids react to the lukewarm refreshments, lead in to a discussion of Revelation 3:15-16.

DATE USED:

Approx. Time

STEP 1: *Tell 'em How Great They Are*   _____
❏ Small Group
❏ Large Group
❏ Fellowship & Worship
❏ Mostly Guys
❏ Extra Fun
❏ Short Meeting Time
❏ Urban
❏ Combined Junior High/High School
❏ Sixth Grade
Things needed:

STEP 2: *Brush with Greatness*   _____
❏ Extra Action
❏ Small Group
❏ Heard It All Before
❏ Little Bible Background
❏ Mostly Girls
❏ Media
Things needed:

STEP 3: *Everything That Hath Breath*   _____
❏ Heard It All Before
❏ Media
❏ Short Meeting Time
❏ Combined Junior High/High School
Things needed:

STEP 4: *Actions Speak Louder Than Words*   _____
❏ Extra Action
❏ Large Group
❏ Little Bible Background
❏ Fellowship & Worship
❏ Mostly Girls
❏ Mostly Guys
❏ Extra Fun
❏ Urban
❏ Sixth Grade
Things needed:

225

SESSION 4

Why Fellowship?

YOUR GOALS FOR THIS SESSION:
Choose one or more

- [ ] To help kids recognize that spending time with other Christians doesn't necessarily have to be a boring or trying experience.

- [ ] To help kids understand why spending time with other Christians is important in building our Christian lives.

- [ ] To help kids establish fellowship opportunities in which they can both draw strength from and strengthen other Christians.

- [ ] Other:_____

Your Bible Base:

Proverbs 27:17
Matthew 18:19-20
2 Corinthians 6:14-18

WHY FELLOWSHIP?

STEP 1

Staying Alive Outside the Hive

(Needed: Prizes)

Instruct group members to stand against the wall at one end of your meeting area. Explain that you're going to play a game called "The Swarm." Select one person to be "queen (or king) bee" of the swarm. The queen (or king) bee must stand in the middle of the room. When you yell, **Swarm,** the rest of the kids must try to get to the wall on the other side of the room without being "stung" (or tagged) by the queen (or king) bee. Those who get stung become "worker bees" and must link arms with the queen (or king) bee. Then, for the next round, the queen (or king) bee and all of the worker bees will try to tag (while remaining linked together) the rest of the group members who are trying to get back across the room. Obviously, the more rounds you play, the larger the "swarm" in the middle will become. Award prizes to the last few remaining kids who haven't been stung.

Afterward, ask the last few remaining "unstung" people: **How did it feel as the "swarm" was bearing down on you?** Get a few responses.

Then ask the entire group: **Has there ever been a time in your life when you felt like you were one of the only Christians around—and that other people were bearing down on you? If so, explain.**

Discuss as a group some reasons why people sometimes feel alone and under pressure as a Christian. For instance, it may seem to some kids that there are no other Christians at their school or workplace. Encourage your kids to discuss some of the struggles they go through when they're feeling alone.

UNIT THREE

Swimming Upstream in a Downstream World

(Needed: Copies of Repro Resource 7, pencils)

Hand out copies of "In the Minority at Majority Junior High" (Repro Resource 7) and pencils. Instruct kids to put an "X" next to the places in their school where, as Christians, they feel like they're in the minority. For example, one of your guys might put an "X" by the picture of the locker room because many guys talk crudely and tell dirty jokes there. One of your girls might put an "X" next to the picture of the lunchroom, where she often eats with a group of girls who gossip and spread false rumors about other girls that they don't like.

When all of your kids are finished, go over the sheet as a group. Then explain: **Most Christians probably feel like they're in the minority at some point in their lives. But to help us avoid that "me against the world" feeling, God has given Christians a solution—other Christians. Let's check out what the Bible has to say about the benefits of fellowshipping with other believers.**

WHY FELLOWSHIP?

STEP 3

Swords, Pyramids, and Lawnmower Blades

(Needed: Bibles)

To make the Bible study a little more interesting, use a "sword drill" approach. The first passage you should call out is Matthew 18:19-20. When the first person to find the passage has finished reading it, ask: **What promise can a Christian take from this passage?** (If two or more Christians get together, God will be there with them.)

How does it make you feel to know that God is with you when you are with other Christians? Allow time for some discussion.

Call out the next passage: 2 Corinthians 6:14-18. When the first person to find the passage has finished reading it, ask: **Do you think this passage is telling Christians to have nothing to do with non-Christians? Why or why not?** Let kids offer their comments.

Suggest that this passage prohibits a cooperation and alignment of thoughts, beliefs, and lifestyles with non-believers. Point out that Jesus didn't treat sinners like the plague—just their sins. In fact, Jesus hung out with the sinners, sometimes even more so then he did with "religious" people.

Ask: **Based on the example of Jesus, who "partied" with non-Christians by attending feasts and social events, what are your feelings about partying with non-Christians in a non-Christian atmosphere?** Let kids discuss their views on this, but don't try to resolve the issue. Instead, simply point out that Jesus did indeed spend time *with* non-Christians, but was never sucked in by them. Also emphasize that Jesus had His "get away" times with fellow believers during which He was strengthened by the support of others.

Have kids form two teams for a "Human Pyramid Challenge." Explain that the team that can build the most levels of human bodies kneeling on top of one another in three minutes will be declared the winner. Emphasize that each level must be held for at least ten seconds to be counted.

After a winning team has been declared, explain that the more support (the number of people on the bottom level) a team's pyramid had, the more potential it had to build more levels. Relate this to the fact that Christians gain both strength and support from other

Christians through fellowship, which then can enable them to build up God's kingdom.

Have your kids grab their Bibles one last time as you call out your last passage: Proverbs 27:17. When the first person to find the passage has finished reading it, ask: **How many of you have ever had to mow a lawn?** After a show of hands, point out that the first part of verse 17, "As iron sharpens iron," indicates that sharpening a piece of iron requires another piece of iron; in this process, both pieces are sharpened.

Ask: **What do you think happens to lawnmower blades as they cut more and more grass?** (The blades get duller and duller, and eventually have to be resharpened by a hard, metallic sharpening wheel.)

Suggest that if a Christian (i.e., a lawnmower) is out in the world ministering to those in need of God (i.e., cutting grass), eventually his or her blades will become dull and will need to be sharpened.

Summarize: **A Christian can get burned out if he or she never gets "resharpened" or revitalized. That's why Christians go to church, attend retreats, and fellowship together. It's this fellowship time that can get Christians back to their "cutting edge."**

The Fun Factor

(Needed: Copies of Repro Resource 8, pencils, slips of paper with group members' names on them)

The idea of spending time with other Christians in order to sharpen each other's Christian walk may sound good to your kids—in theory. Putting it into practice could be another story.

Ask: **In your opinion, how does the fun that Christians have compare with the fun that non-Christians have? Explain.**

Distribute copies of "A Knee-Slapping, Rip-Roaring Good Time" (Repro Resource 8). Give kids a few minutes to work on the sheet. When they're finished, have them hand in their sheets to you. Read the examples that your kids came up with and vote on the best one.

Acknowledge that the examples on Repro Resource 8 are somewhat exaggerated, and that the real issue isn't whether or not every Christian is the life of the party. Instead, the issue is that Christians

share a common bond—their relationship with Jesus—that transcends social makeup.

As a group, brainstorm some ways in which your kids can support each other. If you can't come up with a better idea, you might write group members' names on slips of paper and then have kids draw slips to determine "accountability partners" (making sure you pair up kids who attend the same school). Instruct each person to stick a sticky note with a question mark on it on his or her partner's locker every morning, letting that person know that someone cares about how his or her day at school will go. By the end of the day, each person should stick another sticky note on his or her partner's locker, with either a "happy face" or a "frown face" on it to indicate whether he or she had a good day or a rough day. This can help both partners know how to pray for each other better. Also encourage the partners to share their feelings frequently by talking with each other.

Strength in Numbers

(Needed: Refreshments)

Close the session with a time of group affirmation. This may involve singing some of your kids' favorite songs, as well as a time of sharing and prayer. And of course, you'll want to have some refreshments ready in order to send your kids away in good spirits!

Also try to plan a weekend group activity. An idea that might prove to be fun and interesting would be to have a Saturday night camp out outside the church. Then everyone could attend the Sunday morning worship service together. This activity would be a great opportunity for Christian fellowship.

NOTES

EXTREME CLOSEUP

REPRO RESOURCE 7

In the Minority at Majority Junior High

Below are some illustrations of various areas located throughout your school. If your school is like most schools, there are probably areas where as a Christian, you sometimes feel in the minority. Place an "X" next to any of the places listed below where you feel this way. Feel free to add your own areas at the bottom if there are any we've left out. Be prepared to explain why you feel in the minority in each area.

EXTREME CLOSEUP

REPRO RESOURCE 8

A Knee-Slapping, RIP-ROARING GOOD TIME

Some people believe that Christians don't know how to have a good time. They have some rather strange ideas about what Christians do for fun. Below are some slightly exaggerated examples of some people's ideas of "Christian fun." After reading these examples, come up with a far-fetched idea of your own.

Devin Doolittle
Devin doesn't get out much. He slithers to the family sofa on Friday nights and sometimes doesn't reappear until Sunday morning for church. When no one's around, his favorite thing to do is leave the TV on for several minutes while he turns off all of the other lights in the house. Then, in a moment of unbridled craziness, he turns the TV off and gleefully watches the glow from the TV screen slowly fade into darkness. Sometimes the experience lasts nearly thirty seconds.

Penny Rollzalot
Every Friday after school, as the other kids head off to friends' houses, Penny heads to the bank. There, she cashes in her weekly allowance—a $10 bill—for twenty rolls of pennies. When she gets home, she dumps all 1,000 pennies out of their rolls, starts her stopwatch, and rerolls the pennies as fast as she can. Doing this several times a night, Penny can now boast of rolling 1,000 pennies in under six minutes, as well as making the loudest noise in the offering plate on Sunday morning.

Joe Skripcher
On Saturday nights, Joe likes to randomly open his Bible to a page and guess how many words are on that page. After writing down his guess, he counts the actual number of words on the page. The number of words that his guess is off by is how many minutes he will brush his teeth that night. He's been doing this for a few years now, so he's gotten fairly accurate, usually guessing within ten words. You can imagine how his pearly whites must have glistened the time he forgot to include the footnotes at the bottom of the page in his total and was off by 237 words.

Now you make up a person and his or her idea of a rip-roaring good time.

OPTIONS
SESSION FOUR

STEP 2

Rather than using Repro Resource 7, try another option. Have kids form pairs. Give each pair four small adhesive bandages and a ballpoint pen. At your signal, each pair must do the following *with each person using only one finger:* (1) Unwrap the bandages. (2) Decide in which four areas at school Christian kids are most likely to feel outnumbered, and write the names of those areas on the bandages. (3) Apply the bandages, two per partner. The first pair to accomplish all of this wins. Afterward, discuss as a group the school areas that kids chose and the fact that it was easier to get the needed "first aid" when a partner helped.

STEP 4

Skip Repro Resource 8. Instead, have kids wander around the room. Each person should call out repeatedly the name of his or her favorite TV show. Kids calling out the same show should group together. After half a minute, see how many groups have been formed and how many kids are partnerless. Have kids break up again and mill around. Each person should call out the name of his or her favorite recording artist or band, with groups forming on that basis. After half a minute, see what's happened. Then try it one more time, with kids calling out the initials of their favorite Savior (J.C., one would hope)—and grouping accordingly. After half a minute, all or most kids should be in the same group. (If some aren't, note mentally who they are, but don't make them feel conspicuous.) Use this activity as an illustration of the fact that we may not have much in common—except for our involvement in the group and, ideally, our faith in Christ.

STEP 1

The "Swarm" game won't work well if you have only three or four kids. Instead, conduct an individual competition. Set up a table at one end of the room that will provide a decent-sized working area for each person. At the other end of the room, dump a large pile of some kind of building materials (wooden blocks, Legos, dominoes, or whatever). Explain that the object of the game is to see who can assemble the tallest structure out of the building materials in three minutes. The structures must be assembled on the table, and individuals may carry only one piece at a time. Give a signal and start the timer. At the end of three minutes, give another signal to stop. Measure to see whose structure is tallest and announce the winner. But then have kids take a look at how much they assembled one piece at a time. Say: **If you'd been working together, just think what you could have assembled!** Use this activity as a starting point to get kids thinking about what might be accomplished in their group, one person at a time. Also refer back to this activity in Step 3 instead of using the human pyramid activity.

STEP 4

Rather than drawing names for "accountability partners," have kids commit to *all* of the other people in the group. Offer the locker-notes idea as one suggestion, but then challenge your kids to come up with something they *all* can do to encourage each other on a regular basis throughout the week. Suggestions might include eating lunch together, forming a telephone chain to pass along positive comments, and agreeing to wear the same piece of clothing or jewelry on a certain day to remind kids of each other. Kids may surprise you (and each other) with some of the good ideas they come up with.

STEP 3

Before you start the sword drill, have kids compete in a four-legged race. Divide the group into teams of three. Tie two members of each team together as you would for a three-legged race. Then tie the third person to one of the two in the same manner. You should have one person in the middle who has both legs tied to another person. Have the teams race to see which can get to the other end of the room and back in the shortest amount of time. Award prizes to the winning team. The four-legged race activity should lead naturally into the first passage of your sword drill—Matthew 18:19-20 ("where two or three come together in my name, there I am with them").

STEP 4

Rather than handing out Repro Resource 8, read aloud one or two of the examples on the sheet. Then have kids form groups. Instruct each group to come up with a brief skit that shows another exaggerated example of a Christian having a "fun" time. Encourage kids to be humorous and creative in their skits, but not to be offensive or hurtful. After a few minutes, have each group perform its skit. Afterward, continue the session as written, beginning with the fourth paragraph in Step 4.

OPTIONS
SESSION FOUR

STEP 1

Kids may have heard one too many times that non-Christian peers are "bearing down on" them—as if schools were filled with roving bands of pagans out to corrupt Christians by force. Kids know it's more common for young people to be attracted to "cool" kids and adopt their values in order to be "cool" themselves. To maintain credibility as you discuss peer pressure, avoid assuming that kids feel "swarmed" or "in the minority." First, ask *them* to describe how they feel about being around non-Christians at school. If some of your kids attend Christian schools, get their perspectives, too. If group members don't seem as concerned about peer pressure as the session assumes, address the subject as preparation for the bigger, possibly more hostile, world kids will face as they go to high school, college, and into the work force.

STEP 3

Kids may question the assertion that going to church "sharpens" them. They may see Christian activities as "dulling"— or at least dull. Either skip the Proverbs 27:17 discussion and concentrate on mutual support or be prepared to give concrete examples of how being part of a youth group keeps Christians "sharp." If you choose the second option, share how leading the group keeps you on your toes spiritually. Ask kids who've participated in mission trips, summer camps, or service projects to explain how they were challenged by those activities.

STEP 2

If your kids don't know the Bible because they've just recently gotten involved with your church or youth group, they may be in an excellent position to respect both Christians and non-Christians. When you get to Repro Resource 7, change the instructions a bit. Rather than having kids mark places where they feel "in the minority," have them try to break down all of the locations into "Christians" and "non-Christians." Then discuss what *they* should do in each location. When Christians are around, they can look for encouragement and strength. When non-Christians are around, they need to be aware of setting a positive Christian example and perhaps look for opportunities to invite those friends to the youth group. If group members learn to be more active wherever they are, they are less likely to ever feel in a minority.

STEP 3

The fact that Jesus "partied" with non-Christians is used as a passing comment in the session. But this may be a side of the Son of God that people new to the Bible and your group are unaware of. Just as one example, have group members look up and read Matthew 9:9-13. While they may be amazed that Jesus spent a lot of time hanging out with sinful people, be sure they also realize *why* He did so. Ask: **What did Jesus mean by "It is not the healthy who need a doctor, but the sick"? In what ways can we begin to serve as "doctors" to those around us?**

STEP 1

Provide paper and collage materials for your group members. Ask each person to create a picture of the image that comes to mind when he or she hears the word "fellowship." Encourage kids to be honest. After a few minutes, invite volunteers to share and explain what they came up with. You may find that your kids think of fellowship as an obligatory and boring part of being a Christian. Next, ask group members to think of their best friend and make a list of reasons why that person is their best friend. After a minute or so, invite volunteers to share their reasons. You'll probably find a common thread of "We like to do the same things" or "We have common interests." Say: **If our best friends are people with whom we share interests, and the definition of fellowship is "community of interest, activity, feeling, or experience," why do we say we don't enjoy fellowship with other Christians? Don't we have a lot in common with fellow Christians?**

STEP 5

For your worship time, include songs that are based on the theme of unity and sharing our walk with others. You may also wish to read Matthew 18: 19-20 again. Close the session by thanking God for His promise to be with us, especially when we're in fellowship with other believers.

OPTIONS
SESSION FOUR

STEP 1

No other word sends chills of fear down the spine of a junior high girl quite like the word *cliques*. Some of your girls may belong to a clique; all of your girls are affected by cliques. Ask: **What comes to mind when you hear the word *clique*?** Answers will vary, depending on whether or not your girls are part of a clique. **Why do you think cliques exist?** (For friendship, unity, and identity.) **What does it take to be part of a clique?** Get several responses. Then ask: **When you're not part of a clique—or halfheartedly part of one that doesn't really fit your style or beliefs—how do you feel? Why?** Lead in to a discussion of feeling alone as a Christian.

STEP 4

After your girls have completed Repro Resource 8, say: **It probably wasn't too difficult to come up with something that a boring Christian would do. Now let's come up with a real good time for a real Christian.** Kids often link *don't* or *can't* with Christianity, so it may be a challenge for them to come up with ideas. Encourage them to be as creative and crazy as they can be.

After a few minutes, have volunteers share some of their ideas. Then say: **God didn't create us to be bored or boring. He's a *creative* God who wants us to be creative, enjoy life, and have fun.**

STEP 2

Sometimes guys don't mind being in the minority. If they have confidence in themselves during sports or mental contests, being outnumbered is just another challenge that makes life interesting. So after your group members fill out Repro Resource 7, say: **Suppose we're strategizing how to "take over" the school, but we're in the minority as Christians. What should be our strategy?** Let guys theorize. For example, if the Christian/non-Christian ratio is about 50/50 in English class, they might want to start there. With a little effort, a majority could be achieved. Then they might want to turn their attention to certain areas of the lunchroom, and so forth. Eventually, they might even get around to the locker room. Challenge each guy this week to do at least one thing that will be a positive Christian influence to help counteract something sinful that other people may be doing.

STEP 5

Help your group members plan a special out-of-the-ordinary "guy thing." Let them determine whether it should be a time they will use to get to know each other better, or if they would rather use the opportunity to invite their non-Christian friends to prove that Christians *do* know how to have fun. Challenge them to think big, but you should be aware of the available budget so that they don't plan something they can't actually carry out.

STEP 2

Instead of using Repro Resource 7 as written, let kids *act out* their opinions. Have a volunteer roleplay a roving reporter, narrating his or her walk through the school. The other kids should act like typical students in each of the locations. For example, the reporter might begin by saying, "Here we are, entering Majority Junior High just before classes are about to begin. Let's see what these two girls are talking about." (The "reporter" should then hold the microphone toward two volunteers who will create a typical conversation.) As the reporter roams from room to room, other volunteers should roleplay various students and offer input in character.

STEP 5

As you're sitting around having refreshments, ask your kids to imagine that they are professional church consultants who have just attended an average meeting of your youth group. It is their job to give you some input. Ask your "consultants": **How can this group have more fun on a regular basis? Any group can go out and do stuff, but what would it take for us to have more fun week by week during our meetings?** Let kids respond as "professionals." Keep things lighthearted and fun, but take what they say seriously. Perhaps there are a number of things you can adapt, eliminate, shorten, revise, or "tweak" in some way that would make kids more comfortable. And if they are truly wise consultants, they'll realize that the responsibility of having fun is only slightly up to the leader. Enthusiasm must generate from the group members, or the overall fun level will suffer. (If your consultants come to this conclusion, give them a big bonus in the form of another cookie.)

OPTIONS
SESSION FOUR

STEP 2

Play a "secular" song in which someone promises to "be there" for someone else. Possibilities include "I'll Be There" (Mariah Carey), "I'll Be Your Everything" (Tommy Page), "Bridge Over Troubled Water" (Simon and Garfunkel), "That's What Friends Are For" (Dionne Warwick and Friends), "I'll Be Loving You (Forever)" (New Kids on the Block), "Forever Your Girl" (Paula Abdul), and "Before the Next Teardrop Falls" (Freddy Fender). Ask: **What is the singer promising to do? How might the world be different if every person had that kind of commitment from someone else? On a scale of one to ten—with ten being the highest—how much support do you think most kids in our group get from each other? How could we improve that?**

STEP 5

Before the session, purchase two "recordable" greeting cards—the kind containing a small recording device that captures any spoken greeting you care to put on it. The greeting plays when the card is opened. To close the meeting, have kids form two teams. Put the teams in separate rooms. Give each team a card. Instruct each team to record an encouraging message for the other team—one that pledges support during the coming week. The message may be spoken or sung. Then regather the group and have teams trade cards. Allow kids to pass the cards around so that they can listen to the messages individually.

STEP 1

Replace Steps 1 and 2 with a shorter opener. Have kids form pairs. Instruct the pairs to line up against one wall. Partners must face each other and hold hands. Give each pair a helium-filled balloon with no string. The challenge for each pair is to get its balloon from one side of the room to the other, holding the balloon between the partners' noses. Award a prize to any successful team. Afterward, ask: **What was the secret of winning this game?** (Working together; paying attention to what your partner was doing; going slowly.) **Does anybody put that kind of effort into helping you get from one end of the week to the other? If so, who? What if the members of this group put that kind of effort into helping you? How might your week be different?** Instead of using Repro Resource 7, ask kids where and when during the week it would be best to have another Christian close by—and why.

STEP 3

Skip the 2 Corinthians 6:14-18 reading and discussion. Instead, read Romans 12:10, 13, 15, 16 and relate it to the human pyramid activity. Skip Steps 4 and 5. Instead, put one group member in the middle of the room and have the rest of the group pose supportively around him or her—arms on shoulders, smiling at the person, etc. Take a Polaroid photo of this and give it to the person in the center. Do the same for each group member, giving each a turn in the center. Have kids take their photos home as reminders of the support available in your group. If time allows, choose accountability partners (Step 4) and share the stickly note idea.

STEP 4

Ask volunteers from your church—people of widely varying ages—to come to your meeting to share with your group members why fellowship with other Christians is so important to them. Help your kids see that Christian fellowship is for people of all ages. Before you dismiss your volunteers, give your group members an opportunity to ask them some questions.

STEP 5

If many of your group members come from broken homes, close the session by affirming that Christians are part of the *family* of God. Read Mark 3:31-35. Point out that the bonds and relationships that can—and should—be formed by Christians are every bit as strong as natural family bonds. As a group, sing a couple of hymns or songs that address the topic of the Christian family. (Amy Grant's song "Family" is a good example.)

OPTIONS
SESSION FOUR

STEP 1

Instead of playing "The Swarm," have kids share some examples of times when they felt out of place or "under attack." Especially encourage your high schoolers to share situations they faced when in junior high. List the situations on the board as group members mention them. Then talk about why kids felt the way they did, asking others in the group to share about similar experiences. Finally, discuss what your kids might be able to do to avoid such situations in the future.

STEP 2

Instead of using Repro Resource 7, bring in a large, wall-sized piece of paper on which you've written "Of the Minority in Majority U.S.A." Instruct kids to draw scenes depicting areas of their lives in which they feel they are in the minority. This could include anything from not caring about what brand of shoes you wear in a name-brand-shoe culture to not wanting to be part of a "gossip chain." When the wall is complete, talk about how it feels to be in the minority in such a majority-driven culture. Then ask: **What do you think we can do about this?**

STEP 4

The ironic, exaggerated humor of Repro Resource 8 may be lost on your sixth graders. So instead of using the sheet, simply ask: **What are some things non-Christians do for fun that Christians aren't allowed to do? Do you think it's fair that non-Christians can do things that Christians aren't allowed to do? Why or why not? Do you think non-Christians have more fun than Christians do? Be honest.** Get several responses; then move on to the brainstorming activity at the end of Step 4.

STEP 5

Before the session, you'll need to prepare for each of your group members a list of the unique or special qualities he or she brings to your group's fellowship. As you close the session, share your lists with your kids in front of the whole group. Let your kids know that each of them brings something special to your fellowship. So when he or she is gone, something is missing from your group.

DATE USED:
Approx. Time

STEP 1: *Staying Alive Outside the Hive* _____
❑ Small Group
❑ Heard It All Before
❑ Fellowship & Worship
❑ Mostly Girls
❑ Short Meeting Time
❑ Combined Junior High/High School
Things needed:

STEP 2: *Swimming Upstream in a Downstream World* _____
❑ Extra Action
❑ Little Bible Background
❑ Mostly Guys
❑ Extra Fun
❑ Media
❑ Combined Junior High/High School
Things needed:

STEP 3: *Swords, Pyramids, and Lawnmower Blades* _____
❑ Large Group
❑ Heard It All Before
❑ Little Bible Background
❑ Short Meeting Time
Things needed:

STEP 4: *The Fun Factor* _____
❑ Extra Action
❑ Small Group
❑ Large Group
❑ Mostly Girls
❑ Urban
❑ Sixth Grade
Things needed:

STEP 5: *Strength in Numbers* _____
❑ Fellowship & Worship
❑ Mostly Guys
❑ Extra Fun
❑ Media
❑ Urban
❑ Sixth Grade
Things needed:

SESSION 5

Why Serve Others?

YOUR GOALS FOR THIS SESSION:
Choose one or more

☐ To help kids recognize that serving God often involves serving others.

☐ To help kids understand that faith without actions is dead.

☐ To help motivate and prepare kids to plan and carry out acts of Christian service.

☐ Other:_____

Your Bible Base:

Matthew 25:31-46
Luke 10:25-37
Ephesians 6:7-8
James 2:14-26

WHY SERVE OTHERS?

STEP 1

Bake That Cake!

(Needed: Cake ingredients, utensils, timer)

If possible, begin your meeting in a kitchen area. If it's not possible to meet in a kitchen area, you'll need to bring cake-baking ingredients and utensils, as well as a cake that you've baked before the session. (But don't bring out the cake until the end of the session.)

Ask: **How many of you like to eat cake? How many of you like making cakes?** After kids respond, explain that there is going to be a cake-baking contest, pitting the guys against the girls (if possible). You'll need two sets of ingredients and utensils for baking a cake.

Explain: **When I say, "Go," both teams will have five minutes to get their cake prepared. Ready! Set! Go!**

This five-minute period could be a bit chaotic, particularly if some of the team members have never baked before. Ideally, both teams will start by reading the recipe on the cake mix box and following the instructions. Occasionally, you may want to call out how much time is left. After five minutes, declare a winner based on how how close each team came to completing the recipe. (If you're in a kitchen area, be sure you know how much time it will take the cakes to bake, so you can return to the kitchen to take them out of the oven.)

Afterward, ask: **If both teams had just stood around and not done anything, would the cakes have gotten made?** (Of course not.)

Explain: **Even though both teams had everything that was needed to make a cake, they had to do something to actually make the cake happen.**

UNIT THREE

STEP 2

In Word and Deed

(Needed: Bibles, copies of Repro Resource 9, pencils.)

Ask one of your girls to stand at the front of the room. Say: **Let's say that _____ plans to start working out at the local fitness center. She buys some cross-training shoes, exercise outfits, and a Walkman headset so that she "looks the part." She even reads up on exercises, so she'll know how to do them. Yet with all this preparation, she never actually exercises.**

Ask one of your guys to stand at the front of the room. Say: **Let's say that _____ plans to run for president of the United States. He studies the issues, hits the campaign trail to win voters, and after several long years, is finally elected president. On Inauguration Day, he gets sworn in, making him official. But he does nothing—not one solitary act—as president!**

Point out that in both cases, the people didn't act on what they had prepared themselves to do.

Ask your kids how these examples might relate to Christians who don't serve and act on their faith. If no one mentions it, point out that some people become Christians and start growing and being discipled in the faith, learning more and more about how God wants us to live. Yet with all of God's resources at their fingertips, they don't act on them.

Have kids turn in their Bibles to James 2:14-26. Ask for a volunteer to read the passage aloud. Afterward, say: **James has some strong words to Christians who aren't acting on their faith!**

Ask your kids to reflect on their current spiritual state, answering silently the following questions: **Based on what we've just read, how alive would you say your faith is right now, on a scale of one to ten? What have you done or what are you doing for the kingdom of God?**

Ask your kids what comes to mind when they think of doing "deeds" for the kingdom of God. As kids respond, see if the idea of being a missionary overseas comes up. Ask your kids why some people think that serving God necessarily means going overseas on the mission field. After kids respond, explain that you're going to look at some other options of Christian service besides the mission field.

OPTIONS

EXTRA ACTION

LITTLE BIBLE BACKGROUND

MOSTLY GIRLS

MOSTLY GUYS

JR. HIGH/HIGH SCHOOL COMBINED

242

WHY SERVE OTHERS?

Have kids turn to Matthew 25:31-46. Ask someone to read the passage aloud. Afterward, ask for enough volunteers to fill the parts in the skit "Sheep or Goat?" (Repro Resource 9). Assign the parts and hand out copies of the sheet to the performers. Give volunteers a few minutes to read through the skit before performing it.

When the skit is finished, ask your kids what they would do if God Himself asked them for something to eat, drink, or wear or asked them to visit Him.

After kids respond, ask: **Why do you think some Christians ignore the basic needs of people in society, even though God says that if we do things for these people, in essence, we're doing them for Him?**

After kids comment, say: **It seems that the point God is trying to get across to us is that to serve Him, we must serve others. Let's find out who these "others" are that God is specifically referring to.**

STEP 3

Just Who Exactly Is My Neighbor?

(Needed: Bibles, copies of Repro Resource 10, pencils)

Ask your kids to close their eyes and picture the neighborhood where they live. Ask them if they can name all of their neighbors—not the ones five or six houses down the street, but the ones who live next to them or across the street from them. Go around the room, asking your kids to try to name their neighbors.

Afterward, assign one of your kids to read the story of the Good Samaritan in Luke 10:25-37. But first, have the person read just verse 27. Say: **This man knew Jesus' command to "love your neighbor as yourself." But a couple of verses later, the man asks Jesus, "Who is my neighbor?" Who do you think Jesus was referring to when He said to love your neighbor?** Let kids respond.

Before you have your group member read the rest of the passage, assign some of your kids to play the characters in the Good Samaritan story. These characters might include the man who was beaten and robbed, the robbers, the priest, the Levite, the Samaritan, and the

OPTIONS

- SMALL GROUP
- LARGE GROUP
- HEARD IT ALL BEFORE
- MEDIA
- SHORT MEETING TIME
- URBAN
- SIXTH GRADE

243

innkeeper. (You might even let someone be the donkey if you want.) Have kids act out the passage as the person reads it.

Afterward, discuss with your kids whether or not they think the story defines exactly who our neighbors are. Ask for their conclusions on what this parable is saying. Then point out that instead of nailing down who is and isn't our neighbor, this story indicates that we are to show merciful acts of service to everyone we come in contact with.

Suggest that instead of figuring out which people we have to serve and which people we don't, Christian service is more of an *attitude*. This attitude can be best summed up as being concerned with and acting on other people's interests, and not just our own (Philippians 2:4).

Ask: **In what areas might it be difficult for you to think of other people's needs rather than your own?** Get several responses.

Ask your kids to name some needs that other students at their school might have that they could possibly help meet. Then hand out copies of "Coming Soon to a School Near You" (Repro Resource 10). Allow a few minutes for kids to create a modern-day Good Samaritan example that could happen at their school. After a few minutes, allow each kid to read his or her modern-day parable to the group.

Get Those Hands Dirty!

(Needed: Bibles, previously baked cake [optional])

Refer back to the Good Samaritan passage in Luke 10:25-37. This time, ask your reader to read only the last four words of verse 37 ("Go and do likewise"). Then say: **Jesus didn't say to the man, "Think about this"; He said, "Go and do likewise."**

Explain to your kids the benefits that come from service to others. Have someone read aloud Matthew 25:34 for a glimpse of the inheritance that God promises for us.

Afterward, say: **That inheritance may sound inviting, but what benefits does Christian service have for people *right now*?** Have someone read aloud Ephesians 6:7-8, which promises that "the Lord will reward everyone for whatever good he does."

Let kids discuss their feelings regarding the promises and benefits God gives us both now and in the future. Then ask: **Even with all**

WHY SERVE OTHERS?

of these benefits from God for those who serve others in Christ, why do you think some people are reluctant to serve? (Some people are selfish, and only want to satisfy themselves. Some people believe they are too busy to serve others. Some people may be afraid of being thought of as weird for serving others.)

After some discussion, brainstorm as a group some ways that your group members can serve others. You may want to refer back to Matthew 25:31-46 for a whole list of ideas. Your kids could help out at a homeless shelter or at a soup kitchen by serving meals. They could collect food and clothing to take to a local shelter. You could plan to visit a local nursing home, where your kids could talk with the patients and sing songs to them. You could plan a weekend activity in which your kids could help with a local work team. Rebuilding a fence or a garage, doing yard work, and painting are all options that would no doubt be welcomed by members of your community.

Regardless of the activities your group plans, emphasize that serving God is a constant attitude. And whether it's at home, at school, or with friends, we must be primed and ready to take on the interests of those in need.

Close the session by making your way back to the church kitchen to eat the cakes that have been baking (or simply serve the cake that you baked before the session).

NOTES

EXTREME CLOSEUP

REPRO RESOURCE 9

SHEEP or GOAT?

Setting: Billy and Jane are unwinding from a long day. Billy's sitting in a chair, reading the paper. Jane is on the couch, thumbing through a book.

JANE *(answering the phone)*: Hello. Yes, this is the Goats residence. *(Sits up excitedly)* This is who? You mean, as in Jesus, the Son of God? *(Billy drops the paper, quickly jumping over to the couch where Jane is sitting.)* You say You're coming over? Tonight? Uh, OK, we'll look forward to seeing You. *(Hangs up phone.)*
BILLY: Jesus is coming over? Tonight? To our house?
JANE: That's what He said. Can you believe it? Jesus! *(Both stare around the room and then look back at each other.)*
BILLY & JANE: We've got to clean this place up! *(Both begin frantically straightening furniture, dusting, and vacuuming.)*
JANE: He'll have to eat something. You go get some food ready. I just went grocery shopping, so the refrigerator is full.
BILLY: OK. Can you get out one of my new sweaters? We have to look nice for Jesus. You should wear one of those new outfits you just bought. They're just sitting in the closet. *(Jane nods her head. Then both go back to buzzing around the house, cleaning and preparing. The doorbell rings.)*
BILLY & JANE: He's here! *(Billy tries his best to straighten his clothing, takes a breath, and opens the front door.)*
HUNGRY MAN *(begging in a pathetic voice as he stands in the doorway)*: Good sir, could you spare something to eat and drink? I haven't had a thing in days. Just some bread and water, please.
BILLY *(cutting the man off impatiently)*: I don't have anything to give you. Besides, we're expecting a guest any minute now. So please leave. *(Billy closes the door before the man can respond.)* I'm getting tired of people coming around here begging. Why don't people like that just get a job? *(Jane hands Billy his sweater, which he puts on. Both sit down, waiting for their guest to arrive. The doorbell rings again. Billy runs across the room, then slowly opens the door.)*
COLD MAN *(collapsing on his knees in the doorway, shivering)*: Sir, do you have any clothes to spare? I think I've got frostbite.
BILLY *(quickly pushing the man out the door)*: I'm sorry, we just donated all of our extra clothes to the Salvation Army last week. There's a local shelter just down the street. Why don't you try there? *(Billy blows into his hands, trying to warm up.)* Wow, it's freezing out there!
JANE: It sure is. That guy must be insane to be out with no coat on. Who taught him how to dress? *(Jane and Billy go back to their reading, but frequently check their watches.)* I wonder what's keeping Jesus. *(Doorbell rings again.)*
BILLY & JANE: That's got to be Him. *(Both walk to the door with warm smiles on their faces and open the door.)*
LONELY MAN *(in a sad voice)*: I'm sorry to bother you, kind folks, but I just need somebody to talk to. Today marks one year since my wife left me. Could I come in and—
JANE: You know, there are professionals you should probably talk to. We're not qualified to help you out. We'll pray for you, though. Have a good night. *(Closes the door.)*
BILLY: That's too bad. But I'm glad we're still together. I wonder what's keeping Jesus. It's kind of rude—He hasn't bothered to call or anything to say that He'd be late. *(The phone rings. Billy answers it.)* Hello? Hi, Jesus. Where have you been? . . . That's impossible, we've been here all night.
VOICE OF JESUS: Depart from me, you who are cursed. . . . For I was hungry and you gave me nothing to eat, I was thirsty and you gave me nothing to drink, I was a stranger and you did not invite me in, I needed clothes and you did not clothe me. . . . They also will answer, "Lord, when did we see you hungry or thirsty or a stranger or needing clothes . . . and did not help you?" He will reply, "I tell you the truth, whatever you did not do for one of the least of these, you did not do for me."
(Billy and Jane both have their ears to the phone, but are standing frozen, looking shocked and scared. A loud click is heard on the other end of the line.)

NOTES

EXTREME CLOSEUP

REPRO RESOURCE 10

Coming Soon to a School Near You

OK, so maybe a gang of thieves wouldn't rob and beat up somebody at your school and leave the person lying in the hallway. But there are probably situations that occur every day at your school that are *similar* to the Good Samaritan story.

Create a short story—set in your school—that reflects the basic principle of the Good Samaritan story. Your scenario may be serious or humorous. Take a few minutes to write your story in the space below. Be prepared to share it with the group.

NOTES

OPTIONS
SESSION FIVE

Step 2

Before reading the James passage, try a demonstration of faith and works. Put a water-filled tub or large bucket in the middle of your meeting area. Have a towel handy. Say: **I can walk on water. I can also enable any person in this room to walk on water! I'll give a prize to any person who lets me enable him or her to walk on water right now. You have to leave your shoes and socks on, but I promise they won't get soaked.** See what happens. (You might want to let a couple of group members in on this stunt beforehand if you think no one else will volunteer.) Have volunteers stand in line by the water. Then bring out a tray of ice cubes that you've been hiding. Put the towel on the floor, dump the ice on the towel, and you and your volunteers can walk across the frozen water. After awarding prizes, discuss the difference between believing that it's possible to walk on water and actually doing it.

Step 4

Instead of discussing a theoretical service project, tackle one right in your meeting place. Depending on where you are and what needs doing, you could have group members clean the place up, fold church bulletins, make cards for shut-ins, change diapers in the church nursery, or give a bath to a youth sponsor's dog. If time allows, talk afterward about who was served by the project you undertook.

Step 3

In the context of the good Samaritan story, encourage group members to think of each other as "neighbors." Too often small groups remain small because there's plenty of room for members to "keep their distance" from each other. Unity must begin in your group before it will spread effectively to others at school. If you don't believe your own group is as close as it should be, have everyone share a specific need with the rest of the group. Write all of the needs on the board. Then see if anyone is willing to agree to pray for or attend to those needs in other ways. All those who are willing should sign an agreement.

Step 4

When you're planning service activities, don't forget the individual homes of your group members. Many times the church looks to traditional outlets of service such as those listed in the session. But some of your kids may come from homes that could use help with cleaning, baby-sitting, grocery shopping, or other kinds of chores that your group members could do on a weekend. If your own group members have unmet needs, it's going to be difficult for them to begin meeting the needs of other people.

Step 3

Before the session, you'll need to cut apart four maps of the United States (or another country). Put the pieces of each map into an envelope (so that you have four envelopes). At the beginning of Step 3, have kids form four teams. Give each team one of the envelopes. Have the teams compete to see which one can correctly reassemble its map first. You may be surprised at how little your kids know about areas outside of their region! Afterward, ask: **Do you feel like you have any responsibility to the people in other regions of the country? If so, what is your responsibility? If not, why not?** Compare group members' answers with Jesus' response to the young man who asked Him, "Who is my neighbor?"

Step 4

If you have time at the end of the session, consider involving your kids in an impromptu service project. Take your group to an area near your meeting place that's full of litter. Have kids form teams. Give each team three bags: one to collect cans, one to collect paper, and one to collect other garbage. Set a time limit and let teams collect as much litter as possible. When time is up, see which team collected the most litter. Award prizes, if you wish.

OPTIONS
SESSION FIVE

HEARD IT ALL BEFORE

STEP 3

If you've studied the Good Samaritan recently, skip that passage. Instead, have kids brainstorm a list of "The Five Nicest People in the Bible." (The list might include Jesus, Dorcas, Barnabas, Jonathan, Mary the mother of Jesus, etc.) Discuss how these people served others. (Let kids use a concordance or Bible dictionary to find information about the characters, if needed.) Then brainstorm a list of "The Five Nastiest People in the Bible" (The list might include Satan, Judas, Herod, Pharaoh, Cain, etc.) Discuss the selfishness of these characters. Use your findings to illustrate the fact that servanthood, unlike selfishness, is a quality most people admire.

STEP 4

After hearing at school and in the media about the needs of the hungry, the homeless, victims of war, and others, kids may feel overwhelmed and ready to tune out. Rather than listing all of the world's needs and trying to pick one to address, choose one need yourself before the session. Give the need a human face by bringing in an acquaintance who has firsthand experience with meeting the need—a missionary who has seen famine, a volunteer from a crisis pregnancy center, or someone who has a relative in prison, for example. Ask your acquaintance to talk briefly to the group and to suggest specific ways in which your group could help. Choose one of those ways and concentrate on how you'll carry out your plan during the next few weeks.

LITTLE BIBLE BACKGROUND

STEP 2

The account of the sheep and goats in Matthew 25:31-46 can be a bit scary if this is the first time your group members are dealing with it. Don't rush through it. You'll probably want to do more in response than simply read through Repro Resource 9. Begin by encouraging kids to ask questions of their own. If you don't get much response, then *you* need to ask enough questions to make sure that kids have a clear understanding of what Jesus is saying. Explain that Jesus tells this story not to judge us for the mistakes of our past, but to help us make better decisions in the future. While most people can probably recall past instances in which they could have helped someone but didn't, the important thing to remember is that they begin *now* to see the needs of other people more as Jesus sees them.

STEP 4

For people with little Bible background, the Book of James is an excellent read-through book. First, however, you may need to offer help with the references in Step 2 (James 2:14-26) to Abraham, Isaac, and Rahab. Deal with questions about today's assignment; then ask your group members to read the Book of James in its entirety this week and give you a report on it—in twenty-five words or less—at your next meeting. Most of what James has to say is straightforward and clear. *What* he says is likely to raise some questions, but how he says it makes his book a good one for groups like yours to examine on their own.

FELLOWSHIP & WORSHIP

STEP 1

Before kids arrive, set out bowls of warm water, each with a washcloth and towel, at various places throughout your meeting area. If possible, have enough bowls to be able to pair up your kids and assign each pair a bowl. When kids arrive, set them up with their bowls and have them wash each others' feet. When they're done splashing around, ask what typically comes to mind when they hear someone mention Christian service. If no one mentions it, bring up foot-washing. Say: **Jesus' act of washing His disciples' feet was an example He gave us for serving, but that doesn't mean that's the way we are to serve.** Talk about the many different ways that we can serve Christ through everyday activities. Then ask: **Why do you think God wants us to serve others?** Get several responses. Then move on to Step 2 in the session.

STEP 4

Hand out paper and pencils. Instruct each person to write a psalm of service. If kids wish, they may use Psalm 150 (a psalm of praise) as an example. When everyone is finished, ask volunteers to share their psalms with the rest of the group. Close the session in prayer, thanking God for the opportunities He gives us to serve Him.

OPTIONS
SESSION FIVE

STEP 1

If you don't have enough guys in your group for a girls-versus-guys contest, split your girls into two teams and pit them against each other. You may want to make the contest a bit more of a challenge by having group members bake cakes from scratch, rather than from a mix. Be sure that your girls know that you'll be taste-testing these cakes at the end of the session!

STEP 2

For a group of mostly girls, you'll probably want to make some changes to the skit on Repro Resource 9. Change the character of "Billy" to "Janet." Change the setting of the skit from a living room to a college dorm room. Explain that Janet and Jane are twins who have always done everything together—including rooming together at college. The visitors (the hungry person, the cold person, and the lonely person) may all be other female college students. For the voice of Jesus, you may wish to recruit a male from your church to speak that part. The rest of the skit should work well as written.

STEP 1

Before you assemble in the kitchen, give your guys an unopened Frisbee and ask them to throw it around outside. After they rip open the package and give the Frisbee a couple of tosses, send them to the kitchen for the cake-baking competition. Afterward, ask: **Why didn't you read the instructions before throwing the Frisbee? Why *did* you read the instructions on the box before making the cake?** Point out the importance of reading instructions to learn how to do new things. Unless your group members are convinced they know all there is to know about living a good Christian life, challenge them to keep reading until it becomes as natural to them as throwing a Frisbee.

STEP 2

After you discuss the importance of taking action in the Christian life, have your guys create a slogan that they can use to motivate themselves (and each other) in the future. If time permits, have them make a banner with their new slogan on it to post in your meeting area for a while. Depending on your guys' creative abilities, you might even have them write a song that incorporates the slogan, design sweatshirts that feature it, or do something else to help them remember it on a daily (rather than a weekly) basis.

STEP 1

Begin the session by announcing that you want to play a couple of board games. One should be a game that's familiar to everyone—something that group members open up and start playing right away. The other should be a new or unusual game that no one has ever heard of—but one you're sure that your group members will like. Arrange to leave the room at about the time kids start the second game. See if anyone is willing to read through all of the instructions to learn how to play. Afterward, compare the games to Christian living. Point out that both games can be equally fun, but until we get familiar with another set of rules, one might seem a lot harder than the other. Similarly, we do certain things as Christians that we get used to and that begin to come naturally. But if we carefully read the "instructions" on how to live— the Bible—we may discover new opportunities that are just as good or even better than what we already know.

STEP 4

Change your opening activity from a cake-baking contest to a cookie-baking contest. If you bake a large batch of cookies, all of your group members can have samples—and then they can also have a lot of fun sharing the cookies with other people. Come up with a quick list of possible recipients (your pastor, other church members, your church janitor, etc.), pile into a few cars, and make some on-the-spot deliveries. You've just been discussing how people should take action in their Christian lives. If you now prove that doing so can be a lot of fun, your group members are a lot more likely to "go and do likewise."

OPTIONS
SESSION FIVE

MEDIA

SHORT MEETING TIME

URBAN

STEP 3

To illustrate that the "Who is my neighbor?" question has gotten more complicated since New Testament days, try one of the following activities. (1) Before the session, find a group member or an adult from your church who subscribes to an on-line computer service (such as CompuServe, Prodigy, America Online, eWorld, etc.). Ask the person to demonstrate how the service puts the user in touch with faraway people who can become electronic "neighbors."
(2) Arrange to have an acquaintance fax or e-mail a family photo (with names, ages, etc.) to your meeting place. Pass around the faxed photo for your group members to look at. After using one of these choices, ask: **Who is your neighbor now? Should we try not to find out about people and needs around the world so that we don't have to do anything about them? What do you think Jesus would do?**

STEP 4

Play one or more contemporary Christian songs that issue a call to serve others. Possibilities include "Hollow Eyes" (Petra), "Doer of the Word" (Dan Peek), "Somebody's Brother" (Scott Wesley Brown), "Mountain Top" (Amy Grant), and "Vital Signs" (White Heart). After the song(s), ask: **How did this music make you feel? Let's say the singer or singers come to our meeting two weeks from now and say, "What did you do in response to that song?" What would you like to be able to answer?**

STEP 1

Skip the cake-baking. Before the session, make (or have a few kids make) several signs prohibiting virtually every activity that might take place during a typical meeting ("No Running," "No Eating," "No Sitting," "No Laughing," "No Volleyball," "No Making Fun of the Leader," "No Reading Signs," etc.). Post the signs in your meeting place. As kids enter, appoint a few to help you enforce the rules; anyone caught breaking a rule is sent to "jail" (the corner). If anyone is still at liberty when you're ready to start the meeting, give that person a prize "for being the best at doing nothing." Ask: **Is this what being a Christian is all about—doing nothing?** After listening to replies, move directly to the James passage in Step 2.

STEP 3

Skip Step 3. At the start of Step 4, summarize (or have a volunteer summarize) the Good Samaritan story before reading the last four words of Luke 10:37. Instead of planning a group service project, hand out index cards and pens. Say: **Think of someone at school or in our group whom you've tended to ignore—almost as if you were walking past that person on the road. On your card, write three needs that person might have. Then circle the need that might be easiest for you to meet.** Give kids a minute to pray silently about how they could help meet that need this week.

STEP 1

If you don't have access to a kitchen for the baking activity, try another opener. Ask kids to think about the hardest job they've ever completed—the hardest work they've ever done in their lives. One at a time, have kids come to the front of the room to act out (charades-style) his or her tough job for the rest of the group to guess. After all of the jobs have been guessed, ask: **If you'd just stood around and not done anything, would your job have gotten done?** (Of course not.) Explain: **You had to *do* something to actually complete your job.** Then move on to Step 2.

STEP 3

Before you get into the story of the Good Samaritan in Step 3, pass around several articles (which you've clipped from newspapers and newsmagazines) that deal with international events, preferably ones that involve a need. Give kids a chance to read a few of the articles. Then say: **Jesus tells us to love our neighbors as ourselves. After reading these articles, who would you say our "neighbors" are? Why?** Get several opinions; then take a look at how Jesus responded to the question.

254

OPTIONS
SESSION FIVE

Step 2
Before you read the Scripture references, ask: **What are some problems you see in the world that you would like to have changed? It could any problem from world hunger to the kid sitting next to you in algebra class who always cheats.** List group members' problems on the board as they're named. Then refer back to Step 2 in the session and work through the Scripture passages and questions listed there. When you're finished, come back to your master list. Ask: **From what we've just read and learned, what do you think we could do about these problems?** Encourage kids to come up with practical, realistic solutions. If there's one thing they're particularly excited about, you may even want to adopt it as a group project.

Step 4
As you're brainstorming ideas that your group members could take on as a service project, set up a challenge. Divide your group into two teams—a team of junior highers and a team of high schoolers. Challenge the members of each team to decide on one service project that they could do in the next month. At the end of the month, be sure to get a report of what they decided on and how it went.

Step 1
If you'd rather not have your sixth graders playing around with cake ingredients, try another opening activity. Have kids form two or three groups. Give each group a snap-together model kit. Have the groups compete to see which one can put its model together first. Award prizes to the first group that finishes. Afterward, ask: **If the members of your group had just stood around and not done anything, would the models have been completed?** (Of course not.) Explain: **Even though your group had everything that was needed to build a model, you had to do something to actually get the model built.** Then move on to Step 2.

Step 3
Explore the concept of "neighbors" in a little more detail with your sixth graders. Ask: **Who are your neighbors at home?** See how many kids can name the people who live around them. **Who are your neighbors at school?** See how many kids can name the people they sit next to in class or the kids whose lockers are next to theirs. **Who are our neighbors here at church?** See how many kids can name the people or establishments around your church. **Who are our state neighbors?** See how many kids can name the states that surround yours. **Who are our national neighbors?** See how many kids can name the countries that border yours. Use these questions to lead in to a discussion of Jesus' response to the young man who asked Him, "Who is my neighbor?"

Date Used:
Approx. Time

Step 1: *Bake That Cake!* _____
❏ Fellowship & Worship
❏ Mostly Girls
❏ Mostly Guys
❏ Extra Fun
❏ Short Meeting Time
❏ Urban
❏ Sixth Grade
Things needed:

Step 2: *In Word and Deed* _____
❏ Extra Action
❏ Little Bible Background
❏ Mostly Girls
❏ Mostly Guys
❏ Combined Junior High/High School
Things needed:

Step 3: *Just Who Exactly Is My Neighbor?* _____
❏ Small Group
❏ Large Group
❏ Heard It All Before
❏ Media
❏ Short Meeting Time
❏ Urban
❏ Sixth Grade
Things needed:

Step 4: *Get Those Hands Dirty!* _____
❏ Extra Action
❏ Small Group
❏ Large Group
❏ Heard It All Before
❏ Little Bible Background
❏ Fellowship & Worship
❏ Extra Fun
❏ Media
❏ Combined Junior High/High School
Things needed: